IN AND AROUND
JERUSALEM
For Everyone

THE BEST WALKS, HIKES
AND OUTDOOR SWIMMING

IN AND AROUND JERUSALEM FOR EVERYONE
The Best Walks, Hikes and Outdoor Swimming

Kochav Press
Email: benjietc@gmail.com
Website: https://www.benherskowitz.com/kochav-press

COVER DESIGN: Benjie Herskowitz
PHOTOGRAPHS: Arnold Slyper
BOOK DESIGN: Benjie Herskowitz

ISBN: 978-0-578-63254-4 paperback

First printing 2020

Distributed by
Ktav Publishers & Distributors Inc.
527 Empire Blvd.
Brooklyn, NY 11225-3121
Tel: 718-972-5449, 201-963-9524
Fax: 718-972-6307, 201-963-0102
http://www.ktav.com

Printed in Israel

"Arise, walk about the land through its length and breadth…"

– Words to Abraham in Genesis 13:16

This book is dedicated

to my dear wife

Judy

who has been my hiking partner

from the time our courtship first began.

No hikes have been as meaningful

as those we have done together

in Israel.

IN AND AROUND
JERUSALEM
For Everyone

Contents

The Judean Mountains West of Jerusalem

South of Jerusalem

The Judean Desert and Jordan Valley

North of Jerusalem

Spring-fed Pools and Outdoor Swimming in and Around Jerusalem

Outdoor Trips in Jerusalem Suitable for a Stroller and Wheelchair

Museums and Attractions in Jerusalem

(In alphabetical order)

Location: The Old City and City of David

Aish HaTorah (see page 42)
Address: 6 HaTamid St., Old City

A Look into the Past (see page 51)
Address: By the Western Wall, Old City

Burnt House (Beit Katros) (see page 30)
Address: 2 Tiferet Israel Rd., Old City

City of David Night Show (see page 17)
Address: Ma'a lot Ir David St.

Herodian Quarter Wohl Archaeological Museum (see page 29)
Address: 1 HaKara'im St., Old City

Old Yishuv Court Museum (see page 42)
Address: 6 Ohr HaHayim St., Old City

Temple Institute (see page 30)
Address: 40 Misgav Ladach St., Old City

Tower of David Museum (see page 29)
Address: By the Jaffa Gate

Western Wall Tunnels (see page 51)
Address: By the Western Wall, Old City

Location: Givat Ram

Bible Lands Museum (see page 122)
Address: 21 Shmuel Stefan Wise St.

Bloomfield Science Museum (see page 122)
Address: 3 Museum Blvd.

Israel Museum (see page 122)
Address: 11 Rupin Blvd.

Knesset (see page 121)
Address: Kiryat Ben Gurion

Supreme Court (see page 121)
Address: Sharei Mishpat St.

Location: Other Areas in Jerusalem

Agnon House (see page 138)
Address: 16 Klausner St.

Beit HaRav Kook (see page 153)
Address: 9 HaRav Kook St.

Cable Car Museum (see page 113)
Address: 17 Hebron Rd.

Chagall Windows (see page 145)
Address: Hadassah Ein Kerem

Ein Yael Living Museum (see page 170)
Address: Refaim Valley

First Station (see page 138)
Address: 4 David Remez St.

Friends of Zion Museum (see page 106)
Address: 20 Yosef Rivlin St.

Gazelle Valley Park (see page 173)
Address: Gazelle Valley

Gush Katif Museum (see page 94)
Address: 5 Sha'arei Tsedek St.

Hebrew Music Museum (see page 106)
Address: 10 Yoel Moshe Salomon St.

Herzl Museum (see page 145)
Address: Mount Herzl

Israel Aquarium (see page 170)
Address: 1 km from the Jerusalem Biblical Zoo

Menachem Begin Heritage Center (see page 106)
Address: 6 Sh. A. Nakhon St.

The Museum for Islamic Art (see page 160)
Address: 2 HaPalmach St.

Museum of Italian Jewish Art (see page 106)
Address: 25 Hillel St.

Museum of the Underground Prisoners (see page 153)
Address: 1 Mishol HaGevura St.

Nature Museum (see page 160)
Address: 6 Mohliver St.

Sound and Light Fountain Show (see page 113)
Address: Teddy Park

Ticho House (see page 153)
Address: 10 HaRav Agan St.

Time Elevator Jerusalem (see page 30)
Address: Yitshak Kariv St. 6, Alrov Mamilla Avenue

The Train Theater (see page 160)
Address: Liberty Bell Park

Twin Towers Living Memorial (see page 167)
Address: Arazim Valley of Ramot

Yad LaKashish (see page 153)
Address: 14 Shivtei Israel St.

Yad Vashem (see page 145)
Address: Har HaZikaron

YES Planet (see page 138)
Address: 4 Naomi St.

Attractions
Outside of Jerusalem

(In alphabetical order)

Biblical Museum of Natural History (see page 227)
Address: 5 HaTzaba St., Beit Shemesh

Galita Chocolate Factory (see page 183)
Address: Kibbutz Tzuba

Harel Brigade Monument (see page 233)
Address: Har Hadar

Israel Police Heritage Museum (see page 227)
Address: 9 Virginia St., Beit Shemesh

Kiftzuba Amusement Park (see page 183)
Address: Kibbutz Tzuba

Stalactite Cave Nature Reserve (see page 227)
Address: Close to Beit Shemesh

Tzuba Winery (see page 183)
Address: Kibbutz Tzuba

Yellin House at Motza (see page 207)
Address: Motza

Location: South of Jerusalem

Deer Land Park (see page 248)
Address: Close to Kibbutz Kfar Etzion

Gush Etzion Heritage Center (see page 248)
Address: Kibbutz Kfar Etzion

Gush Etzion Winery (see page 248)
Address: Gush Etzion Junction

Lone Oak Tree (see page 248)
Address: Just outside the town of Allon Shvut

"The Exotic Animal Experience" at Sde Bar (see page 241)
Address: Sde Bar

The Workshop Gush Etzion (see page 248)
Address: Rosh Tzurim

Location: The Judean Desert and Jordan Valley

Botanical Garden (see page 279)
Address: Kibbutz Ein Gedi

Canaan Tours at the Dead Sea (see page 262)
Address: Sonol Gas Station, Kfar Adumim

Eretz Bereshit (Genesis Land) (see page 261)
Address: Yishiv Alon

Jordan Valley Monument (see page 285)
Address: Jordan Valley

Moshe Castel Museum (see page 303)
Address: 1 Kikar HaMuseon, Ma'ale Adumim

Museum of the Good Samaritan (see page 262)
Address: Off Route 1 shortly after the entrance to Kfar Adumim

Oren Farm (see page 285)
Address: Netiv HaGedud in the Jordan Valley

Park Shamir (see page 303)
Address: By the central entrance to Ma'ale Adumim

Ptil Tekhelet (see page 261)
Address: Kfar Adumim

Location: North of Jerusalem

Psagot Wineries (see page 289)
Address: Kokhav Ya'akov (but moving)

Ancient Shilo (see page 289)
Address: Shilo

Map Showing Location of Hikes in the Judean Mountains West of Jerusalem

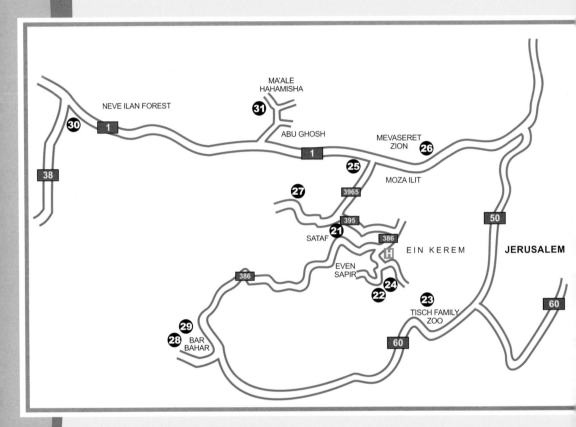

21 Ancient Agriculture in Sataf; **22** The Schvil Hamaayanot and Yad Kennedy Memorial; **23** The Springs of Emeq Refaim; **24** To Ein Kerem via Ein Hindak and the Ein Kerem National Park; **25** Castel National Park; **26** The Unusual Cave Formations in Nahal Halilim; **27** To the Tzuba Spring and Crusader Ruins of "Belmont" on Tel Tzuba; **28** The Spring of Ein Hod and Crusader Castle at Hurvat Beit Itab; **29** The Beautiful Nahal Katlav; **30** Outpost 21 via the Historic Burma Road; **31** The HaHamisha Forest and Ein Kfira Spring

Map Showing Location of Hikes in the Judean Desert

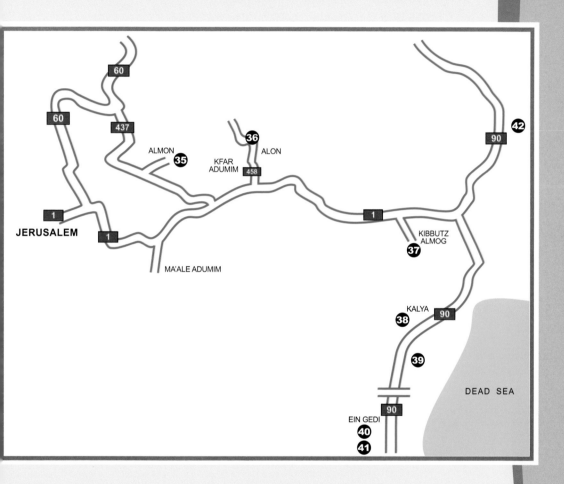

35 Ein Prat Nature Reserve; **36** Ein Mabu'a; **37** Nahal Og; **38** Qumran; **39** Enot Tsukim/ Ein Feshkha; **40** Nahal David, Ein Gedi Spring and Ancient Synagogue; **41** Ein Gedi – Nahal Arugot; **42** Qasr el Yahud National Park

ISRAELITE PERIOD *(1000 – 586 BCE)*

1000 BCE	King David conquers Jerusalem from the Jebusites
970 BCE	King Solomon becomes king
965 BCE	Solomon begins building the Temple
931 BCE	Division of the Jewish Kingdom
722 BCE	Assyrians conquer Samaria. Many refugees flee to Jerusalem
715 BCE	Reign of Hezekiah

BABYLONIAN AND THEN PERSIAN PERIODS *(586-322 BCE)*

586 BCE	Jerusalem conquered by the Babylonians (Nebuchadnezzar) and the First Temple destroyed
539 BCE	Cyrus conquers the Babylonian Empire
538 BCE	Cyrus allows the Jews to return to Jerusalem
516 BCE	Second Temple built in the 6th year of Darius the Great
458 BCE	Ezra's Aliyah
445 BCE	Nehemiah appointed governor of Judah and rebuilds Jerusalem's walls

HELLENISTIC PERIOD *(332-141 BCE)*

332 BCE	Alexander the Great conquers Judea
323 BCE	Death of Alexander the Great and beginning of struggle between his heirs
167 BCE	Maccabean revolt
164 BCE	The Maccabees capture Jerusalem and rededicate the Temple

HASMONEAN PERIOD *(140 BCE – 63 BCE)*

140 BCE	The Great Assembly proclaims Simon as high priest, commander and leader

ROMAN PERIOD *(63 BCE – 324 CE)*

63 BCE	Pompey conquers Jerusalem
40 BCE	The Roman Senate appoints Herod "King of the Jews" and provides him with an army
19 BCE	Herod begins expanding the Temple Mount and rebuilding the Temple
30 CE	Jesus crucified
70 CE	Roman forces destroy Jerusalem and the Second Temple
132 CE	Bar Kochba Revolt

OF JERUSALEM

BYZANTINE PERIOD *(324- 638 CE)*
324	Emperor Constantine reunites the Empire
325	Church of the Holy Sepulcher built
614	Persians capture Jerusalem
629	Byzantines recapture Jerusalem

FIRST MUSLIM PERIOD *(638-1099 CE)*
638	Caliph Omar conquers Jerusalem
661	Jerusalem under Umayyad Dynasty
687	Dome of the Rock built on the site of the Temple
750	Jerusalem ruled under the Abassid Dynasty
969	Fatimid Caliphate

CRUSADER PERIOD *(1099-1187 CE)*
1099	Crusaders capture Jerusalem and establish the Kingdom of Jerusalem

AYYUBID PERIOD *(1187-1259 CE)*
1187	Saladin captures Jerusalem from the Crusaders after the Crusader defeat at Battle of the Horns of Hittin
1229-1244	Crusaders briefly recapture Jerusalem twice

MAMLUKE PERIOD *(1260-1516 CE)*
1260	Jerusalem raided by the Mongols. The Mongols are defeated by the Egyptian Mamlukes
1267	Nachmanides in Jerusalem

OTTOMAN PERIOD *(1516-1917 CE)*
1517	Ottoman Empire captures Jerusalem
1537-1541	Suleiman the Magnificent rebuilds the walls of Jerusalem
1831-1840	Muhammad Ali of Egypt takes over city

BRITISH MANDATE *(1917-1948 CE)*
1917	The British capture Jerusalem in World War 1

THE STATE OF ISRAEL
1948	State of Israel established. Jerusalem divided by armistice line between Israel and Jordan
1967	Jerusalem reunited during the Six Day War

TIME: About 2-3 hours

DISTANCE: 4.25 km

TYPE OF WALK: Circular

DIFFICULTY: Easy walking

STARTING POINT:
City of David Visitors Center. There is a shop for hot and cold drinks and snacks, WC's, and a few chairs and tables for picnicking.

PUBLIC TRANSPORT:
The closest stop on the light rail is City Hall. From here it is about a thirty minute walk to the Dung Gate via the Jaffa Gate. There are buses to the Western Wall Plaza, including from Binyanei Ha'umah (enter "Western Wall" into Moovit) and from here it is a few minute's walk to the Dung Gate. There are also buses to the Jewish Quarter parking lot (which is a private parking lot), and from here it is about a ten minute walk to the Old City Dung Gate. From the Dung Gate turn left along Ma'ale HaShalom and then take the first turn on the right. Shortly on your left is the attractive entrance to the City of David Visitors Center.

1 The City of David

T he City of David entered into Jewish history almost three thousand years ago when King David captured the fortress from the Jebusites. For hundreds of years its whereabouts was unknown, and only relatively recently did archaeologists discover its location and begin digging and uncovering its past. It is now the most exciting place in Jerusalem for reliving the city's early history. Plus, wading through Hezekiah's tunnel with friends or family is a lot of fun!

Planning your visit to the City of David:

The City of David is open from 8 am–5 pm Sunday to Thursday, and from 8 am–2 pm on Friday. Tickets can be bought up to two hours prior to closing. Entry to Hezekiah's Tunnel is up to one hour prior to closing. Keep your entrance ticket for entering the water system and the Shiloah Pool.

The best way to explore this site is with a group tour. They are also in English and start from the Visitors Center. The tour includes the 3-D movie, the important archaeological features and Hezekiah's tunnel, and lasts two or three hours depending on whether you go through the tunnel. There are several tours a day. They can be booked on line or by calling 972 77 9966 726 or *6033.

You can also tour the City of David on your own. There is no charge to view the archaeological ruins, although there is a charge to enter the Secret Tunnel – and this is highly recommended. The 3-D movie is also definitely worth seeing. You receive an assigned time for an English or Hebrew viewing. The movie lasts about fifteen minutes. There is a charge.

From the end of the Secret Tunnel you have two options. You can wade through Hezekiah's tunnel. This will take about thirty minutes and is a lot of fun, especially if you are with a group. You will need appropriate footwear and a flashlight. You can buy a small but quite adequate flashlight at the gift store at the Visitors Center. The maximum height of the water is indicated on the wall by the entrance to the tunnel and is about 1.5 feet. However, this is only towards the beginning and end of the tunnel; in most of the tunnel the water is much shallower.

Another option is to go through the dry Canaanite tunnel instead of Hezekiah's tunnel. This is the circular tour described here. The tunnel is lit up and takes about five minutes to walk through. Going this route is highly recommended as there are fascinating things to see when you exit the tunnel. If the rest of your party decides to go through Hezekiah's Tunnel, you can meet up with them at the Shiloah Pool.

OVERVIEW

THE CITY OF DAVID – FROM DAVID TO NEHEMIAH

Jerusalem is mentioned in the Book of Joshua (Joshua 15:63). It was then a massively fortified Canaanite city occupied by the Jebusite tribe. Joshua was able to defeat the kings of the Canaanite cities on the mountain ridge, thereby establishing a foothold in the country, but was unable to capture Jerusalem because of its topography and formidable fortifications.

The city is bounded on its eastern side by the steep Kidron Valley and on its western side by the Central Valley (also known as the Tyropoeon Valley). The Kidron Valley is clearly evident today, but the Central Valley is difficult to envisage from the City of David as it became filled with debris over the centuries. However, if you walk a short distance to the Givati Parking Lot Excavation, you can readily appreciate that there was once a valley outside the entrance of the City of David. The Kidron and Central Valleys met south of the City of David, so that the city was surrounded by steep valleys on all but its northern aspect.

The Canaanite city obtained its water from the gushing Gihon Spring. This spring was located outside the main walls of the city on the west bank of the Kidron Valley. To assure that they had a continuous supply of water, the Canaanites built a reservoir, now called the "Canaanite Pool," adjacent to the spring. Also, to protect their water supply pool during a siege, the Canaanites enclosed the spring with a tower and the pool with walls projecting from the city wall (see picture on next page). Access to the pool was via steps located between the walls.

The Canaanites also constructed an underground "Secret Tunnel" that began from inside the city to access the water supply system. This tunnel still exists today, and you can walk through it to the area of the Canaanite Pool. From here you can see the ruins of the projecting walls that enclosed the pool and the ruins of the tower that protected the spring.

Only a portion of water from the spring was diverted to the Canaanite Pool. The rest was led via an underground tunnel, the "Canaanite Tunnel," along the western bank of the Kidron Valley, to a second pool just beyond the southern walls of the city. Water for agriculture was led

FREE SHUTTLE:
There are free one-way and return shuttles from the all-day parking lot at the First Station to the Western Wall Plaza. The entrance to the parking lot is at the beginning of Derech Bethlehem opposite the Dan Boutique. The shuttle also stops at Mount Zion, the Jewish Quarter and the Old City walls. The shuttle leaves on the hour and every twenty minutes thereafter from 8 am–8 pm on Sunday, Tuesday and Wednesday, from 7 am–8 pm on Monday and Thursday, and on Friday from 8 am until 1 hour before the beginning of Shabbat. There is no shuttle on Shabbat.

DRIVING DIRECTIONS AND PARKING:
Enter "City of David" into Waze and click on "City of David Ma'alot Ir David Street." Karta Parking (חניון קרתה) on Yitzhak Kariv St. is a short distance from the Jaffa Gate.

off by pipes at intervals from this tunnel into the Kidron Valley. You can also walk along this tunnel today, as it is now dry.

How did King David, the second king of the Jewish kingdom, manage to capture the city? Its walls would have been extremely difficult to breach, to the extent that the Jebusites boasted that even the blind and lame stationed on its walls could defend it. The Bible relates that David said to his soldiers "*Whoever smites the Jebusites and reaches in the tzinor…*"(II Samuel 5:8). The word "*tzinor*" means a pipe or channel. Biblical commentators of the past were unable to understand this, but we now know about the Canaanite water supply system. It is possible that Joab, a nephew of King David who volunteered for this task, climbed through this system. This enabled him to enter the city and open its gates. For his bravery, he was promoted to become David's general (I Chronicles 11:6).

Following his capture of Jerusalem in about 1000 BCE, David made it his capital. It was not a big city at that time, and probably had a population of no more than about five hundred to seven hundred people.

The protective walls of the Jebusite city. The tower to the right protected the Gihon spring.
The walls projecting from the main city walls on the left surrounded the "Canaanite Pool"
(Picture courtesy of the City of David)

The City of David was not included within the Old City walls built by Suleiman the Magnificent in 1535 CE, and knowledge of its whereabouts was lost. Everything you see displayed at this site has been revealed by recent and still ongoing archaeological excavations.

The first ruins you see on entering this site are the foundations of "The Large Stone Structure" at the most northern end of the city and at its highest elevation. It is has been suggested that this was King David's palace. We do know for sure that it functioned as a royal administrative center several hundred years after King David, as clay seals were found in the ruins belonging to officials mentioned in the Bible who lived at the end of the First Temple period.

Major changes in the City of David were made by King Hezekiah, the 13th king of Judea, who reigned from about 715 to 686 BCE. Judea had become a powerful nation and Hezekiah formed an alliance to break away from the Assyrians, then the dominant power in the Near East (see the essay "Who was King Hezekiah?" on page 18). He also prepared Jerusalem for a possible retaliatory siege by the Assyrians. The fortifications around the Gihon Spring were a potential source of weakness if the city was to be besieged. He therefore diverted water from the spring to a pool on the southern slopes of the City of David. A channel was dug into the rock and the entrance to the spring from the Kidron Valley was blocked off. This channel is known as Hezekiah's Tunnel. It still flows with water and you can walk along its full length (533 meters). How Hezekiah managed to accomplish the technological feat of two teams working from either end of the tunnel joining up is still a matter of admiration and debate.

Warren's Shaft System is a shaft discovered in 1867 by the British archaeologist and engineer Captain Charles Warren, who found a vertical underground shaft leading from the Canaanite Pool into the city. Initially, it was assumed that this was part of the Canaanite water system, but it later became apparent that it is a completely natural shaft. The Canaanites probably had no knowledge of it and their Secret Tunnel was a few meters above it. Hezekiah's workers probably discovered it a thousand years later. They realized that they could use it for removing debris and they were the ones who lowered the Secret Tunnel to its present level.

Hezekiah's tunnel ends today at the Byzantine Pool of Siloam. This was part of a church complex built here on the mistaken belief that it was the site of the original Siloam Pool. However, if you continue walking you will soon come to the Second Temple remains of a section of the original "Shiloah (Siloam) Pool" into which Hezekiah's Tunnel drained. This pool may also have been used as a mikvah by pilgrims visiting the Temple Mount.

The area around the Shiloah Pool was close to the main southern entrance of the city. Steps were built within the Central Valley for the use of pilgrims ascending to the Temple Mount, and these led from the Shiloah Pool to the outside wall of the Temple Mount. The original steps from Second Temple times have recently been exposed by archaeologists and it will soon be possible to ascend on this road as at the time of the Temple.

Start your tour by walking up the stone steps directly opposite the ticket office to the "Beit Hatzofeh Lookout" to appreciate the topography of the City of David.

To the east can be seen the steep Kidron Valley and on the opposite side of the valley you can see the mainly Arab village of Silwan. Beyond this is the Mount of Olives and at its top the Seven Arches Hotel. To the north is the Temple Mount. Between the City of David and the Temple Mount is an area known as the Ophel, although much of it cannot be seen from this vantage point. This was a residential area in First Temple times and many refugees from the northern Israelite kingdom settled here following its fall to the Assyrians. You can clearly see the steps leading up to the now blocked Triple and Double Gates, the main entrance and exit gates for the Temple Mount. The northern wall of the City of David was located just beyond the observation area on which you are now standing.

The movie theater is just below the observation plaza. Viewing the movie is highly recommended. After the movie, descend by the metal steps to the "Large Stone Structure" located beneath the wooden platform of the Visitors Center.

You are now looking at foundation stones dated to the time of King David and that may have been part of his palace, the "House of Cedars," built for him by Hiram king of Tyre as described in II Samuel 5:11. The building was probably used as an administrative center in late First Temple times. Two bullae (clay impressions used for sealing documents) that belonged to high-ranking officials during the reign of King Zedekiah and whose names are mentioned in the book of Jeremiah were found in the ruins. King Zedekiah was the last king of Judah.

Continue down the steps to the "Royal Quarter" (area G), a residential area for royal officials and notables during First Temple times. The picture on the next page and the diagram in the brochure provided will be helpful in identifying the various structures.

The "Stepped Stone Structure" **A** in front of you is likely a retaining wall built to support the "Large Stone Structure." Houses were later built on top of this wall. "The House of Ahiel" **B** is a four roomed, two storied First Temple period dwelling belonging to a well-to-do family. The building was given this name because shards of pottery bearing Ahiel's name were found here. There is also a model of his home in a glass-covered case a bit further along. "The House of the Bullae" **D** is a narrow room beneath the House of Ahiel that was probably used for archives, as fifty-one seals were found here bearing names of people who lived towards the end of the First Temple period. The documents burned when the Babylonians destroyed the city in 586 BCE and only the bullae were left. "The Burnt Room" **C** is a room that was found filled with a layer of ash from the Babylonian destruction. Underneath the ash were smashed shards of pottery and expensive furniture.

On top of the "Stepped Stone Structure" is a section of wall ("Nehemiah's Wall") **E** built by Nehemiah in 445 BCE after the Jews returned from the Babylonian exile. Follow it along to the left and you will see that it merges into a Hasmonean tower. The ruins of area G are below Nehemiah's Wall, so that these buildings would have been outside the walls of the city during Second Temple times. This would explain why they are still relatively intact. Nehemiah probably built his wall on top of the slope rather than using the Canaanite wall lower down because rocky debris from the Babylonian destruction made access to the

original wall difficult. The population of the city was also quite small, so that only a small area needed enclosure. The location of Nehemiah's Wall remained the location of Jerusalem's "First Wall" for over five hundred years.

Clay figurines have been found in this and in other archaeological digs in Jerusalem, with more than 1500 being discovered in the City of David alone. These corroborate the words of Jeremiah: "The number of your gods, Judah, is like the number of your cities" (Jeremiah 2:28). It is likely that many inhabitants of Jerusalem during the First Temple period adhered to some Jewish rituals but also worshiped pagan gods (this is called syncretism). Lack of faithfulness to the one God was a major theme of the Biblical prophets.

> **Continuing, you will soon come to a small brown hut. At this point it is possible to return to the Visitors Center by turning to the right. However, most people will turn to the left and will follow the sign "To the Water System (Warren's Shaft) and Hezekiah's Tunnel" to visit the ancient water supply system.**

> **Despite what the sign says, you will not be walking in Warren's Shaft but rather "The Secret Tunnel" built by the Canaanites. About halfway down the descent of the tunnel you will see a lit-up space on your left and a sign indicating that this is an opening into Warren's shaft. Warren's Shaft is a natural shaft now believed to have had nothing to do with the Canaanite water system.**

> **At the bottom of the tunnel is the "Canaanite Pool." This was a reservoir cut into bedrock by the Canaanites. It is now dry and has been so since Hezekiah built his tunnel. However, prior to this it was fed from the adjoining Gihon Spring. You can see where a channel opened into the reservoir on its far wall.**

> **Proceed further and you will come to the ruins of "The Spring Tower" – the protective Canaanite tower built around the Gihon Spring. The spring can no longer be seen as it is underneath the far wall of the Spring Tower. Prior to Hezekiah's Tunnel being built, it would have been seen as a pulsating stream of water.**

This is the spot where Solomon came on his father's royal mule when he was anointed monarch of the kingdom (I Kings 1:38-39). You can view on the wall a short silent movie with music that shows how the towers and walls were built over the water system. This is helpful for understanding the layout of the ruins. There is a button switch on the wall that activates the movie, or you can ask the attendant.

You now have two choices – to go through Hezekiah's Tunnel or the Canaanite Tunnel. Wading through Hezekiah's Tunnel is a fun experience. But to see things of interest, take the Canaanite Tunnel.

> **Wading through Hezekiah's Tunnel: Make sure you have a flashlight and appropriate footware for this approximately thirty minute walk. Towards the end of the tunnel, on the rock wall on your left, there is a copy of the inscription engraved here when the two parties digging from opposite ends of the tunnel met up. When this inscription was discovered in the late 19th century, thieves cut it out of the wall, and damaged it in the process. The Ottoman authorities found the thieves, retrieved the inscription, and took it to Istanbul, Turkey, where it is now on display in a museum.**

> **Walking through the Canaanite Tunnel: The entrance to this tunnel is by the entrance to Hezekiah's Tunnel. It is a dry tunnel, takes five minutes or so to walk through, is well lit up, and an adult can walk through it comfortably. In ancient**

times, this tunnel led off from the Canaanite Pool. You can see the exit point to the right of the pool.

Continuation of the walk after exiting the Canaanite Tunnel:

After exiting the Canaanite Tunnel there is a turn off to a WC on your left. At the intersection after this, turn right onto the "Upper Trail" to the Shiloah Pool.

Note the following as you walk along:

❖ **Sections of the outer wall of the Canaanite city**
The Canaanite wall was a massive wall on the bank of the Kidron Valley made of large field rocks embedded in bedrock. It was subsequently repaired, probably by King Hezekiah. *"And he took courage and built up all the wall that was broken down, and raised it up to the towers...* (II Chronicles 32:5). Ruins of houses can be seen on the steep incline above the wall.

❖ **A copy of the inscription found in Hezekiah's Tunnel**
This is a second copy of the inscription found when the two parties digging Hezekiah's Tunnel met up. It is written in Palaeo-Hebrew, which is an ancient form of Hebrew.

❖ **The "Weill Excavations"**
You will see these caves adjacent to a wooden structure. They have been identified in the past as the burial caves of the House of David. However, there is considerable doubt as to whether this is truly the case. The Book of Kings tells us that David was buried in the City of David: *"And David slept with his fathers, and was buried in the City of David."* (I Kings 2:10). We also read that Nehemiah built his walls near the sepulcher of David: *"After him Nehemiah... repaired until opposite the sepulchers of David and until the [man]-made pool..."* (Nehemiah 3:16). However, there is considerable doubt that these two caves are where David was really buried, since they do not show the elaborate features usually associated with First Temple burial chambers, especially those used for monarchs. These particular caves may have been used for storage. There are also other traditions as to where King David was buried, such as on Mount Zion, although this also is disputed. It is also possible that David's descendants were buried in another location and not in the same burial chamber as David. In sum, this is a controversial issue (see the essay "Is King David really buried on Mount Zion?" on page 77).

❖ **The Meyuhas House**
This house was built by the Meyuhas family in 1873. Leaving the safety of the Old City and building a home here was a brave thing to do at that time. The family was forced to flee during the Arab riots of 1936 and they currently live in Western Jerusalem, although a Jewish family is living in the house.

The trail comes to an end at a gate. To open the gate, press the button by the side of the gate. You are now on the road Pardes Rimonim. This will lead you down the hill to the entrance to the Shiloah Pool close to the next intersection.

"Hezekiah's Tunnel" and the "Upper Trail" end at two different pools. Hezekiah's Tunnel exits at the "Byzantine Pool of Siloam," which is part of a Byzantine church complex built in

A section of the Shiloah Pool of Second Temple times

the 5th century. To see the true Shiloah (Siloam) Pool of Second Temple times, you will need to continue down the steps. If you have come by the "Upper Trail," you will come immediately to the Second Temple Shiloah Pool. You will need your entrance ticket to enter into this pool section.

Hezekiah's pool was built to the south of the City of David, between the outer wall of the City of David and a new wall that enclosed the Western Hill. It was destroyed by the Babylonians, but rebuilt by the Hasmoneans. The pool was expanded by Herod, and the ruins before you are from this time. The Romans covered it over after the Jewish Revolt. Archaeologists have revealed only a section of the Shiloah Pool. The remainder is buried in the adjacent garden and has not been excavated yet as it is in private church property. The nature of the steps suggests that it may have been used as a ritual bath for pilgrims. The Water Libation ceremony was performed here during the Feast of Tabernacles. The pool is of significance to Christians as it is believed that this is where Jesus cured a man of blindness when he bathed in its waters (John 9:4-7).

There are a number of ways to get back to the Visitors Center from the Shiloah Pool.

1. A popular option is to walk along the "Central Drainage Canal" and this is included in your admission. It takes about twenty to thirty minutes. This underground canal was built by King Herod in Second Temple times to drain water that collected in the Central Valley during the rainy season. Its entrance is adjacent to the Byzantine Pool of Siloam and it exits at the Givati Parking Lot Excavation, from where you cross the road to the Visitor Center.

The first part of this route is on the "Western Stepped Road" which is a small section of the road used by pilgrims to ascend from the southern entrance of the city to the Temple Mount. This "Pilgrimage Road" is currently being excavated and eventually you will be able to walk its entirety to outside the Temple Mount. When pilgrims used this road it was not underground, but over the centuries the Central Valley became filled with debris. The excavations are being carried out in a large tunnel beneath people's homes. When completed, this is likely to be one of the foremost tourist sites in Jerusalem.

2. Take a shuttle back to the Visitors Center outside the entrance/exit to the pool area. The attendant at the pool may arrange this for you. There is a small charge for this as it is not included with your admission.

3. Walk along the road Pardes Rimonim. This is a very pleasant, somewhat steep ascent. Turn left from the entrance/exit to the pool area. At the next intersection turn left onto Pardes Rimonim. It is marked by a red arrow. You will pass Jewish and Arab residences on the way. The road is closely surveyed by cameras. After about fifteen minutes you will arrive at the Visitors Center.

Activites of Interest:

City of David Night Show: The City of David has special and regular activities including the Hallelujah Night Show which is projected onto the antiquities of the City of David using state-of-the-art technology. Booking needs to be done in advance and can be done from their website. The free shuttle from the First Station operates conveniently to get you to the show. The show is not wheelchair accessible.

2 An Introduction to The Old City

This introductory walk to the Old City visits its Jaffa Gate entrance and sections of the Christian and Jewish Quarters. A rooftop lookout provides a wonderful view over all four quarters of the city. During the walk, you will learn about some of the contributions of King Hezekiah, the Romans, the Crusaders and the Ottomans to the physical layout of ancient Jerusalem.

OVERVIEW

WHO WAS KING HEZEKIAH?

The name King Hezekiah comes up a lot when touring Jerusalem's Old City and the City of David. This king not only had an impact on the history of Judea, but also on the physical layout of Jerusalem.

Hezekiah was the 13th king of the Kingdom of Judah. He reigned from about 715 to 686 BCE. The biblical Book of Kings looks favorably on his reign in that he abolished idol worship throughout his kingdom and strengthened the institution of the Temple at the expense of private altars (II Kings 18:1).

The Assyrian empire was then dominant in the Near East and Hezekiah was witness to the destruction of the northern Israelite Kingdom and the exile of the northern tribes by the Assyrian King Sargon II in about 722 BCE. Many Jews from the northern kingdom managed to escape exile and settled in Jerusalem

and other cities in Judea. As a result, Jerusalem experienced a large population increase.

Judea had become the most powerful country between Assyria and Egypt, and when the Assyrian king Sargon died, Hezekiah saw this as an opportune time to throw off the Assyrian yoke. This was strongly opposed by the prophet Isaiah who appreciated that Jerusalem's isolation, being on the mountain ridge and distant from the main highway, accounted for its security; but his advice was ignored.

Aware that he might soon have to face the full strength of the Assyrian empire, Hezekiah strengthened the defenses of Jerusalem. Its Western Hill, including what is now called Mount Zion, contained two new residential areas outside the city walls. He enclosed these two

areas with an extension of the city wall. The northern approach to the city had always been its weakest point, since it lacked any natural topographical defenses, and Hezekiah built a new and stronger northern city wall close to the existing one. The "Broad Wall" viewed on this walk is a small section of this new northern defensive wall.

He also ensured that the population of Jerusalem would have sufficient water during a time of siege by digging an underground tunnel from the Gihon Spring in the Kidron valley to a new pool, the Siloam Pool. The Gihon Spring had been fortified since the time of the Canaanites, but it was still a potential area of weakness. Following the tunnel's construction, the Kidron Valley approach to the Gihon Spring was blocked off, thereby depriving an attacking army access to water.

As Isaiah had predicted, Hezekiah's allies, including Egypt, did not come to his aid when Assyria attacked Judea. Some deserted the alliance and paid tribute to Sargon's son and successor Sennacherib, while others, including the Egyptians, were defeated in battle.

Sennacherib unleashed destruction on forty-six Judean cities and their surrounding villages, including the well-fortified city of Lachish. By 701 BCE the city of Jerusalem was under siege. Despite his opposition to Hezekiah's campaign, Isaiah prophesied that the city would not be conquered and that Sennacherib would die: "*Therefore, thus says the Lord concerning the king of Assyria: He shall not come into this city, nor shoot an arrow there.....*" (Isaiah 37:33).

This is indeed what happened: "*And it was that very night, an angel of God went out and struck down 185,000 of the Assyrian camp. The rest arose in the morning and behold – they were all dead corpses*" (II Kings 19:35).

Jerusalem was saved, although much of Hezekiah's kingdom lay in ruins. Assyrian sources describe Hezekiah as remaining a vassal of the Assyrians and paying heavy tribute, but they make no mention of Assyria entering Jerusalem. Hezekiah died a few years after this and was succeeded by his son Menasseh. As Isaiah had also foretold, Sennacherib would soon die, being murdered by his sons.

TIME: Allow at least 3.5 hours, and about half a day if visiting museums or churches

DISTANCE: Just over 9.5 km

TYPE OF WALK: Circular

DIFFICULTY: An easy walk.

STARTING POINT: The Jaffa Gate of the Old City. There are WC's by the entrance to the northern section of the Ramparts Walk.

PUBLIC TRANSPORT: There are bus stops close to the Jaffa Gate. The closest stop on the light rail is "City Hall" — about a five to seven minute walk to the Jaffa Gate.

DRIVING DIRECTIONS AND PARKING: Enter "Jaffa Gate" into Waze, and click on "שער יפו ירושלים." The closest parking is Karta Parking. Enter "חניון קרתה" into Waze. This is only a short distance from the Jaffa Gate.

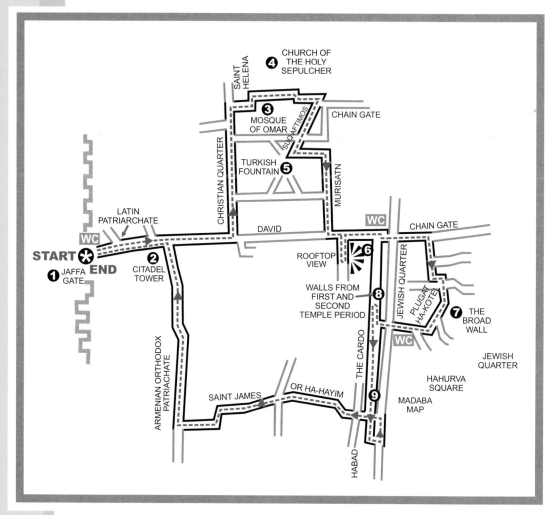

1. First part of the walk:

Before entering Jaffa Gate, look at the magnificent wall in front of you, surrounding the Old City, that was built by Suleiman the Magnificent during the Ottoman period.

Jerusalem fell to the Ottoman Turks in 1517 CE, and the sultan, Suleiman the Magnificent, began constructing this city wall in 1537, possibly because of concern that Christian Europe would mount another Crusade to capture Jerusalem, although such a Crusade never materialized. The city wall was in ruins during the previous rule of the Mamlukes. Suleiman built his new wall on the remains of walls built during the early Muslim and Crusader periods, although the foundations of some of the western sections of his city wall were much older than this. Mount Zion and the City of David were outside the city walls since the early Muslim period and were not included within Seleiman's walls.

The city wall was constructed in a medieval style with towers, turrets and portholes, and was meant to be impregnable. The floral and geometric patterns on the wall and gates were probably meant to enhance the spiritual significance of the city.

Enter the Old City via the Jaffa Gate ❶.

Jaffa Gate is so named because the road to and from Jaffa was from this gate. Jaffa was an important port for the Holy Land from ancient times. The Arabic sign above the gate credits Suleiman with beginning the construction of the gate in the Islamic year 945, or 1538 in the Gregorian calendar. Unlike the other eight gates into the city, Jaffa Gate is not part of the façade of the city wall but faces north towards Jaffa Rd. The gate is called Bab al-Khalil in Arabic, which means "Gate of the Friend," since the road from here also leads to Hebron. Abraham is buried in Hebron and is regarded by Muslims as being the beloved of God.

Note the defensive features of this gate. The porthole above you on entering the gate allowed defenders to pour noxious fluids onto an enemy that had breached it. The gate is also in the form of an L, which would have slowed down an enemy's entry into the city.

Nowadays, cars have a more direct way of entering the city than making this L-turn, and they have the German Kaiser Wilhelm II to thank for this. Politics can make strange bedfellows. The Turks (Muslims) and Germans (Lutherans) were allies, and in 1898 the Kaiser visited Jerusalem. No effort was spared by the Turks to make his visit an impressionable one. A section of the wall adjacent to the gate was knocked down and part of the moat surrounding the Citadel was filled in so that the Kaiser could enter the city on horseback wearing his tall helmet. (By contrast, General Allenby entered Jaffa Gate humbly on foot following the Turks surrender of the city to the British during World War I). How far the moat previously extended into the square can be seen from a shallow channel of paving stones in the square.

Crossing Omar Ibn Al-Khattab Square, the following can be seen:

❖ Two Turkish-style gravestones in a small, enclosed area just before the Tourist Information Center. A popular legend holds that they are the graves of two construction engineers for the wall who were beheaded by Suleiman. Suleiman was displeased that Mount Zion and the Tomb of David had been left outside the city wall. He may also have been worried that they would build a similar wall for someone else! Nevertheless, they were buried close to the walls they had built in appreciation for their work.

❖ To the left of the square, two stores beyond Latin Patriarchate St., is a very beautiful alley with hints of its former class. The alley is entered through an arch with the word "Versavee" above it. In the 1800's, the East New Imperial Hotel on this alley was regarded as the classy hotel of Jerusalem.

As you proceed across the square, a tower can be seen on your right at the northeast corner of the Citadel ❷.

When you enter the city through the Jaffa Gate, you are actually standing on top of a hill with a valley on either side. Outside the city and beneath the entrance to Jaffa Gate is the beginning of the Hinnom Valley. Inside the city is the gradual descent towards the Central or Tyropoeon Valley. The Hasmonean John Hyrcanus I was the first to build a fortress on top of this hill. It was part of the city wall and provided protection to the westward expansion of the city, as well as the western gate into the city. Herod considerably improved the fortress. He also erected a large and magnificent palace close to the fortress and adjacent to the western city wall in what is now the Armenian Quarter.

There are no remains of Herod's palace, although one of the towers is still standing within the Tower of David complex. The fortress originally had three towers, one of which he named after his dead and beloved brother Phasael, another after Mariamme his former wife whom he had put to death, and the Hippicus tower was probably named after a friend who was commander of the cavalry. When the Romans conquered Jerusalem, they left the towers standing as a monument to their prowess. Rebelling Jews destroyed Herod's palace during the revolt.

The tower still standing is probably the Phasael Tower. Only the foundations of the two other towers remain. The lower stones of this remaining tower are Herodian, as can be seen from their beveled edges. The upper building blocks appear different and are medieval additions. This was once a massive construction, and what remains is now only a bit more than half the size it was at the time of Herod. The upper part of the towers contained lavish living quarters with pools and baths.

The fortress was restored during the Byzantine period, severely damaged during the Persian invasion of 614 CE, and rebuilt again by the Mamlukes. The dry moat around the Citadel was added by the Crusaders. The rest of the Citadel is Ottoman and was built by Suleiman the Magnificent based on its previous Crusader design. The minaret was added by

Herod's fortress and palace by the western wall of the city
(Photo courtesy of the Tower of David Museum)

the Ottomans in the 16th century. The Citadel remained a Turkish military installation until the time of the British conquest.

It now very appropriately contains a museum showing the history of Jerusalem – appropriate because this fortress has played a significant part in Jerusalem's history.

Proceed straight ahead to the Arab shuk on David St.

2. The next part of this walk will bring you to the Christian Quarter and the courtyard of the Church of the Holy Sepulcher. If you would like to shorten the walk, continue along David St. and pick up the walk at the next section:

Take the first street on your left, Christian Quarter St. Turn right onto St. Helena Rd, which is signposted as being in the direction of the Church of the Holy Sepulcher. Follow the curve of the street past the Mosque of Omar ❸, go under the arch, and then down the steps to the courtyard of the Church of the Holy Sepulcher ❹.

What is a mosque doing in the Christian Quarter and so close to the Church of the Holy Sepulcher? Tradition has it that when the Moslem Caliph Omar ibn al-Khattab entered Jerusalem after the surrender of the Byzantines, the Patriarch offered him the right to pray in the church. He refused, explaining that if he did so he would need to confiscate the church and turn it into a mosque. Instead, he prayed outside the church and the "Mosque of Omar" was later built on the spot where he prayed. The present mosque dates to the 15th century; the 12th century mosque was destroyed in an earthquake.

According to Christian tradition, the Church of the Holy Sepulcher is the site of Jesus' crucifixion, burial and resurrection. It is the most sacred site for all Christian denominations and sects except for Protestants who dispute the church being at the correct location. Golgotha, where Jesus was crucified, was at that time outside the walls of Jerusalem. After the Bar Kochba Revolt, the Roman Emperor Hadrian razed the city and rebuilt it as a Roman city called Aelia Capitolina. He also built a temple at this site, now within his city, dedicated to the goddess Venus, possibly to cover up the cave in which Jesus had been buried and thereby prevent early Christians from visiting it.

During the rule of the Roman emperor Constantine the Great, Christianity became legalized in the Roman Empire instead of being a persecuted religion. Constantine subsidized a visit to Aelia Capitolina by his mother Helena, who was a devote Christian. She put much effort into locating the site of Jesus' crucifixion and burial. Digging underneath Hadrian's temple, Helena's workmen discovered Jesus' tomb and the three crosses on which he and the two criminals had been crucified. On Constantine's orders, shrines were built above these, and he built a church for this complex. This would become the Church of the Holy Sepulcher. The church subsequently suffered damage from earthquake, fire and Arab destruction. Repairs were made, but when the Crusaders conquered Jerusalem in 1099, they found the church in need of extensive renovations. They therefore rebuilt the church and moved the entrance to its western side, where it is today.

The two gateways and facade of the church are therefore of Crusader origin. You can also see a small wooden ladder under the second window to the right, which has been there for over two hundred years. How so? The Muslims blocked the entranceway on the right when they captured the city from the Crusaders, and they only permitted the church to open on special holidays. The ladder by the window was used to bring food to the monks locked inside. The church has been managed by six Christian churches since the decree of the Ottoman Sultan Osman III in the 18th century and they have been unable to agree what should be done with the ladder!

After viewing the entrance to the Church of the Holy Sepulcher and possibly entering it, exit the courtyard through the small archway on the right side of the wall ahead.

Continue straight ahead for a short distance, and then turn right under an elaborate arch into Suq Aftimos, the Aftimos Market.

The Greek Orthodox Patriarchate built up this area at the beginning of the 1900's as part of their Muristan Complex. Muristan is Persian/Turkish for hospital, and it was called this because a Crusader church and hospital for pilgrims run by the Knights Hospitaller, a Christian military order, was located here. It is now a typical Old City market and restaurant area.

Continue to the elaborate-looking fountain ❺.

The Turks erected this fountain in 1898 in honor of the visit of Kaiser Wilhelm. It is located on the path the Kaiser took from Jaffa Gate to the nearby site where the Lutheran Church of the Redeemer would be built. The Kaiser laid the cornerstone for this church.

Just before the fountain take the first left and exit this area by another arch onto Muristan Rd. Turn right and pass through vaults above which is the sign of an eagle. This was the symbol of the German Empire; these vaults may have been part of a construction the Kaiser intended to build. This is obviously as far as he got. Exit Muristan Rd. by turning left onto David St.

3. Continuation of the walk into the Jewish Quarter:

Just before the metal roof over David St. where it becomes a vaulted one, turn right onto Habad St. for a rooftop view of the Old City ❻. After passing a few stores you will see a grey metal stairway on the left that leads to the rooftops. From this vantage point, you have a wonderful view of the Temple Mount and all four quarters of the Old City. Climb up the steps and platforms to the highest point for the best view.

Behind you as you face the Temple Mount and to your left are the spires and domes of the churches of the Christian Quarter. In front of you and on your left are the roofs of the Muslim Quarter. In front of you to your right is the Jewish Quarter with its newer buildings, and behind you are the houses of the Armenian Quarter.

When did these four quarters come into being? They were already established in the Mamluke period, were in place during the Ottoman period, and were officially recognized by the British during their Mandate. Nevertheless, these neighborhoods have always been mixed. There are mosques in the Christian Quarter, and churches in the Via Dolorosa in the Muslim Quarter. Jews have also lived in the Moslem and Christian Quarters. Walking in the Moslem Quarter, you may notice Israeli flags fluttering on Jewish buildings.

In the distance on the Mount of Olives Ridge you can see three projections. To the far left is the water tower of the Hebrew University on Mount Scopus. A bit further to the right is the Augusta Victoria Complex, which was built by the German Kaiser as a hostel and sanatorium for German pilgrims. It now includes the Augusta Victoria Hospital providing specialty medical care. To the right of this, in the village of A-Tur, you can see the spire of the Russian Church of the Ascension where Christians believe that Jesus ascended to heaven after his resurrection. To the right of this is the Mount of Olives Jewish cemetery and above it is the Seven Arches Hotel.

Return to David St. and turn right. This road soon turns to the right, and then turns almost immediately to the left where it becomes Chain Gate St.

Take the next alleyway/street on the right (the street after Jewish Quarter Rd.), which is Plugat Hakotel St. Follow the turns of this alleyway and soon before you, protected by black metal railings, is the Broad Wall ❼.

This wall was built by King Hezekiah in the late 8th century BCE in anticipation of an attack by the Assyrian king Sennacherib – and a siege did happen. From the map displayed on the retaining wall behind the Broad Wall you can appreciate that Hezekiah's wall protected the northernmost expansion of Jerusalem, which by that time had expanded to the middle of today's Jewish Quarter. Throughout its history, the northern approach to Jerusalem has been its most vulnerable, as the Kidron and Hinnom Valleys provide natural protection for the rest of the city.

The city wall Hezekiah built was broad (seven meters in this section) and tall (eight meters). The curve is because of the topography of the valley. To your right, notice that the Broad Wall cuts through the ruins of a house. To complete the wall, Hezekiah had to demolish some houses, and this house may well be one of the buildings that the prophet Isaiah referred to when he said disapprovingly: *"You counted the houses of Jerusalem and you demolished the houses to fortify the wall"* (Isaiah 22:10).

Follow the railings to the right and at the corner turn right. The row of red tiles on the street indicates where the First Temple wall continues underneath the street. Go under the brick arch on the continuation of Plugat Hakotel St., passing the dormitory of Yeshivat Netiv Aryeh. Very soon you will reach a T-junction with Jewish Quarter St. Ahead and just slightly to your right are steps leading down through an open black gate to The Cardo.

The word Cardo in Latin means "heart" and the Cardo was the heart of the Roman city Aelia Capitolina. Jewish Jerusalem was destroyed by the Romans after the Great Revolt of 70 CE. After the Jews revolted again during the Bar Kochba Revolt, the emperor Hadrian obliterated all Jewish vestiges of Jerusalem and rebuilt it as a Roman city. It was built in a typical Roman grid fashion. The central Cardo was the main marketing thoroughfare and it bisected the city from Damascus Gate in the north to Zion Gate in the south. The southernmost part of the Cardo was completed in the Byzantine period, probably to link up the Church of the Holy Sepulcher to the Nea Church.

This section of the Cardo was part of the Roman city of Aelia Capitolina

Having no bulldozers, builders in the past built new structures on top of the old, so that the levels of streets in Jerusalem progressively rose. Based on the Byzantine Madaba map of Jerusalem (see next page), Israeli archaeologists suspected that the Cardo was in this location. They dug down and they found it.

Turn right when you reach the level of the Cardo and you will come to two well-like structures in the center of the street ❽.

These are exploratory shafts dug by archaeologists. At the bottom of the first shaft is a continuation of the First Temple wall. Within the second shaft are First and Second Temple walls. Continue a bit further along the Cardo and on the left are more remains of the First Temple wall and at its side is a Hasmonean Second Temple wall.

Their continuation underneath the road is indicated by red tiles for the First Temple wall and black tiles for the Hasmonean wall. These walls indicate the northernmost limit of the city in First Temple and Hasmonean Second Temple times. On top of the walls is a Roman column from the time of the Cardo. We will soon see a lot more of these columns. This part of the Cardo was used later by the Crusaders as a market.

Retrace your steps and walk along the Cardo, now in a southerly direction. There are many quality stores here. When the stores end, continue ahead under a brick arch to a wider section of the Cardo.

Outdoor malls are not a new invention. From here it is possible to visualize how the Cardo would have looked in Byzantine times. On each side of the road was a walkway at a slightly higher level than the road. Pillars extended the length of the Cardo and supported a roof covered with tiles that provided shade and protection from the rain for pedestrians and shoppers. In a section where the pillars are reasonably intact, a wooden frame has been placed on a few of the pillars to demonstrate how the roof covering would have looked. On your right, notice a very realistic mural of the Cardo of Byzantine times. In the left lower corner is an image of the mayor of Jerusalem, Teddy Kollek, and his two architects, all dressed appropriately for the times. This joke is rather hollow, though. In Roman and Byzantine times, Jews would not have been allowed to enter the city, and this would no doubt have included Teddy Kollek. On your left are mosaic representations of typical stores of that period.

Go through the passageway ahead to view a replica of the Madaba Map ❾ on the wall in a small section of the Cardo.

The Madaba map was discovered in Madaba in Jordan in 1884. It was part of a mosaic floor of a church from 6th century Byzantine times and showed a map of Israel, Jordan, and parts of the Negev. The map of Jerusalem provides a bird's eye view of the location of the important Christian institutions in Byzantine Jerusalem, although it is not drawn to scale. (Byzantia is the name given to the eastern part of the Roman Empire that became Christian at the time of the emperor Constantine the Great).

The map is titled in Latin "The Holy City of Jerusalem." The site of the destroyed Temple is not on the map since it had no importance to Christianity. In fact, its destruction confirmed the degradation of the Jews and the validity of Christianity. Interestingly, in ancient times, east was upwards, since east was considered the prime direction. The Magnetic North Pole was not discovered until 1831 by James Clark Ross, a commander in the British Navy. This makes it a bit tricky trying to orientate yourself to the buildings in the map.

The Cardo is represented by the central line with pillars on either side. In the center of the map is an upside-side-down 3-D representation of the Church of the Holy Sepulcher. To the left (i.e., to the north) is the Damascus Gate. A single column can be seen within the Damascus Gate. Damascus Gate is known in Arabic as Bab el Amud (translated as "Gate of the Column"). In the Roman period there was a single column just inside the gate. This probably supported a statue of the Roman emperor. To the far right (south) of the map is the Church of Holy Zion (Hagin Sion Church), which is where the Dormition Abbey is today. At the right-hand end of the Cardo is the Nea Church. The ruins of this church can be seen today adjacent to the Jewish Quarter parking lot.

Continue through another passage ahead to the open part of the Byzantine Cardo. Exit the Cardo by taking the stairs up to Jerusalem Quarter Rd.

The pillars of the Byzantine Cardo

4. Continuation of the walk as a circular one to the Jaffa Gate:

Cross over the Cardo by the walkway on your left and continue ahead to Ohr Ha-Hayim St. This road becomes St. James St. At its end, turn right onto Armenian Orthodox Patriarchate Rd. and this will lead you back to Jaffa Gate.

Nearby Places of Interest:

The Tower of David Museum and **The Sound and Light Spectacular** is located in the medieval citadel known as the Tower of David, which is close to Jaffa Gate. It contains exhibits on the history of Jerusalem. The exhibits are in the medieval guardrooms and present the main events of the city's history in a chronological sequence beginning with the Canaanite period and continuing until Jerusalem became the capital of the State of Israel. The museum is open 9 am–4 pm (9 am–5 pm in August), 9 am–2 pm on Friday (until 4 pm in August), and 9 am–4 pm on Saturday (until 5 pm in August). Tours are offered in English Sunday to Thursday at 11 am, and on Friday at 11 am. There are no tours on holidays or holiday eves. The tour is included in the admission price. You can sign up on line for this. In the event you have no escort guide, you are provided with a complementary audio guide. This has thirty-five stops and takes sixty to ninety minutes. A large part of the exhibition is accessible for people with mobility problems and wheelchairs. There is also a tour of the remains of King Herod's Palace and the Kishle in English every Friday at 10.00 am. The Sound and Light Night Spectacular at the Citadel presents the story of Jerusalem through virtual reality images. It runs for forty-five minutes. There is a charge. Book online or reserve in advance by calling (02) 626-5333 or *2884. Times of the show are also provided at this phone number. Tickets on the night of the show are subject to availability. The show is wheelchair accessible.

The Western Wall: Cross Hurva Square, and at its far left is Tiferet Israel Rd. Continue straight and go down the steps on Ma'alot Rabbi Yehuda HaLevi. This leads to the security check for the Western Wall.

Herodian Quarter Wohl Archaeological Museum at 1 Hakara'im St: Turn into Hakara'im St. from the Hurva Square and you will soon see the museum on your right. Before a building project begins in Israel, an archaeological dig is usually carried out first, if there is a possibility of ruins being present. The ruins of upper-class mansions and houses belonging to priests from the Herodian period were discovered here. On completion of the archaeological dig, the ruins were preserved and Yeshivat Hakotel was built on top of the ruins. The museum demonstrates the considerable wealth of the priestly class at the end of the Second Temple period. These mansions are believed to have belonged to priests because of their location, their splendor, and the many ritual baths within the homes. Almost all of the floors were covered with mosaics. Some of these can still be seen, as well as some stucco paintings on the walls. The exhibits show stone utensils, used by the priests because they did not transmit ritual impurity. Notice also the figurines found on location, evidence that idol worship was rife within the city. The museum is open Sunday to Thursday 9 am–5 pm, and Fridays and festival eves 9 am–1 pm. Their phone number is: (02) 625-5906.

The Temple Institute at 40 Misgav Ladach St., off Tiferet Israel Rd. The museum researches into the Jewish Temples of the past and prepares for the Temple of the future. The results of their research are shown. Vessels and instruments that could be used in a rebuilt Holy Temple are displayed: scale models of the Second Temple, the outer Altar, the Ark of the Covenant, and oil paintings portraying daily life in the Holy Temple. There is a gift shop specializing in publications, films and educational material about the Temple. The museum is open Sunday to Thursday 9 am–5 pm, Friday 9 am–12 pm, and is closed on Shabbat and Festivals. There is an admission charge. Their phone number is: (02) 654-1255.

The Burnt House (Beit Katros) at 2 Tiferet Israel Rd. This house was burnt down when the Romans destroyed the city in 70 CE. A stone weight was found here with the Aramaic inscription "D'Bar Katros" – which means "belonging to Bar Katros," and this enabled identification of the owner of the property. The Talmud is not at all flattering about Bar Katros and other priestly families: "...Woe unto me from the House of Katros, woe unto me from their quills... for they are high priests, their sons are treasurers, their son-in-laws are executives, and their servants beat people with sticks (Pesachim 57a). The Talmud considered these priests to have abused their positions, an indication of the corruption of the priesthood at that time. Also shown in the museum are the personal effects of a young lady, including the sword that might have killed her. A bone from her arm was also found. Her bone was buried, but there is a photo shown of how they found it. A movie is also shown. Tickets can be purchased at the door or a combined ticket obtained at the Wohl Archaeological Museum. The museum is open Sunday to Thursday 9 am–5 pm, Friday 9 am–1 pm, and is closed on Shabbat and holidays. Their phone number is: (02) 626-5906.

Time Elevator Jerusalem at Yitshak Kariv St. 6 on Alrov Mamilla Avenue. Enter a time capsule and take a twenty-five minute journey into 3000 years of Jerusalem's history. You truly get the feeling that it is you rather than the screens on all sides that are moving. Simultaneous translations are available in Hebrew, English and other languages. Open Sunday to Thursday 10 am–5.20 pm and Friday 10 am–2 pm. There is an admission charge. Tickets must be purchased in advance through their box office or web site. Their phone number is (02) 264-8381 and e-mail maalit1@ terminal-jerusalem.co.il.

3 The Jewish Quarter –
COMMUNITY BUILDING, DESTRUCTION AND RENEWAL

The Hurva Synagogue

TIME: About two hours of walking, but half a day if visiting synagogues and museums

DISTANCE: 3 km

TYPE OF WALK: Circular

DIFFICULTY: An easy walk.

STARTING POINT:
Bus stop adjacent to the (private) northern parking lot for the Jewish Quarter at Tiferet Yerushalayim Square. The walk can finish at either the Jaffa Gate or the starting point.

PUBLIC TRANSPORTATION:
Several buses stop at the Jewish Quarter parking lot. Enter "חניון הרובע היהודי הצפוני" into Moovit.

PARKING:
Karta Parking is on Yitzhak Kariv St. close to its intersection with highway 60. This is just a short distance from the Jaffa Gate. Enter "חניון קרתה" into Waze.

Groups of Jews have been settling in Jerusalem from the Jewish diaspora for the last 750 years. Upon arrival, they invariably built a Synagogue, and these Synagogues provide a window into the Jewish communities that immigrated here. Two weeks after the State of Israel was declared, the Jewish Quarter was captured by the Jordanians and systematically destroyed. Following the Six Day War and the reunification of Jerusalem, the Jewish Quarter was rebuilt and many of its damaged Synagogues restored. As we admire the old-world beauty of the streets and alleys of the Jewish Quarter, we will attempt to take ourselves back in time to the Jewish communities that settled here.

Sephardim, Ashkenazim, Hasidim, and Perushim/Misnagdim

Over the last seven centuries, four groups of Jews emigrated to Palestine from the Jewish diaspora. "Sephardim" came from Spain, Portugal and North Africa, and "Ashkenazim" from northern and central Europe. In the 18th century, the Ashkenazi community was split by the development of a new revivalist movement called *"Hasidism"* that followed the teachings of their leader Rabbi Yisrael Baal Shem Tov and adopted a more spiritual and kabbalistic approach to Judaism. Ashkenazim who rejected these new ideas and followed Hasidism's chief opponent, the Vilna Gaon, were called *"Perushim"* or *"Misnagdim."*

Although Jews were coming from different countries, they observed the same Torah laws, with various differences in customs, lifestyles, and wording of prayer. Until fairly recently, these communities kept somewhat apart in terms of where they lived and where they prayed. Much of this can be explained by comfort level, but it was indirectly promoted by the *"kollelim"* (plural of *kollel*).

There were almost no economic opportunities in Jerusalem. Plus, these Jews came to Jerusalem specifically to engage in Torah learning. They were therefore supported financially by donations from their country of origin via the kollelim. Nevertheless, there was a strong unifying factor for all four communities in that they all believed in the value of living in Palestine. Many of the followers of the Vilna Gaon also held that their moving to this country would further the redemption of the Jewish people from their dispersion and lead to the eventual coming of the Messiah.

RECREATING THE HISTORY OF THE JEWISH QUARTER THROUGH ITS SYNAGOGUES

Prior to the destruction of Jerusalem by the Romans there was no such thing as a Jewish Quarter as the city was totally Jewish. Following the destruction of Jerusalem in 70 CE, Jews were banished from the city, and this remained the situation for several hundred years. There was a small Jewish community in today's Muslim Quarter during the First Muslim Period, but it was totally destroyed during the Crusader conquest of 1099 CE.

The beginning of today's Jewish Quarter can be dated to 1267 CE, when the Ramban (Nachmanides), the great Biblical commentator and leader, arrived in Jerusalem after being expelled from Spain following his successful debate against the apostate Jew, priest Pablo Christiani. The Ramban had always held that making aliyah to Israel was a Biblical command and that the practice of Judaism in Israel was at a much higher level than in any other country. Nevertheless, to emigrate from Spain alone without his family at the age of seventy-two was an incredibly brave thing to do. Jerusalem was then in ruins as a result of the Mongol invasion of 1244. The Mongols had been defeated by the Mamlukes, and the Mamluke sultan encouraged the Ramban to restore a Jewish Quarter.

Arriving in Jerusalem seven years after the defeat of the Mongols, the Ramban found only two Jews living in the city. Not discouraged, he converted an abandoned building on Mount Zion into a synagogue and gathered a minyan (prayer quorum) for Sabbath prayers. The Ramban Synagogue visited on this walk is not the Ramban's original synagogue, but dates to a later period when Jews moved inside the city walls following a dispute with Christians over property rights on Mount Zion. The new synagogue continued to bear his name because of his contributions to the community. For some time, this was the only synagogue for the two thousand or so Sephardi and Ashkenazi Jews in Jerusalem.

Did you notice a mosque close to the Ramban Synagogue and wondered what it was doing there? A prominent Jew had a disagreement with the community and converted to Islam. His mother was so annoyed with the community that she

FREE SHUTTLE:
There is a free shuttle both ways from the parking lot at the First Station to Dung Gate. Enter into Waze "First Station Parking Lot." After three hours, there is a charge for parking. There is free parking just beyond the gas station and adjoining parking lot on Emek Refaim St. with no time limit.

The shuttle bus leaves on the hour and every twenty minutes thereafter. Buses operate on Sunday, Tuesday and Wednesday 8 am–8 pm, Monday and Thursday 7 am–8 pm, and Friday 8 am to 1 hour before Shabbat. There is no shuttle on Shabbat.

The interior of the Yohanan ben Zakai Synagogue, one of the Four Synagogues

dedicated her house, which was very close to the courtyard of the synagogue, to the Muslim religious authorities to build a mosque. This mosque would cause considerable problems for the synagogue and eventually led to its closure.

The Ottomans captured Jerusalem from the Mamlukes in 1516 and the Ottoman sultan encouraged Jewish families previously expelled from Spain and Portugal to settle here. However, in 1589, the Ramban Synagogue was closed down by the Turkish governor of Jerusalem because of its proximity to the mosque and the community was left without a place of worship. The building was converted into a stable and then used for other functions to the point that people no longer remembered it as a place of prayer. It was only after the Six Day War that it was converted back again into a synagogue.

To accommodate the growing Sephardi community, the first of the Four Sephardi synagogues, the Yohanan Ben Zakai Synagogue, was built in the early 1600's. For some time, there had not been a functioning synagogue in the city and people were praying privately.

The Ashkenazi community was extremely small and their synagogue was the Menachem Zion Synagogue in the

Ashkenazi neighborhood, north of the former Ramban Synagogue. This was the synagogue of the "Shelah Hakadosh," the first Ashkenazi Chief Rabbi of Jerusalem who came to Jerusalem in 1622. However, he was hounded by the Ottoman authorities and forced to flee.

The Ashkenazi population increased in 1700, when Rabbi Yehuda Ha-Hasid arrived from Poland with a group of about one hundred disciples. He and his followers believed that their coming to Jerusalem would hasten the coming of the Messiah. They immediately borrowed money from local Arabs to build a Synagogue. However, Rabbi Yehuda died tragically a few days later and the group soon found itself in financial straits and unable to repay the loan. After twenty years the Muslim lenders lost their patience and burnt the synagogue and its forty Torah scrolls. Ashkenazi Jews were forced to flee the city and were banned from returning to Jerusalem. The courtyard of the destroyed synagogue became known as the "Hurvat Rabbi Yehuda Ha-Hasid" (Rabbi Yehuda Ha-Hasid's ruin).

Ashkenazi Jews did not return to the city until 1816, when a small group of followers of the Vilna Gaon obtained permission from the Egyptian ruler Mohammad Ali to move from Tzfat to Jerusalem. They collected enough money to repay the Ashkenazi community's debts and rebuilt the Menachem Zion Synagogue on the edge of the Ashkenazi courtyard.

This small synagogue was eventually unable to accommodate the growing Ashkenazi community and Sir Moses Montefiore obtained permission to erect a new building. This was completed in 1875 on the original site of Rabbi Yehuda Ha-Hasid's building. This imposing domed structure was officially called "Beit Ya'akov" after Baron Jacob (Ya'akov) Rothschild, but it was popularly known as the "Hurva" (ruin). It rapidly became the center of the non-Hasidic Ashkenazi community.

This beautiful synagogue was blown up by the Jordanians a day before the surrender of the Jewish Quarter in May 1948, and it once again became a ruin. After the Old City was liberated in 1967, only one arch of the synagogue was rebuilt, and this arch became a symbol of the Jewish Quarter. However, in 2010, a replica of the original building was built using photographs and original building plans from the central planning office in Istanbul, and this synagogue is now once again the Jewish Quarter's main Ashkenazi place of worship.

Hasidic Ashkenazi Jews began moving to Jerusalem in the early 1800's. Their synagogue, also a very impressive building, was called *Tiferet Israel* and it was inaugurated in 1872. It too was destroyed during the 1948 War of Independence and is presently in ruins, although there are now plans to rebuild it.

Many Jewish Quarter buildings were destroyed or severely damaged by the Jordanians after the 1948 War of Independence. After the Six Day War, a special agency was tasked with rebuilding the Jewish Quarter with the aim of recreating its quaintness, while at the same time constructing modern, comfortable living accommodation. As you stroll through the Jewish Quarter, you will almost certainly agree that these aims were admirably achieved.

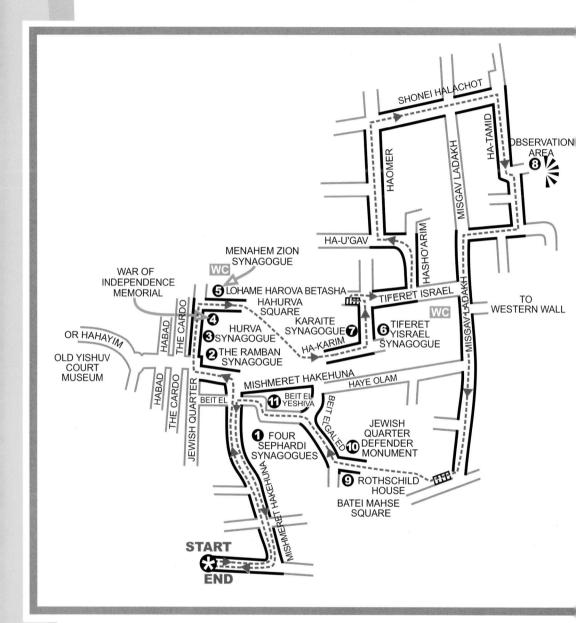

Walk towards the Sephardic House Hotel on Mishmerot Ha-Kehuna St. at the north-eastern end of the parking lot and this street will take you to the Four Sephardi Synagogues ❶ on the right-hand side of the road. They are worth entering. (For admission details see page 42).

The Four Sephardi Synagogues are a group of four interconnected synagogues built at different times. Their entrances are below ground level, since the Muslim authorities required synagogues to be built in a lowly state. They were severely damaged by the Jordanians after the 1948 War of Independence but were rebuilt after the Six Day War. The arks and other furniture were brought from old synagogues from Spain and Italy, but apart from this the recreated interior is that of former times.

The first synagogue you will enter is the Yohanan ben Zakai Synagogue, named after the Second Temple sage Rabbi Yohanan ben Zakai. It was the chief synagogue for the Sephardi community and was also used for important community events. It is still used as such by the Old City Sephardi community. Note the double ark at the front, which is similar to and may have been inspired by the double ark of the Ramban Synagogue. Note also the shofar and jug of oil on a ledge on the right-hand wall. The synagogue has a tradition that they will be used to announce and anoint the Messiah, although these are not the originals that were placed here.

Continuing straight ahead from the entrance brings you to the Eliyahu Ha-Navi Synagogue. According to a tradition, it received this name because one year there were only nine men present for prayers on the eve of Yom Kippur, until an old man appeared to complete the quorum. At the end of the service they looked around to invite him to break the fast, but he had disappeared. They realized that this had been none other than Elijah the Prophet. The synagogue was built in the early 1600's, around the same time as the Yohanan Ben Zakai Synagogue, and may have been used initially as an academy. In its left-hand corner is a large alcove with steps leading to "Elijah's Cave" where there is a chair reserved exclusively for the prophet. There is also a "Groom's Chair" probably brought here by Spanish exiles in the 16th century. The ark is not the original but was brought from an historic synagogue in Italy. Otherwise, except for the decorations around the ark, its original style has been maintained.

The "Middle Synagogue" was built in what was originally the courtyard between these two synagogues and was used for prayer when extra space was needed. The photographs on its walls show the original decorations of the synagogues and the destruction discovered when people returned after the Six Day War.

The last synagogue to be built here was the Istanbuli Synagogue, built by immigrants from Constantinople/Istanbul in Turkey in the 1700's. It is the largest of the four synagogues.

After exiting the synagogues, turn right on Meshmeret Ha-Kehuna St. After passing under the arch you are in Ha-Hurva Square and the Hurva Synagogue ❸ is in front of you. The Ramban Synagogue ❷ is at the southwest corner of this synagogue, below ground level, and is also in front of you. It was built below ground level for the same reason as the Four Sephardi Synagogues. There are usually yeshiva students studying inside the building, but this should not deter males from walking down the steps and paying an unobtrusive visit.

From inside the synagogue you can see that there are twin Torah arks. Most synagogues have only one ark. This arrangement is probably because of the row of pillars in the middle of the building. The double ark allows all worshippers to see at least one of the arks. The pillars were "borrowed" from the Byzantine Cardo. This type of reuse has been a common practice in the Old City.

From the Ramban Synagogue go to the back of this building to Jewish Quarter Rd. and turn right towards the "Courtyard of the Ashkenazim." The Ashkenazi community used to live around this courtyard. You will soon pass the entrance to the Hurva

Synagogue ❸. If you wish, you can enter this building, and even take a tour. There is a charge for both (see page 42 for admission details).

The Hurva Synagogue was the main Ashkenazi non-Hasidic synagogue until the fall of the Jewish Quarter in 1948. In the early years of the British Mandate, Sir Herbert Samuel was appointed the first British High Commissioner of Palestine. On Shabbat Nachamu, the Sabbath following the fast of Tisha B'av that commemorates the destruction of the two Jewish Temples, he was honored during the Sabbath service, in this synagogue, with *maftir* (the honor of being called up to the Torah, that is followed by reading the *haftarah*, a section of the Prophets.) The *haftarah* of Shabbat Nachamu begins with the words "*Be consoled my people....*"(Isaiah 40:1-26), which describes the rebuilding of Jerusalem. The entire congregation of the synagogue became very emotional and wept when he began his chanting since he was perceived as being an agent of this prophecy. The synagogue was blown up by the Jordanians after the 1948 war. After the reunification of Jerusalem, it was left in ruins and only its arch was rebuilt to memorialize its history. Recently, the synagogue has been completely rebuilt.

At the corner of Jewish Quarter Rd. and the next street on the right, Lokhamei HaRova BeTashakh St., is the War of Independence Memorial ❹. It contains photographs and also an excellent and quite moving movie about the battle for the Jewish Quarter during the War of Independence.

Did you know that when the defenders of the Jewish Quarter surrendered, there were only twenty to twenty-five fighters remaining? The Jordanians were so embarrassed that it had taken their fighters so long to beat such a small number of combatants, that they took additional civilians as prisoners of war to increase the numbers. The movie is in Hebrew, but subtitles are available in four languages, including in English.

On the other side of Lokhamei HaRova BeTashakh St. are stairs that lead up one floor to a plaza. The restored Menachem Zion Synagogue ❺ is on the left of the plaza.

The Menachem Zion Synagogue was constructed in the 1600's and was the first synagogue to be built by the Ashkenazi community. It was rebuilt by the followers of the Vilna Gaon when they returned to Jerusalem in the early 1800's. Also on this plaza, ahead of you, is the Eitz Chaim Yeshiva. This was once the largest yeshiva in Jerusalem. However, it relocated close to the shuk in Nachla'ot in 1937 because of the Arab riots. During the time of the British Mandate, there were periodic Arab riots from 1920 onwards. As a result of this, many people moved out of the Old City, and the Jewish Quarter became considerably reduced in size.

Turn right on Lokhamei HaRova BeTashakh St. in the direction of Ha-Hurva Square. On reaching the Square, cross it diagonally towards the right to Hakara'im St. by the Wohl Archaeological Museum. Walking along this road, you will see the ruins of the Tiferet Yisrael Synagogue ❻ ahead of you.

This synagogue was built by Hasidic Ashkenazi Jews in 1843. It was an impressive domed building, as the Hasidic Jews no doubt wanted their synagogue to be as imposing as the Hurva. It also was blown up by the Jordanians shortly after the surrender of the Jewish Quarter during the War of Independence.

The Karaite Synagogue ❼ is on your left, and it too can be visited (see page 42 for admission details).

One of the many quaint alleys in the restored Jewish Quarter

The Karaite Synagogue is the oldest functioning synagogue in Jerusalem. According to the tradition of the Karaites, it was built in the 8th century CE by their founder Hakham Anan ben-David after he left Babylon to settle in Jerusalem.

Karaite Jews do not accept the authority of the Oral Law as developed in the Mishnah and Talmud by the Jewish sages, but only that of the Bible, including the Prophets and Writings. Because of this, their laws and customs often differ significantly from the practices of Rabbinic Judaism. Nevertheless, the movement has always been very Zionistic. Jerusalem was the international center for Karaites during the First Muslim Period between the 9th to 11th centuries CE when they constituted the majority of Jews in Jerusalem.

Karaite Judaism was once a very influential movement. When Maimonides moved to Alexandria in Egypt, for example, he came to a predominantly Karaite community. Nowadays, it is a small and diminishing community, with about thirty thousand to fifty thousand Karaites living in Israel and a few small communities in other countries. Their main center is in Ramla, and there is also a Karaite community in Ashdod. This synagogue was damaged in 1948 but restored by the Karaite community after the Six Day War.

Go down the steps at the end of this road and at the bottom of the steps turn right onto Tiferet Israel St. Take the second left onto Hasho'arim St. just before the arch.

Almost immediately Hasho'arim St. forks into two. Take the left-hand street, Ha-U'gav Rd., and then the first street on the right after this, which is Ha'Omer St. This street winds under a series of arches. When it comes to a junction with Shonei Halakhot St. turn right and walk down the steps on Shonei Halakhot St. At the end of this road you will come to a large plaza overlooking the Western Wall. But don't take all your photos here, as there are better ones to come!

By the railings at the end of the plaza, take the steps up Ha-Tamid St. and you will soon come to a lookout area **❽** that provides a superior view over the Western Wall.

Continue along Ha-Tamid St., passing the Aish Hatorah World Center on your left. It is possible to go up to their Rooftop Observation Deck (see page 42 for admission details).

Immediately after the Aish Hatorah building, the street turns sharply right and continues up several flights of steps. [The narrow alley after the Aish Hatorah building on the left goes down to the Western Wall]. At the T-junction, turn left on Misgav Ladakh St.

Continue on Misgav Ladakh St. and cross Tiferet Israel St. On your left are the ruins of St. Mary's Hospice of the German Knights built by the Order of the Teutonic Knights during the Crusader Period. You will also pass the Temple Institute on your right.

Continue along Misgav Ladakh St. and pass under the arch of the Montefiore Hall. At the end of the street, at the T-junction, climb up the stairs on the right and this will bring you to Batei Mahse Square and **❾** the Rothschild House.

The land for this square was purchased by a Dutch and German kollel in 1857 for building "batei mahse" (sheltered housing)" for the poor. Apartments for rent were at a premium in the Jewish Quarter because of its rapidly increasing population, and when they became available, they were quickly snatched up, even though they were extremely small and of poor quality. This particular project elicited a lot of excitement as Jews were beginning to build on land they had bought, including outside the Old City, as a result of a change in Ottoman law. A number of apartment buildings were built within this square. Each apartment had two rooms, a kitchen and a hall, which was considered luxurious. The open space around the buildings was also unique for the Jewish Quarter. The apartments were alloted by lottery, with preference being given to Torah scholars: one third to members of the kollel, one third to Jews from Austro-Hungary, and one third to poor Jews regardless of origin. People were permitted to stay in their apartments rent-free for three years. The Jordanians destroyed the buildings after the surrender of the Old City in 1948.

The building on the west side of the square, the Rothschild House, was a particularly nice apartment building. It was built in 1871 with a donation from Baron Wilhelm Karl de Rothschild of Frankfurt. It was restored after the Six Day War. The Rothschild coat of arms can be seen at the center of the building. The pillars displayed in the square are from Second Temple times, although this is not their original location.

Go down the street to the left of the Rothschild House to a western entrance to the square and you will see an arch on which is engraved in Hebrew "Sheltered housing for the poor on Mount Zion." Then return to the square.

To the right of the square on a wall just before the steps is a plaque with a quotation from the prophet Zechariah: *"Old men and old women will once again sit in the streets of Jerusalem, each with his staff in his hand because of advanced age, and the streets of the city will be filled with boys and girls playing in the streets"* **(Zechariah 8:4-5).** Come here when the adjacent school is out and you will see the fulfillment of this prophecy.

Exit the square via the alleyway to the right of and adjacent to the Rothschild House, and you will soon come to the Jewish Quarter Defenders Monument **❿**.

The Rothschild House in Batei Mahse Square

This is a monument to the forty-eight people who died in defense of the Jewish Quarter during the War of Independence. They were buried in a communal grave in this spot, as it was impossible to take them outside the city during the conflict. After the war, the Jordanians refused to permit their internment. Following the liberation of the Jewish Quarter in 1967, they were reinterred on the Mount of Olives.

Turn right on Gal'ed St. and continue under a series of arches. At the next three-way intersection, turn left onto Beit-El Rd. This will lead you back to Mishmerot Ha-Kehuna St.

Are you ready to see one more religious building? At the corner of Beit-El Rd. and Mishmerot Ha-Kehuna St. is the Beit El Yeshiva **⓫**. You will easily recognize it because of its elaborately decorated silvery door. It was established in the mid-1700's as a prayer and kabbalist center for studying the kabbalistic works of the Ari Hakodesh who was born some two centuries earlier in what is now the Old Yishuv Museum. The building was restored after the Six Day War and is once again being used by married men for the study of kabbala.

To return to the bus stop at Tiferet Yerushalayim Square, turn left on Mishmerot Ha-Kehuna St. and this will lead you past the Four Sephardi Synagogues to the Jewish Quarter Parking lot. Alternatively, to go to the Jaffa Gate, cross over the Cardo on the steps to Ohr Ha-HayimSt. This road passes the Old Yishuv Museum, which you may well wish to visit (see next page for admission details). Ohr Ha-Hayim St. becomes St. James St. At its end, turn right onto Armenian Orthodox Patriachate Rd., and this will lead you directly to the Jaffa Gate.

Additional Details about Visiting the Synagogues and Old Yishuv Court Museum:

The Four Sephardi Synagogues at 18 Beit El. These synagogues are open for visitors during daylight hours from Sunday to Thursday. There is an entrance charge. The synagogues are open for worshippers on Friday and Shabbat free of charge. Their phone number is: (02) 628-0592.

The Hurva Synagogue: This synagogue has a very beautiful interior. Its Torah scrolls are contained within the world's tallest ark. You can also walk on the veranda of the dome for a 360 degree view of Jerusalem. The synagogue is open for visiting from 9 am–5 pm Sunday to Thursday, and 9 am–1 pm on Friday. The admission charge includes an audio-guided tour. A guided tour is also available for an additional charge. Their phone number is: 02-626-5906

The Karaite Synagogue on HaKara'im St. A movie about the Karaite community is shown. The synagogue is open Sunday to Thursday from 8 am–2 pm. There is an entrance fee. Their phone number is: (050) 573-3723.

Aish Hatorah on 6 HaTamid St has 50-minute tours that include the stunning chandeliers of the main hall, the roof that overlooks the Western Wall and Temple Mount, other roofs in the Old City, a model of the Temple, and multimedia presentations. Tours are from 9 am–5 pm Sunday to Thursday and should be booked in advance by calling (073) 229-3536. There is an entrance charge.

Old Yishuv Court Museum at 6 Ohr Ha-Hayim St. This museum is open Sunday to Thursday from December to February from 10 am–3 pm, and from March to November from 10 am–5pm. On Friday and festival evenings it is open from 10 am–1 pm. It is closed on Shabbat. There is an entrance fee. Their phone number is: (02) 627-6319. The courtyard was owned by the Weingarten family; Rabbi Weingarten and his wife lived in one of the adjoining rooms prior to the War of Independence. Returning to the building after the Six Day War, the family decided to turn it into a museum to display how people lived during the Ottoman period and British Mandate. The building is about five hundred years old. Two very old synagogues are also located in the courtyard and are part of the museum. One is named after Rabbi Isaac Luria, otherwise known as the "Holy Ari," who, according to local tradition, was born in one of the rooms of this house. The Ari was the most important leader of the kabbalists of Tzfat during the 16th century. The Ohr Ha-Chaim Synagogue is next to the Ari Synagogue. It was established in the 1700's as part of the yeshiva of Rabbi Haim Ben Atar from Morocco. Many Sephardi students studied in his yeshiva, and this is where he wrote his Biblical commentary Ohr Ha-Chaim; hence the name of this street.

4 The Jerusalem Archaeological Park, Davidson Center and Western Wall

TIME: Allow 2-3 hours

STARTING POINT:
The ticket office for the Jerusalem Archaeological Park adjacent to the Dung Gate. It is marked "Ticket Office and Tourist Information Center."

DIRECTIONS BY PUBLIC TRANSPORT:
There are buses from the Central Bus Station to Dung Gate. Enter "Dung Gate" into Moovit. Buses also stop at the Jewish Quarter parking lot (which is not a public parking lot), only a short distance from Dung Gate. Enter "חניון הרובע היהודי הצפוני" into Moovit.

FREE SHUTTLE FROM THE FIRST STATION: See page 9

PARKING: The closest parking is Karta Parking on Yitzhak Kariv St. close to its intersection with highway 60. This is just a short distance from the Jaffa Gate. Enter "חניון קרתה" into Waze.

ADMISSION: The Archaeological Park and Davidson Center are open Sunday to Thursday 8 am–5 pm, and on Friday and holiday eves 8 am–2 pm. They are closed on Shabbat and Jewish holidays. There is an English tour at 11am and Hebrew tour at 3 pm for an additional charge. On Friday and holiday eves, the Hebrew tour is at 9 am and the English tour at 11 am. An audio tour can be rented. Their phone number is: *4987.

The Jerusalem Archaeological Park is one of the foremost archaeological sites in the city. This short walk visits the Davidson Center, views the former southern gates of the Temple Mount, and explores the ruins of a main street of Jerusalem from Second Temple times. The walk ends at the Western Wall (the Kotel). Since they cover the same topic, the Overviews for this walk and for the Temple Mount can be studied together (see page 52).

OVERVIEWS

ENLARGING A MOUNTAIN – HEROD'S TEMPLE MOUNT

The Temple Mount had become too cramped for the number of pilgrims visiting Jerusalem, the Temple itself was in need of repairs, and the magnificence of the mansions in the Upper City were putting God's residence to shame. Thus, when Herod the Great proposed renovating the Temple compound and enlarging the Temple Mount, the Jewish people responded enthusiastically.

The Temple he built became one of the architectural wonders of the Roman world, and pilgrims and tourists came from throughout the Roman Empire to admire it. The Holy of Holies was covered with gold plate that dazzled from afar and the rest of the Temple was overlaid with white marble. The floor of the Temple Mount was tiled with blue-tinged marble that gave the impression of a moving sea of water. States the Talmud:

"One who was not privileged to see Herod's Temple never saw a magnificent building" (Bava Basra 4a).

All that remains of Herod's construction are the walls of his Temple Mount, and one cannot but be amazed at his boldness.

But how did he manage to enlarge a mountain?

The Hasmoneans had previously extended the Temple Mount and Herod enlarged it even further by creating an artificial platform around the mountain. The eastern side of the Temple Mount could not be extended because of the steepness of the Kidron Valley, but it was possible to extend the other three sides. To the west, Herod extended the Temple Mount platform into the Central or Tyropoeon Valley and the intervening space was filled with landfill. The southern aspect of the platform was extended using multiple arches.

Its northern aspect was expanded by joining the Antonian Hill to the Temple Mount and filling the area in between with landfill. The Antonia Fortress was on the Antonian Hill and it overlooked the Temple Mount. Its purpose was not only to protect the Temple Mount, but also to enable Herod to control the worshippers in the Temple. When completed, the Temple Mount platform had been doubled in size and was now equivalent in area to about twenty soccer fields.

The walls of this enlarged Temple Mount needed to be strong enough to prevent the entire edifice from collapsing and this was done by enclosing the platform with huge ashlars (a cut stone block). Each limestone block was of variable width and length but had a fixed height of one meter. The largest weighed over six hundred tons, although most were about twenty-eight tons. Each ashlar was decorated with a characteristic inset margin and smooth surface and was quarried and cut to fit exactly into its designated place.

The width of the wall of the Temple Mount was made up of three ashlars. Each was slightly inset one on top of the other to give the wall a slight pyramidal effect. The height of the wall was thirty-two meters from street level, although sections were even taller than this. Its foundations in the Central Valley, for example, were dug into bedrock for an additional twenty meters, giving the walls in this section a total height of fifty-two meters, or about seventeen stories. The foundations of this section can be seen when walking along the underground drainage tunnel that extends from the Davidson Center to the Pool of Siloam.

Herod also built a Royal Portico or basilica in the southern section of the Temple Mount. It is called the Royal Portico, not because it was for Herod's personal use but because of its grandeur. In fact, it may not have been completed by Herod's death. It consisted of four rows of columns, the southernmost columns being interwoven into the southern wall of the Temple Mount, thereby creating three large covered walkways that extended the full length of the southern wall. Its pillars were massive and topped with Corinthian capitals. It was used for administrative and financial purposes, including changing money and buying sacrifices. The Sanhedrin also met here at the end of the Second Temple period.

Access to the Royal Portico was via Robinson's arch, a large and impressive stairway and overpass that led from the main road in the Central Valley directly into the Royal Portico. A small part of this overpass is still visible. Non-Jewish visitors could enter into the Royal Portico, since it was not directly connected to the rest of the Temple Mount. There are no remains today of this basilica other than the tops of some of its columns. The al-Aqsa Mosque occupies some of the area in which it once stood.

The internal design of the Temple was left unchanged, although Herod increased its height. Priests specially trained in building were used for its renovation. So great was the enthusiasm of the people that it was completed within eighteen months, although the expansion of the Temple Mount took longer. Throughout all these renovations, the Temple service continued uninterrupted.

The Temple that Herod built lasted for less than a hundred years, but the Temple Mount he constructed has lasted over two thousand years. So solidly was it built, that the Romans were able to dislodge only a few upper ashlars after destroying the Temple.

HOW NOT TO WIN A GREAT REVOLT

The Great Revolt began seventy years after Herod's death and resulted in the destruction of the Temple and the razing of Jerusalem.

Herod the Great had run a semi-independent state and was trusted by Rome. During his reign, he managed to squeeze together a modus vivendi between the Jewish people and Rome by a combination of ruthlessness at any sign of dissent to his rule and accommodation to the messianic yearnings of the population. This included renovating the Temple on the Temple Mount. No one would be able to copy this; not his son Herod Antipas, who was eventually fired by Rome, nor the procurators subsequently appointed by Rome. Eventually, the country would descend into chaos.

A number of factors can be identified as leading to the revolt.

Some of the procurators were corrupt and insensitive to Jewish practice. The procurator Gessius Florus, in particular, almost goaded the Jews into revolt. He persuaded Nero to strip the Jews of Caesarea of their citizenship so that they were at the mercy of the Greco-Roman population. When the Jews revolted, their revolt was mercilessly put down. Three thousand and six hundred Jews were killed by his troops when they jeered at him. Jewish elders were flogged and crucified.

Religious and messianic zeal were also rife among much of the population. The Jewish group most active in this struggle was the Zealots who advocated armed revolt against Rome. Another violent group called the Sicarii directed their violence against Jews who supported Rome. These groups no doubt imagined that following a successful war, Rome would tolerate an independent Jewish State. Parties advocating restraint, such as the Pharisees and Saducees, were not powerful enough to prevent descent into conflict.

The revolt broke out in 66 CE and lasted seven years. It was initially successful. The Roman garrison in Jerusalem was overrun. A Syrian legion sent to Palestine was defeated in Beth Horon and six thousand Roman troops were killed. These victories led many Jews to believe that Divine help would be forthcoming in their struggle, just as at the time of the Hasmoneans. However, Rome could not permit the secession of a single Roman province, and it now called upon the capable leadership of the general Vespasian, who brought with him four legions and a force of sixty thousand men.

Vespasian's initial efforts were directed at the Galilee where the Zealots were most active, and he overran their main fortresses of Gamla and Yodfat. Following their defeat, many of the Zealots fled to Jerusalem and took over the struggle against Rome from within the city. Vespasian was called to Rome to become emperor, but his son Titus continued the siege of Jerusalem.

Within the city, Jewish groups fought each other for control of the direction of the revolt. One group of Zealots even burnt the city's food supply to encourage the population to continue the struggle! Titus was in no hurry to capture

Jerusalem, preferring to wait while the Jews killed each other. Only when the Romans closed in on the city did these warring factions unite. After a seven month siege, the walls of Jerusalem were breached and the Temple destroyed.

Following their victory, Roman retribution under Titus was fierce. Almost the entire city was ransacked and burned. Much of the population, some of whom were pilgrims who had come to Jerusalem at an inopportune time, died of hunger, disease or by the sword, while others were sold into slavery.

The last Jewish stronghold to fall was Masada, which was occupied by the Sicarii under the leadership of Elazar ben Yair. When they saw their position was hopeless, the nine hundred and sixty defenders of the fortress committed suicide rather than fall into Roman hands.

During the siege of Jerusalem, the leader of the Pharisees, Rabbi Yochanan ben Zakai, escaped from the city and persuaded Titus to allow him to set up a Rabbinic academy in the city of Yavne. Within this academy, the Rabbis began the task of adapting Judaism to the absence of a Temple and its rituals. The focus of the religion turned to adherence to Biblical Law and its Oral traditions and to the role of the synagogue in Jewish worship. The Orthodox Judaism practiced to this day is a testament to the momentous accomplishment of these Sages.

THE WALK

It is recommended to visit the Davidson Center first. It is located in a former Umayyad Palace. Two movies are presented and both are worth watching. The first movie is in alternating Hebrew and English and presents the accomplishments of the archaeologists who worked at this site. There is also a movie in the movie theater, also in alternating Hebrew and English, describing a visit by a villager from the Galilee to Herod's Temple. If you are on a guided tour, you may be shown the virtual model of Jerusalem, and this will provide you with an appreciation of the layout of the Temple. Archaeological finds from this site are also displayed in the Center

After exiting the Davidson Center, visit the ruins of the Umayyad Palace.

The Umayyad Palace was built as an administrative center by the Umayyad caliphate (661-750 CE) during the Early Muslim Period. It was erected on top of Byzantine ruins. Building blocks salvaged from Second Temple and Byzantine times were used in its construction. (The "borrowing" of ashlars has been a common practice in Jerusalem throughout the centuries). The buildings were erected around a central courtyard, now delineated by cypress trees. The Umayyads also built the Dome of the Rock on the Temple Mount and rebuilt the al-Aqsa Mosque.

Walk past the Umayyad Palace. Where the Ottoman wall encircling the Old City meets the southern wall of the Temple Mount there is a fortified tower built by the Crusaders. This tower marks the eastern corner of the defensive wall erected around the city by the Crusaders following their conquest of Jerusalem in 1099. The section of Ottoman wall you see in front of you was built on top of remains of the outer wall of the Umayyad palace and Byzantine remains.

Go through the double archway in the Ottoman wall to the top of the Ophel, which is the area between the City of David and the Temple Mount.

The Hebrew word "*ophel*" means to rise or climb, and the area was so-called because pilgrims would ascend to the Temple Mount from lower in the city. King Solomon used this area for administrative buildings, and he constructed earth-filled terraces with retaining walls. This may account for another name for this area, the "Milo," — which means to fill. This name is first found in the book of Kings (I Kings 9:15). Until the Muslim Fatimad period, the Ophel was within the city walls. In Second Temple times it was occupied by the common people and was known as the "Lower City." This is in contrast to the "Upper City" on the other side of the Central Valley towards Mount Zion, which was where the wealthy people lived. Pilgrims coming to the city for festivals received free hospitality from Jerusalemites, and many stayed in the Ophel. Public buildings were also erected here for their use.

From where you entered this area, you will see a wooden path that descends into the Ophel. The ruins, which include ritual baths and a cistern, are labeled. When you reach the bottom, return to the plaza adjacent to the Temple wall either via the wooden path that runs parallel to the one you have just taken, or go a bit further and ascend via a path that leads to the Triple Gates. On the way, you will pass First Temple ruins.

There are two sets of gates set into the southern wall of the Temple Mount called the Huldah Gates. The one furthest from you is the Triple Gate. It is likely that its central gate was closed except during Festivals and entrance was through the side gates. To the left of the Triple Gate is the Double Gate used for exiting the Temple Mount. Only one gate of the Double Gate is now visible, as the other gate is hidden by the Crusader tower.

The Triple Gate with its reconstructed steps

48

The gates from Herod's time were replaced during the Early Muslim period in the 7th and 8th centuries, and blocked up during the Fatimad period when the southern Temple wall became the protective wall for the city. Nevertheless, the underground tunnels from the gates to the Temple Mount still exist.

What is the significance of the name 'Huldah Gates'? One explanation is that the prophetess Huldah was buried close by. Burials were not carried out within the city walls, but King David and his descendants and the prophetess Huldah are exceptions. Another explanation is that the word "huldah" means a gopher in Hebrew, and the ascent to the Temple Mount through an underground passage resembled that of a gopher.

Although the usual entrance to the Temple was through the Triple Gate, mourners would enter through the Double Gate and exit through the Triple Gate. This would obviously be noticed since it was against the flow and everyone would wish the mourners "May He who resides in this house console you" (Babylonian Talmud, Middot 2:2). Similar words are still used when Jews go to mourners' homes to comfort them.

Below the gates are the stairways used by pilgrims to enter and leave the Temple precincts. The steps by the Double Gate have been restored, while those by the Triple Gate are reconstructions. The steps are alternately broad and narrow, 90 cm and 30 cm respectively. This slowed the pilgrim's walking and provided dignity to his/her ascent and descent. The stairway for the Double Gate is wider than for the Triple Gate. This is because this was an exit gate, and the steps needed to be able to handle a rush of people at one time.

Retrace your steps through the Umayyad palace and make your way towards the southwest corner of the Temple Mount. Notice the huge corner ashlars with their typical Herodian features of an inset margin and smooth surface placed here to strengthen the wall.

How did Herod's builders put such massive building blocks in place so accurately, ashlars that in some instances were over five hundred tons? We have no written records describing this particular project, but we know quite a bit about Roman building methods. The Temple Mount is on a mountain, but it is not the highest mountain in the area. The blocks were quarried at a higher elevation and placed onto horizontal wooden poles for moving. Special carts pulled by oxen may also have been used. The ashlars were then lifted to their designated position using earthen ramparts, pulleys, and levers. The final fine positioning was achieved by placing small leaden balls underneath the blocks. The placement of each ashlar was so accurate that mortar was never needed.

Go down to the main street of Herodian Jerusalem. Six meters or so of debris had to be removed to expose the original street. Prior to removing the debris, ground level was at the same level as the protrusion of Robinson's Arch from the wall.

There are a number of interesting things to view on this street:

❖ On entering the street, you will see three stones on the ground. One of them has engraved on it an incomplete inscription in Hebrew reading *"Lebeit hatekia lehachr[iz]" – "[Belonging] to the trumpeting chamber to [declare]."* This stone is a replica, the original being in the Israel Museum. These stones were originally part of a southwestern tower of the Royal Portico reinforced during the Great Revolt and were thrown into the street by Titus's soldiers. The beginning and end of the

Sabbath were announced from this tower with the blowing of a trumpet or shofar.

The Jewish Sabbath was taken seriously by Jerusalem residents. The Talmud relates that *"On Friday afternoon six blasts were sounded, the first as a signal for people to stop performing work in the fields, the second sounded a little while later to stop work in the city and to stop from doing business, the third to kindle the Sabbath lights. After the third blast, the blower of the shofar would leave enough time to roast a small fish or enough time to attach bread to the wall of an oven and bake it there, and then he would sound a tekiah, a teruah and another tekiah [these are types of musical notes on the shofar] – and the rest time of Sabbath had arrived"* (Shabbat 35b).

❖ The remains of Robinson's Arch can be seen as a ledge protruding from the wall. This ledge was discovered by Edward Robinson in 1838 (hence its current name). He assumed it was the remains of a bridge that crossed the Central Valley to the Upper City. However, no evidence of such a bridge was found. It turns out that this was not a bridge but an overpass supported on arches that led from the western side of the Herodian street directly into the Royal Portico on the Temple Mount.

❖ The remains of four stores can be seen on the left of the street. Coins, stone weights and storage jars were found inside the stores, although these are not on display here. A lower section of Robinson's Arch rested on the roofs of these stores. A short section of a stairway can be seen just past the ruins of the stores, and this provided a passageway from the Herodian street to the Upper City.

❖ Finally – the very obvious pile of ashlars lying on the street. This is more or less how Israeli archaeologists found them when they excavated here in 1968, although they did push them into a pile so they could uncover the remains below. They are not lying here because of the passage of time, but because Titus' army dismantled the top of Herod's wall during its destruction of the city.

After exiting the archaeological park make your way to security for the Western Wall and enter the Western Wall plaza. There are separate prayer areas for men and women. Since the destruction of their Holy Temple, this is where Jews have come to mourn its destruction and to pray, since this was the closest point outside of the Temple Mount to where the Holy of Holies used to be.

Jews were not allowed to enter Roman and Christian Jerusalem except on the Fast of the 9th of Av, the day commemorating the destruction of the two Temples, when they were allowed to pray by the Western Wall. During the British Mandate, prayer at the Western Wall became a political issue as the Arabs tried to halt it. After the Six Day War, Moshe Dayan, the Chief of Staff for the Israel Defense Force, reached an agreement with the Arab Wafq that they would continue to have jurisdiction over the Temple Mount while Jews would continue to pray at the Western Wall. Jews would be allowed to enter the Temple Mount but not to pray there. Following this accord, houses close to the Western Wall were knocked down to create the large plaza that exists today.

Nearby Places of Interest

From the Western Wall plaza, consider two activities - the Western Wall Tunnels and the Reality Tour of the Temple ("A Look into the Past"). Both need to be booked in advance.

Western Wall Tunnels: *The Western Wall was used as a garbage dump during the Islamic period, just as the Temple Mount was used for garbage by the Christians. Suleiman the Magnificent in the Ottoman period identified the current Western Wall area and cleared it. The Mamlukes in the 14th and 15th centuries wished to elevate the importance of the Temple Mount. They therefore created a new street level by building arches within the Central Valley, and mosques and institutes of learning were constructed close to the Temple Mount. Hence, this part of the Arab quarter is built on a platform supported on arches. After the Six Day War, the area was excavated and debris cleared out from between the arches and the street level of Herodian times was revealed. Much of interest was discovered. The site is open from Sunday to Thursday from 7 am until late at night, Friday 7 am–12 pm, and Saturday evenings based on reservations. It is closed on Shabbat. Tours can be booked on line through the website of the Western Wall Heritage Foundation or by calling its call center at 972-2-627-1333. This is open Sunday to Thursday 8:30 am–7 pm. There is an admission charge.*

A Look into the Past *at the Western Wall Plaza uses advanced virtual-reality technology and special goggles to provide a 360-degree perspective of Herod's Temple. It is open Sunday to Thursday 10 am–11 pm, Friday 9 am–12 pm, and is closed on Shabbat. A session can be booked on line through the website of the Western Wall Heritage Foundation or by calling: 972-2-627-1333 from Sunday to Thursday 8:30 am–7 pm. There is an admission charge.*

5 On The Temple Mount

The Temple was destroyed almost two thousand years ago, but the Temple Mount is still considered holy in Judaism. There are two aims to this walk. Firstly, to understand the main Muslim buildings on the Temple Mount. And secondly, to conjure up the Temple that once stood here based on the structures that are currently standing, historical information and archaeological findings.

Visiting the Temple Mount

The Temple Mount can be visited by non-Muslims Sunday to Thursday 7:30 am–11 am, and also 1:30-2:30 pm during the summer. It is closed to visitors on Muslim holidays, and there may be restrictions during the month of Ramadan. Times can be confirmed by calling (02) 622-6250.

The procedure for ascending is to go to the southern security station close to the Dung Gate. Do not wait in the regular line for the Western Wall as there is a

Herod's Temple from the model at the Israel Museum

special entrance for ascending the Temple Mount to the right of the women's entrance. Unless you are with a group, **you will need to show the police a government-issued ID card.**

People who are part of a group can walk wherever they like other than Muslim holy places, such as the Dome of the Rock and al-Aksa Mosque, and they are not escorted by the police. Jews who wish to be led by a religious guide and directed where they may or may not walk according to Jewish law join a group and are escorted by the police. The guide may give a short speech of encouragement in Hebrew halfway during the walk. Other than this, no explanations are provided.

The Waqf insists, and the Israeli police are compliant with this, that no religious articles can be brought onto the Temple Mount. Also, if you engage in any religious activity, such as praying, the police may remove you from the Temple Mount. Cameras are permitted. Backpacks, leather shoes, etc., can be left at one's own risk in unlocked trunks by the Dung Gate before ascending.

TIME: About 1.25 to 1.5 hours

DISTANCE: About .75 km

TYPE OF WALK: Circular

DIFFICULTY: A very easy path.

STARTING POINT: The southern security station for the Western Wall close to the Old City Dung Gate

HOW CAN THE TEMPLE MOUNT BE HOLY TO JUDAISM WHEN THERE IS NOTHING JEWISH THERE ANYMORE?

There is no remnant of the Temple on the Temple Mount. To all intents and purposes, this is a large Islamic prayer area. Why then does Judaism regard the Temple Mount as being holy?

This page is not the first to ask this question. Even before the Islamic period, this topic was discussed in the Talmud, and Rabbinic discussion continued into the Medieval period. However, the bottom line is that Jewish law has ruled that the Temple Mount has extreme holiness, even today.

The concept of holiness is an important one in Judaism, and much of Jewish practice is directed at bringing holiness into this world. Thus, time can become holy in Judaism – for example the Jewish Sabbath and Jewish holidays. Space can become holy – namely the Holy of Holies within the Temple. An object can become holy, such as a sacrifice designated for the Temple. A place, the land of Israel, can become holy. The Torah describes God Himself as being holy (Leviticus 11:44). A Jew achieves holiness by imitating God and adhering to His covenant and in so doing he becomes part of His "*holy nation*" (Exodus 19:5-6).

It is impossible to define precisely the nature of holiness since it is a metaphysical concept. The best one can say is that holiness is a separation from the normal functioning of this world by restrictions and limitations that impart a sense of being in contact with the Divine. Or, that holiness is a means of bringing God's transcendence into this world by means

He has delineated. Thus, the holiness of time, space, and place are achieved by means of commands that separate them off from their regular functioning.

The Temple Mount is holy in Judaism even in the absence of the Temple because God's Presence emanates from this mountain. God's Presence was tangible in Solomon's Temple to the extent that the priests were unable to continue their work because of the glory of God (Kings 1 8:10-11), and aspects of this holiness never disappeared. This places a heavy responsibility on those visiting the Temple Mount. In fact, the Chief Rabbinate of Israel has ruled that Jews should not walk on the Temple Mount at all. However, there are Orthodox Jews who disagree with this ruling, including prominent Rabbis from the modern orthodox camp, who feel that as long as the holiness of the Temple Mount is fully respected it is permissible to ascend the Temple Mount, as did influential Rabbis in centuries past.

Maimonides, the important Medieval expert on Jewish law (who visited the Temple Mount) writes in his halachic work the Mishnah Torah: "*In spite of the fact that the Holy Temple is now in a state of destruction as a result of transgressions, one is nonetheless obligated to conduct himself with reverence, just as he would have done when the Holy Temple was standing. One must enter only into the permissible areas. One must not sit in the area of the courtyard, and one must not be frivolous in the direction where the eastern gate stood... Although the Holy Temple is currently in a state of destruction, its sanctity remains"* (Mishnah Torah, Book of Divine Service, Laws of the Chosen House 7:7).

To walk on the Temple Mount, Jews need to be ritually pure. One may attempt to explain what ritual impurity and its conversion to ritual purity are all about, but in the final analysis they are the requirements made by the Torah to elevate the sanctity of the Sanctuary. The reality is that for the last two thousand years, ritual impurity has had minimal bearing on Jewish life since the Jewish people have had no Temple. It is impossible to achieve the degree of purity necessary to walk on the area where the Temple was formerly located except by means of purification with the ashes of a red heifer (Numbers 19:13) - something that currently does not exist. However, it is possible for males to become sufficiently ritually pure to ascend the Temple Mount and to walk in areas beyond where the Temple complex once stood, by immersing beforehand in a mikvah (ritual bath). Women can also ascend the Temple Mount, although the situation is more complicated than for men because menstruation renders women ritually impure.

Details: There is a reliable kosher renovated mikvah for Jewish men and women in the Old City at 11 HaOmer St. No appointment is needed. There is a charge. Their phone number is: (050) 632-3960.

Details about the immersion process for Jewish males and females are available on the website of the Temple Institute.

When ascending the Temple Mount, gentiles and Jews are encouraged to wear non-leather shoes as a sign of respect for the Temple Mount. Modest dress should be worn. If, for example, your knees are exposed, the police will provide you with an outer garment to cover them.

HEROD'S TEMPLE

Herod's Temple was the last Temple to be built on the Temple Mount, being constructed on the foundations of the previous Temple. Nothing remains of it, since it was burnt to the ground by the Romans in 70 CE during the Great Revolt. Nevertheless, it is possible to figure out where the Temple and its courtyards once stood from descriptions in the Mishnah, the writings of the Jewish historian Josephus who lived at the time of its destruction, and from the work of archaeologists.

It is difficult to appreciate this nowadays but in former times the Temple Mount looked more like a mountain. At its very top was the Holy of Holies, located where the Dome of the Rock now stands, and the Temple was reached through courtyards at progressively higher levels. It is likely that the Central Platform for the Dome of the Rock built by the Muslims is now at a slightly lower level than that of the Temple, as the Temple's foundations were destroyed by the Romans. Conversely, ground level beyond the platform is now at a higher level than formerly because of the accumulation of debris over the centuries.

The Temple, and this was also the case for the Sanctuary in the wilderness, faced towards the west and people entered from the east. Pagan temples may have faced towards the east, from where the sun rises and from where gods were thought to appear in the morning. It is no coincidence that the Jewish Temple faced in the opposite direction.

The first court that pilgrims entered was the Court of Women. This was so called because it was the furthest court that women could enter, and not because it was exclusively for women. Women would stand on the roof of the porticos around this court to avoid intermingling of the sexes.

Fifteen semi-circular steps led from the Court of Women to the Court of the Israelites. These steps were located where the steps onto the Central Platform are now. Between the two courtyards was a large and elaborately decorated bronze gate called the Niconar Gate, named after the family that donated it. This gate was usually open so that people could follow the proceedings in the Temple Court. The Fifteen Psalms of Ascent (Psalms 120-134) were sung by the Levites on the steps, and rituals such as the cleansing of the leper and purification of women after childbirth were performed in front of the steps.

The Court of the Israelites and the next level up, the Court of the Priests, were narrow courts. Jewish men could enter the Court of the Israelites to watch the Temple proceedings. The Court of the Priests was solely for priests, although males who were not priests would enter this court to lean on their animal sacrifice and thereby symbolically offer themselves to God via their offering. At the center of the steps between the two courtyards was a small platform, the "*duchan*," from which the Levites sang psalms.

At a higher level still was the Temple Court (*azarah*), and this was where the Altar was located. The Altar was a square structure with a ramp at its southern side. Animals for sacrifice were slaughtered at the base of the altar and brought to the top of the Altar via the ramp.

Steps led from the *azarah* to the Temple. The Temple consisted of three sections – the entrance Porch ("ulam"), the Holy ("heichal"), and the Holy of Holies ("debir"). At the time of the First Temple, the Holy of Holies contained the Ark of the Covenant, and God's Presence was most manifest between the wings of the golden cherubim that covered the Ark.

When Solomon's Temple was inaugurated, the Bible describes, "*The cloud had filled the house of the Lord and the priests were not able to remain and perform the service because of the cloud, for the glory of God filled the House of the Lord*" (Kings 8:10-11). To this day, Jews turn in the direction of the Holy of Holies during individual and communal prayer.

There is a Rabbinic tradition that the Ark of the Covenant was hidden by Josiah, the king of Judea, to prevent the Babylonian king Nebuchadnezer from capturing it and taking it to Babylon (Tosefta, Sotah 13:1 and Kareithot 5b). It has not been located since, and during the Second Temple times the Holy of Holies was completely empty.

A short distance from the Temple and its courts was the Soreg, which was a low decorated brick wall that surrounded the Temple and that functioned as a barrier beyond which only Jews in a state of purity could go. Signs in various languages warned Gentiles not to proceed further on punishment of death. One of these stones engraved in Greek was found as part of an Old City building and is now in a museum in Istanbul, Turkey. A fragment of another sign is in the Israel Museum.

It is difficult to know what the Jewish people thought of Herod's Temple. On the one hand, the expansion of the Temple Mount was needed because of overcrowding, and this project was approached enthusiastically by the Jewish people. The many non-Jews who came to this tourist site brought knowledge of monotheism to the Roman Empire. On the other hand, it was built by a murderer, a protege of Rome, and a king of Edomite stock who was detested and hated by his Jewish subjects. There is a description of the Temple in the Mishnah, but surprisingly this description is of the pre-Hasmonean Second Temple and not Herod's, though the Mishnah was written after the destruction of Herod's Temple. Our knowledge of Herod's Temple is therefore based mainly on the writings of the Jewish historian Josephus.

THE TEMPLE MOUNT AS A MUSLIM PILGRIMAGE SITE

The First Muslim Period in Jerusalem began in 638 CE when the caliph Omar ibn al-Khattab, the second caliph after the death of Muhammad, took over the city from the Byzantines. One of the most powerful caliphs in history, he considerably expanded the territory ruled by the caliphate. He cleaned up the Temple Mount, which had been left as a garbage site during the Christian period and built a mosque to the south of the Foundation Stone. Other than this, he had little interest in Jerusalem or the Temple Mount.

The Islamic empire was subsequently ruled by three dynasties. The Umayyad dynasty came to power in 661 CE and Jerusalem was held in considerable esteem by the Umayyad caliphs.

It is related in the Koran that Mohammad was told to take his horse El Burak to the "*remotest mosque*" or "*al-Aqsa*," and it is from here that he went up to heaven to meet the prophets Moses, Elijah and Jesus. In 682 CE, fifty years after Muhammad's death, there was a crisis for succession of leadership of the Islamic empire following the assassination of Ali, the fourth caliph and husband of Muhammad's daughter Fatima, and this resulted in Muslims in Syria and Palestine being unable to go on pilgrimage to Mecca.

The Temple Mount was considered to be "*The remotest sanctuary*" during the Ummayad dynasty, and it would become the third holiest site to Sunni Muslims after Mecca and Medina. (The Temple Mount was never a holy site for Shiite Muslims). It was probably also during the Ummayad dynasty that the Final Judgment foretold by the Koran was given a geographic location – the Temple Mount – based on Jewish and Christian ideas.

The 5th Umayyad caliph, Abd al-Malik, completed the Dome of the Rock in 692 CE. This imposing structure was built on the site of the Jewish Temple, and as the most prominent building in Jerusalem it demonstrated the preeminence of Islam over the other monotheistic faiths. His sons built the al-Aqsa Mosque at the site of Omar's original mosque. The al-Aqsa Mosque has had to be rebuilt several times since, mostly because of earthquake damage. Much of the current building dates from 1929. The capital of the Umayyad dynasty was Damascus, but they also built an imposing palace in Jerusalem. The ruins of this palace can be seen in the Archaeological Park.

The significance of Jerusalem and the Temple Mount (Haram al-Sharif) to Muslims was used as a rallying call by Haj Amin al-Husseini, the Mufti of Jerusalem, during the British Mandate as a response to the perceived threat of Zionism and his fears that the Jewish people would once again attempt to rebuild their Temple.

WALKING ON THE TEMPLE MOUNT

This walk is around the interior perimeter of the Temple Mount. The descriptions provided are not intended to provide a comprehensive discussion of all the buildings on the Temple Mount, but only those structures most relevant to Jewish history.

Ascend the Temple Mount via the Mughrabi Gate ❶.

The Mughrabi Gate is the only entrance through which non-Muslims are permitted to enter the Temple Mount. Archaeological excavations and clearing of debris from the Western Wall Plaza revealed that this gate is directly above another gate, Barclay's Gate. Barclay's Gate was built in the Herodian period and its stone lintel is visible from the women's section of the Western Wall Plaza. This and another western gate, Warren's Gate, provided entrance to the Temple Mount from street level in Second Temple times and underground passageways with steps led up to the Temple Mount.

Barclay's Gate has been blocked up since the 10th century, and the Mughrabi Gate was built above it in the 12th century at the new ground level. The ground level of Second Temple times has now been exposed by archaeologists, and this is why the Mughrabi Gate now needs to be entered by a ramp. The wooden entrance ramp that you are walking on is supported on stilts and is a temporary structure, as the previous embankment collapsed in 2014 and no agreement has been reached between Jordan and the Israeli authorities as to a more permanent bridge.

After entering the Temple Mount, you will see Corinthian columns ❷ on your right. This is all that remains of Herod's Royal Portico (see the essay "Enlarging a Mountain – Herod's Temple Mount" on page 44).

The first building seen on your right with a grey dome is the al-Aqsa Mosque ❸. It is the third holiest site for Sunni Muslims. Its interior, which dates from the 12th and 14th centuries, is reported to be extremely impressive. King Abdullah I of Jordan (1882–1951) was assassinated in this mosque by a Palestinian while attending Friday prayers because of suspicion he was about to make peace with Israel. Entry is permitted only to Muslims.

The al-Aqsa Mosque means the "*farthest mosque*," and it commemorates Muhammad's ascent to heaven. It began as a large wooden prayer house, but has been rebuilt a number of times by caliphs from different dynasties after it was destroyed by earthquakes. The present structure was built by the Fatimad caliph and dates from 1035 CE, although there have been renovations and repairs since then, some as late as the last century. Some of the wooden

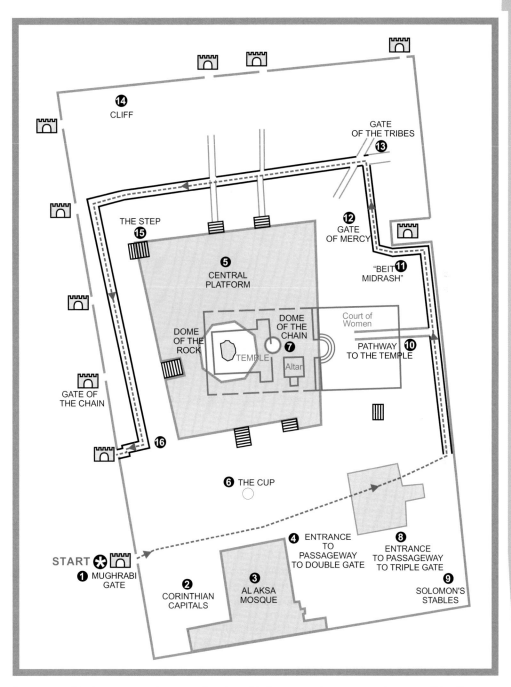

beams used in its construction are of cedar of Lebanon and cypress and may well be "re-cycled" beams from First Temple times. Similar wooden beams can be seen discarded by the Gate of Mercy (to be seen shortly), and they have been carbon dated to as early as the 9th century BCE.

In front of the entrance to the al-Aqsa Mosque you can see the entrance to a tunnel ❹ dating from Second Temple times. This was the main passageway for pilgrims exiting the Temple Mount.

Entrance to the exit tunnel from the Temple Mount to the Double Gate

The underground tunnel, now under the al-Aqsa Mosque, dates from the time of Herod, and it provided the main exit from the Temple Mount via the Double Gate in the southern wall of the Temple Mount. Only one of these two gates is now visible from outside the Temple Mount, as the other gate is hidden by a Crusader tower. The passageway has domed stone ceilings, two of which are adorned with carvings of geometrical designs with foliage, and are supposed to be quite beautiful. They can no longer be viewed as the Waqf does not permit entrance to non-Muslims.

To your left looking towards the Central Platform ❺ can be seen "The Cup" ❻, which is a large washbasin surrounded by a green metal grid. It was built by the Mamlukes in 1320 CE and is in the form of the Sultan's coat of arms.

The Cup is a washbasin for Muslims to wash their hands and feet. It is now connected to the water mains, although this is relatively recent. Prior to this, water was obtained from water cisterns hewed into the rock of the Temple Mount. There are about thirty-seven known cisterns on the Temple Mount, some of which are extremely large. One is known to have held about two million gallons of water. Many were initially quarries for Temple Mount building that were later plastered over to hold water. They were fed by surface water from the Temple Mount and an aqueduct system, initially built during the Hasmonean period, that brought water from a spring south of Bethlehem (see the essay "Supplying Water to Thirsty Jerusalem" on page 133). Herod considerably improved upon this system and also extended Solomon's Pools. Solomon's Pools are reservoirs south of Bethlehem fed by spring and run-off water. The aqueduct system entered the Temple Mount via Wilson's Arch, which is a bridge over the Central or Tyropoeon Valley. This arch is now below ground level, but can be viewed on a tour of the Western Wall Tunnels. An abundance of water was a necessity for the Temple, as sacrificing animals was a bloody affair. During the Second Temple period, blood was washed away from the altar from water issuing from its base.

Just past the Cup in the direction of the Central Platform was the Soreg, a short barrier that delineated the Temple area in which non-Jews were not permitted to enter.

Walking along, you will see on your left a short stairway leading to the Central Platform. Through the arches you have a direct view of the Dome of the Chain ❼, which looks like a miniature version of the Dome of the Rock.

According to legend, the Dome of the Chain is on the spot on which either King David or King Solomon had a chain that magically resolved disputes. This building probably stands where steps leading to the Porch of the Temple were once located. The arches on the four sides of the platform were built by the Muslims shortly after they drove out the Crusaders.

After passing the entrance to the al-Aqsa Mosque you will see on your right the exit of another tunnel ❽ built by Herod that led from the Triple Gate in the southern Temple Mount wall onto the Temple Mount. There is an iron roof over its opening. This tunnel provided the main entrance way for pilgrims ascending the Temple Mount.

Further along and also to your right is a flat area in the southeast corner of the Temple Mount. This is the roof of a new mosque built by the Muslims in Solomon's Stables ❾. Its entrance is by the southern wall.

Solomon's Stables were not built by King Solomon. It is an underground area that is part of Herod's extension of the Temple Mount platform. The platform was built on arches, and the spaces between were not filled with earth, as this would have created too much pressure on the outside wall. The empty areas between the arch supports were used by the Crusaders as stables. The Muslims have recently cleared this area and turned it into a below-ground mosque. This was probably done to "fill up" unoccupied areas on the Temple Mount and thereby prevent any future Jewish encroachment. No permission was requested to do this and the Israeli authorities apparently paid no attention to what was happening or turned a blind eye. During the mosque's construction, the Waqf carted away dozens of truckloads of dirt without any archaeological oversight and tipped them in the nearby Emeq Tzurim National Park. Numerous artifacts from First Temple times and onwards have been discovered by sifting through the dumped dirt and this park has become an archaeological site.

Turn left when you reach the eastern wall of the Temple Mount. You cannot see this because its height obstructs your view, but the eastern wall is built above the Kidron Valley and facing the Mount of Olives. A large part of the eastern wall of the Temple Mount reaches to bedrock and dates from First Temple times. The wall was lengthened when Herod expanded the Temple Mount platform and the northern and southern sections of this eastern wall are Herodian.

Between you and the Central Platform is an olive grove. The Court of Women was located within this grove. Continue walking until you come to a path ❿ that provides a direct view of the Dome of the Rock. This would have been the main entranceway into the Court of Women.

If you are with a religious Jewish group, you will probably stop at this point for people to contemplate, since before you was the main entrance for pilgrims into the Court of Women and from here to the rest of the Temple compound. Between the Court of Women and the next court up, the Court of the Israelites, were fifteen semi-circular steps and the beautifully decorated bronze Gate of Niconar. The steps in front of you leading to the Central Platform are probably where these fifteen steps were located, although the present-day steps are not the original semi-circular steps.

Continue walking along the periphery of the Temple Mount and you will soon see the sealed Gate of Mercy ⑫ on your right. The threshold of this gate is below the surface of the plaza. This is the only eastern entrance to the Temple Mount and has been sealed off since medieval times.

This gate has significance in the traditions of Judaism and Christianity. It is called Sha'ar HaRachamim ("Gate of Mercy") in Jewish sources and the "Golden Gate" by Christians. It was probably built by the emperor Justinian in the 520's CE on top of the ruins of a previous gate. It was sealed by the Muslims in 810 CE, opened by the Crusaders, and closed again by Saladin when he came to power after defeating the Christians. Suleiman the Magnificent built the gate as part of his city wall in the Ottoman period but also left it sealed.

Why the openings and closings? An answer may relate to Jewish and Christian eschatology. There is a tradition based on writings from the Biblical prophets that the Messiah will enter Jerusalem from the Mount of Olives through the Gate of Mercy, and this is also the Christian tradition regarding Jesus. Tradition also holds that the resurrection of the dead will commence on the Mount of Olives and the Final Judgment will take place in the Kidron Valley below this eastern wall. Blocking the gate could delay these events. Notice wooden planks at the bottom of the gate. They were left here following repairs to the al-Aqsa Mosque. They are extremely old and have been carbon-dated to First Temple times.

At the northeast corner of the Temple Mount is the Gate of the Tribes ⑬. The Israel Defense Force entered the Temple Mount through this gate in 1967 when they re-united Jerusalem during the Six Day War.

Follow the path to the left so that you are now walking parallel to the northern border of the Temple Mount. For those concerned about ritual purity it is now possible to approach closer to the Central Platform, as its edge is quite far from the location of the Soreg and Temple compound. The wall around this part of the Central Platform is medieval, although there are also Herodian foundation stones visible. There is no longer a northern wall for the Temple Mount and Muslim educational institutions are located where it once stood.

At the northwest corner of the Temple Mount is a building on top of a cliff ⑭. This is where the Fortress of Antonia was located.

It is likely that King Solomon built a fortress by the northern wall of the Temple Mount, since its northern approach was not protected by topographical features, and this fortress would have been used by later Judean kings. The Hasmoneans also had a fortress here. The fortress built by Herod was called the Fortress of Antonia and was named after his close friend Mark Antony. The historian Josephus describes the structure as follows: *"It was the work of King Herod and crowning exhibition of the innate grandeur of his genius."*

Part of the cliff was cut away and the fortress built on the remaining rock. It appeared like a tower with four towers at each corner and it dominated the Temple Mount. Its northern wall was surrounded by a moat. Six hundred Roman soldiers were in this fortress/palace. Their function was to police the Temple Mount and in effect maintain Herod's control over it. The fortress was connected to the Temple Mount by a passage. Herod filled in the valley between the fortress and Temple Mount so as to enlarge the northernmost part of the Temple Mount platform.

Turn left along the perimeter of the western wall. The cloisters along the wall were built in the 13th century, but it is likely that cloisters like this existed along the entire periphery of the Temple Mount during Second Temple times, except adjacent to the southern wall where the Royal Portico stood.

Be sure to look at the base of the first set of steps ⑮ at the north-west corner of the Central Platform. Note that they look different from the rest of the blocks in the steps. They are also not parallel to the Central Platform, but parallel to the eastern Temple Mount wall.

This row of steps is of pre-Herodian stone. Archaeologists think that these ashlars were part of the corner of the pre-Herodian western and northern walls of the Temple Mount. The dimensions of the Temple Mount before the Hasmoneans extended it are known from a Mishnah in the chapter of Middot. Thus, the location of the pre-Hasmonean Temple Mount can be located from these corner stones. Moreover, knowing that the Even Ha-Shtiya (Foundation Stone) in the Dome of the Rock is where the Holy of Holies once stood permits location of the position of the Temple. From this information we can derive the position of the Soreg, and from this we can derive the area that still has extreme holiness in Judaism.

As you walk along the western wall of the Temple Mount, you are passing the Western Wall Tunnels on the other side of the wall and then the "Kotel" or "Western Wall." At the next stairway on your right, you can peer through the open door of the Dome of the Rock, and if your vision is good you may be able to see the lights of a chandelier that illuminate a large rock. The gold covering of the dome of the building, incidentally, is fairly recent.

The Dome of the Rock is not a mosque but a shrine built over the rocky projection of the top of the Temple Mount. This stony projection is called by Muslims the "*Sakhrah*." Muslims believe that it is from here that Muhammad paid a night visit to heaven accompanied by the angel Gabriel. Also, according to their beliefs, Israfil – the angel of the trumpet – is responsible for sounding his horn on Judgment Day. The Dome of the Rock was completed by the Ummayads in 692 CE on the site where the Holy of Holies was located.

The Holy of Holies was built above the rocky top of the highest point of the Temple Mount and this rock is known in Hebrew as "*Even Ha-Shtiya*." According to a Talmudic tradition, the creation of the world began from the *Even Ha-Shtiya*, and this is where Adam, Cain, Abel and Noah offered sacrifices. This is also the rock of Mount Moriah where Abraham began offering up his son before being stopped by an angel. The *Even Ha-Shtiya* has never been accorded any special holiness in Judaism and almost all the rock, except for its very top (¾ of a fingersbreadth above the ground), was covered up during the construction of the Second Temple to build the foundations for the Holy of Holies. The *Even Ha-Shtiya* was completely covered up when the Dome of the Rock was converted into a church during the Crusader period. It was then converted back into a Muslim shrine during the rule of Saladin and the *Sakhrah* was exposed again, as it is to this day, some seven feet above ground level.

Exit the Temple Mount through the Gate of the Chain ⑯. It is the custom among Jews to walk backwards towards the gate and to continue to face the location of the Holy of Holies until the last moment.

The Gate of the Chain is an impressive gate built by the Crusaders. It is at the end of the Street of the Chain, which is an extension of David St. that begins close to the Jaffa Gate. There was also a gate here in the Second Temple period, but it was below the current gate, and was accessed by Wilson's Arch over the Central Valley.

To return to the southern security station for the Western Wall Plaza where you started this walk, continue along Chain Gate St., take the first turning on the left, Ha-Kotel St., and this will bring you to the security station. Alternatively, continue along Ha-Kotel St. to reach the Dung Gate.

Nearby Places of Interest
Temple Institute – *see page 30 in chapter 2.*

6 The Northern Rampart of the Old City Wall and the Via Dolorosa

This circular walk views the Old City Christian Quarter from the northern rampart of the city wall, and continues along the ramparts to Lions' Gate. It then proceeds to the Via Dolorosa and the Stations of the Cross. For Christians this walk is a means of experiencing the suffering of Jesus on his way to crucifixion. For non-Christians, it is a means of appreciating the contributions of Christian institutions to this city, of discovering the Roman basis to the Old City, and for viewing remains of Jewish Jerusalem, now underground, prior to Jerusalem's construction as a Roman City.

The Christian Quarter developed around the Church of the Holy Sepulcher, which is where Christian tradition holds that Jesus was crucified, buried and resurrected. Jesus died in a Jewish city expanded and beautified by Herod the Great, although it was then under Roman control. Jewish Jerusalem was destroyed during the Great Revolt and replaced by a Roman city called Aelia Capitolina by the Roman emperor Hadrian in around 130 or 135 BCE. Hence, some sites identified with Jesus in the past are in fact ruins of Aelia Capitalino and were built more than a hundred years after his death. To locate vestiges of the Herodian city in which Jesus walked, one has to look below ground level.

Via Dolorosa Friday Procession. Each Friday at 3 pm there is a Via Dolorosa Procession led by the Franciscans that starts from the First Station of the Cross inside the courtyard of the Omariyya School on the Via Dolorosa a short distance from the Lions' Gate. The Procession visits each of the Fourteen Stations of the Cross and ends at the Church of the Holy Sepulcher.

TIME: Half a day. When planning this walk bear in mind that many of the churches are closed in the middle of the day

TYPE OF WALK: Circular. You can also make this a two-way walk along the rampart by returning to your starting point from Lions' Gate. It is possible to descend from the ramparts at a number of places, but once you have left you cannot get back on except from Jaffa Gate

DIFFICULTY: An easy walk.

STARTING POINT:
The ticket office for the rampart walk is just inside the entrance of Jaffa Gate and has the sign "Ticket Office, Information, Daily Tours." A ticket is valid for two days for the two ramparts, northern and southern. The ramparts are open from Saturday to Thursday 9 am–4 pm during the winter and from 9 am–5 pm during the summer. They are closed on Fridays. There is a WC by the entrance gate to the northern rampart.

DRIVING DIRECTIONS AND PARKING:
Enter "Jaffa Gate" into Waze, and click on "שער יפו ירושלים". The closest parking is at Karta Parking. Enter "חניון קרתה" into Waze. This parking lot is only a short distance from the Jaffa Gate.

PUBLIC TRANSPORT:
Many buses stop just a few minutes from Jaffa Gate. The nearest light rail stop is outside City Hall and is about a seven minute walk to the Jaffa Gate.

OVERVIEW

ABOUT THE CHRISTIAN QUARTER

Jesus was crucified in about 30 CE during the prefecture of Pontius Pilate. His trial was held in the Praetorium, the seat of the Roman governor. He was led from there, with two men who were accused of being criminals, to be crucified on a rocky mound outside the city called Golgotha. The name Golgotha comes from the Hebrew gulgoleth, meaning a skull, because the mound resembled a human skull. It was formerly a quarry and this was where the Romans crucified common criminals. Permission was requested to bury him in a nearby tomb built into the rock, rather than leaving his body in the open as was the usual practice with criminals.

However, when the tomb was checked three days later it was empty. According to Christian tradition he is considered to have risen from the dead, re-appeared to his disciples forty days later, and then ascended to heaven.

Golgotha is therefore where Jesus was crucified, buried and resurrected. After his death, his disciples, all of whom were Jewish, formed a messianic group based on belief in his resurrection and eventual re-appearance as the Messiah.

Following the Great Revolt, Jerusalem was completely destroyed, and after the Bar Kochba Revolt the emperor Alieus Hadrian rebuilt it as a Roman city, which he called Aelia Capitolina in his own honor. A pagan altar was built on the Temple Mount and a shrine to Venus at Golgotha, which was now within this new Roman city.

When Christianity became the quasi-official religion of the Roman Empire under the emperor Constantine who had converted to Christianity, he asked his mother Helena to travel to Jerusalem to find the site of Jesus' death and to reestablish Jerusalem as a Holy City. What she found were the ruins of a Roman city and not the ruins of the earlier Herodian city. However, this did not deter her. She supervised digging under the paving of Hadrian's Roman temple, and found the crosses, on which Jesus and the two thieves had been crucified, as well as Jesus' tomb.

Constantine built two connected churches on this site – a great basilica over Golgotha and a rotunda over Jesus' tomb. These buildings were consecrated in 335 CE, and as Constantine and his mother

One of the triumphal arches built by Hadrian now in the Alexander Nevsky Church

intended, Jerusalem became a popular site for Christian pilgrimage. In effect, this mother and son pair were setting the stage for Roman Palestine to become a Christian country; much of the country had been otherwise empty of Jews from the time of the Bar Kochba Revolt.

The Church of the Holy Sepulcher has been destroyed and rebuilt a number of times. It was destroyed by fire by the Persians in the 3rd century CE, and by the Fatimad caliph in 1009 CE during the Early Islamic Period. It was rebuilt again between 1027 to 1028 CE by an agreement between the Fatimids and the Byzantine Empire. When the Crusaders conquered Jerusalem in 1099 they found the church unsuitable for use because of earthquake damage. They refurbished it and unified the chapels, although the structure they built was smaller than the Byzantine one. The facade of the church seen today is from the Crusader period. When the Muslims defeated and expelled the Crusaders, they left the church intact.

Via Dolorosa means "Path of suffering," and Christian tradition holds that this is the path trodden by Jesus on his walk from his trial at the Praetorium to his crucifixion at Golgotha. The first Ten Stations are on the Via Dolorosa, and the last Five are in the Church of the Holy Sepulcher. This particular route dates from the 13th century. Prior to this, the Byzantine tradition was to walk from the Kidron Valley to Mount Zion and then to Golgotha. The ancient paving stones seen in the Convent of St Anne's and on the Via Dolorosa are from the time of Aelia Capitolina and not from the time of Jesus.

The Christian Quarter contains many churches, the seats of the Patriarchs of the various Christian denominations, Christian hospices, schools and businesses. Most of the churches seen on this walk date from the early 1900's. The Ottoman Empire at that time was weak, and there was growing interest among the European powers, particularly Russia, France, Germany, Austria and Great Britain, to gain a foothold in Palestine as an entry point to India and the east and because of the importance of the Suez Canal. Much of this penetration was achieved under religious pretexts.

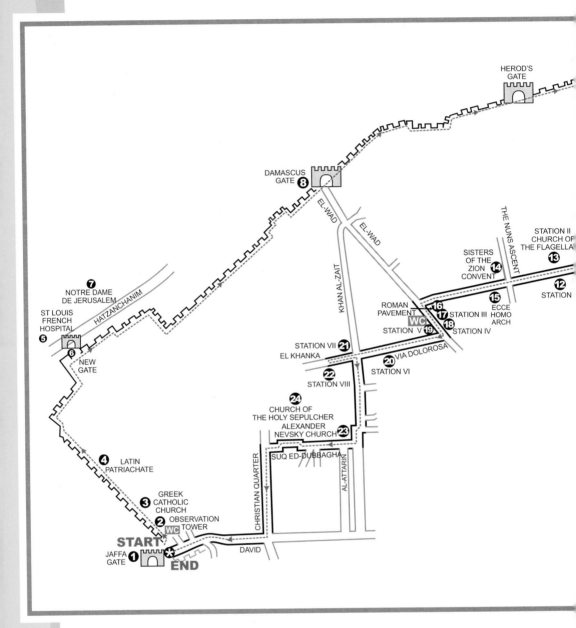

THE WALK

Street names in the Old City can be confusing. They are in three languages. The English name may be the same as the Arabic name, but different from the Hebrew name. Israeli maps may follow the Hebrew name. To avoid confusion, I follow the English name on the street sign.

Follow the sign to the northern Ramparts Walk.

The wall around the Old City and its ramparts were built between 1537 to 1541 CE, by Sultan Suleiman the Magnificent, during the Ottoman period. Looking at the magnificence

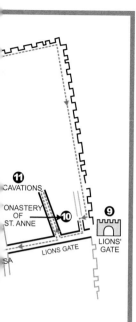

of this wall, one might imagine that Jerusalem was a central location for the Ottoman Empire. However, this was far from being the case. Rather, Suleiman may have been concerned that Charles V of Spain would organize another Crusade to take control of the Church of the Holy Sepulcher. The walls and gates were built on the foundations of the previous Crusader wall, which were built on even earlier foundations. Therefore, as for the previous Crusader wall, Suleiman's wall did not include the City of David or Mount Zion.

The first stop after entering the rampart is the Observation Terrace ❷. This is above the Jaffa Gate and from here you have an excellent view of the Tower of David complex. (For an explanation of the Jaffa Gate ❶ and the Citadel tower see Chapter 2 "An Introduction to the Old City" on pages 21 and 22.)

As you walk along the rampart, the first religious building you will see within the Old City has a pointed tower and balcony and belongs to the Greek Catholic Church ❸.

A faction of the Greek Orthodox Church broke away from their main body in the 18th century and joined the Catholic Church. It is called the Melkite Greek Catholic Church, and its members constitute the largest Christian community in Israel.

The next tower has pointed gables and displays the white and yellow flag of the Vatican. This is the seat of the Latin Patriachate ❹.

The Latin Patriachate is the highest Catholic functionary in the Holy Land. This position was terminated after the Crusaders were expelled from Jerusalem by the Muslims, but was reestablished in 1847.

At the northwest corner of the city wall, you will walk around the white dome of a family mosque, one of the few mosques in the Christian Quarter. Outside the city wall you can see a building with turquoise shutters, the Saint-Louis French Hospital ❺. This hospital is run by nuns for the terminally ill of all faiths.

You will now pass over the New Gate ❻. Also outside the city wall is the hostel Notre Dame de Jerusalem Center ❼. This hostel and the Saint-Louis French Hospital were built by the Christian community, but were physically separated from it after Israel's War of Independence.

Unlike the other seven gates into the city, this gate was constructed fairly recently, in 1889. The Christian community requested its construction from the Ottoman authorities so they could have easier access to the Christian institutions outside the city walls. After the 1948 War of Independence, access to these institutions was no longer possible and this remained the situation until the Six Day War.

Inside the Old City and just beyond the New Gate is the compound of the Franciscan Order. Their symbol is the Jerusalem Cross, a large central cross and four smaller crosses in its four quadrants. Following the fall of the Crusader Kingdom, the Franciscans elected to remain in Jerusalem to protect the interests of the Catholic Church.

Continue along the ramparts until you are above the Damascus Gate ❽. This gate marks the entrance to the city from Damascus and Nablus (Shechem). From the platform you have an excellent view of the Dome of the Rock on the Temple Mount.

Since the 10th century, this gate has been called in Arabic "Bab el-Amud" (the Gate of the Column) because of a tall monumental column that once stood in the plaza outside the gate when it was part of the Roman city of Aelia Capitolina. The column likely supported a statue of the Roman emperor.

Continue along the rampart. Shortly you will pass over the entrance to Zedekiah's Cave.

Zedekiah's Cave, or King Solomon's Quarries as it is also known, is a vast cave complex beneath the Old City. It was used as a quarry, probably beginning during the First Temple period, and many of Jerusalem's finest buildings were built from its stone. It is now used for cultural and music events.

Opposite to the Post Office building outside the walls you will walk over Herod's Gate. This gate was built by Suleiman and has no connection to King Herod. However, the remains of a magnificent triple gate built by Herod have been found beneath the Damascus Gate.

As the ground elevation rises you have an excellent view of the Mount of Olives Ridge. This ridge extends 3.5 Km from Mount Scopus in the north to the slope of the Kidron Valley in the south. The Mount of Olives is one of its three peaks. Three towers on top of the ridge can be easily identified.

To your left can be seen the concrete water tower of the Hebrew University on Mount Scopus. To the right of this is the tower of the Auguste Victoria Compound, named after the wife of the German Kaiser Wilhem II. It was built by the Kaiser in 1910 as a hostel, hospital and church for German pilgrims to Palestine. It now includes the Augusta Victoria Hospital providing specialty medical care. Further along to the right, in the village of A-Tur on the Mount of Olives, is the Russian Church of the Ascension. Christian tradition considers this to be the site of Jesus' ascent to heaven and the burial place of John the Baptist.

Outside the north-east corner of the city wall can be seen a magnificent building of white limestone which houses the Rockefeller Museum.

This museum, opened in 1938 with funds provided by the American philanthropist John D Reckeller Jr., was the official museum of the British Mandate. It contains thousands of antiquities unearthed by excavations during the mandate period. It is now an extension of the archaeology section of the Israel Museum.

Continue along the eastern rampart. Outside of the wall is the Kidron Valley. Shortly before the rampart walk comes to an end by the Lions's Gate ❾ descend to the road. This will lead you to Lions' Gate Rd.

The Lions' Gate is the only functioning gate in the Old City's eastern wall. It was built by Suleiman the Magnificent in the 16th century. Near the top of the gate are two leopards (often incorrectly identified as lions). The stones may have been "borrowed" from a Mamluke structure, as the leopard was the symbol of the Mamluke sultan Baybars.

The Via Dolorosa from the Lions' Gate:

Walk along Lions' Gate Rd. to the entrance to the Monastery of St. Anne ❿, which you will see shortly on your right. Within the monastery, head towards the excavations ⓫ at the far end of the compound. You can descend into the ruins, which are labeled.

You are now looking at the ruins of two reservoirs separated by a dam. They have been identified as the Pools of Bethesda, where Christian tradition holds that Jesus performed the miracle of healing a sick man (John 5:29). The pools were then outside the city walls, and they remained so until the construction of the Third Wall, which was completed during the Great Revolt of 87-95 CE. They may have been part of a healing complex in the Roman period that contained a temple to Aesculapius, the Roman god of healing. A Byzantine basilica, the Church of St. Mary of the Probatice, was built over a pagan temple on the central dam in the 5th century, with the length of the church being supported by pillars within the pools. Ruins of this church can be seen on the dam.

The adjacent Church of St. Anne was built by the Crusaders in the 12th century, being named after Hanna (Anne), mother of Mary, the mother of Jesus. According to a tradition, Mary was born near here in her parent's home. The church was destroyed after Saladin's conquest of Jerusalem in 1187, and he converted it into an Islamic educational institute. It was subsequently abandoned. In 1856 it was donated to Napoleon III by the Ottoman sultan because of his help in the Crimean War. It still belongs to the French government and is administered by the Missionaries of Africa, known as the "White Fathers" because of their white robes.

Continue down Lyons' Gate Rd. to the First Station ⓬, which is on your left. You will see a metal circle on the wall with a Latin number on it – in this case number I – near the top of the flight of stairs to the Omariyya School. This station is closed except on Fridays when it is open as part of the Friday Procession.

This station is thought to be the site of the Praetorium, where Jesus appeared before Pontius Palate within the Antonia Fortress. There is now a school where this fortress was formerly located. The fortress was built by Herod the Great to replace an earlier Hasmonean fortress. The Roman garrison within it policed the Temple Mount to prevent disturbances.

The Second Station of the Cross ⓭, the Franciscan Church of the Flagellation, is on the other side of the road. Enter into the garden. Christian tradition holds that this is where Jesus was abused by Roman soldiers after being condemned to death. There are two churches on either side of the garden entrance. Both were built in the early 1900's on the ruins of earlier Crusader and Byzantine churches. The church to the right is the Church of the Flagellation and over its entrance are thorn-like decorations representing the crown of thorns placed on Jesus to humiliate him. The church on the left marks the place where the cross was imposed upon him.

Across from the garden entrance is the Terra Santa Museum. A fifteen minute movie can be viewed in the museum. It is also in English and artfully incorporates into the movie the Roman archaeological ruins found here. The movie is a useful introduction to the Via Dolorosa. It presents the history of Jerusalem in Jesus' time and later, and describes the path that Jesus is believed to have taken to Golgotha. The museum is open 9 am–5 pm. There is a charge to enter the museum. Their phone number is: (058)550-2736.

Continue along the Via Dolorosa in the direction of El-Wad Rd. to the Sisters of Zion Convent ⑭. The entrance to the convent is at the corner of The Nun Ascent and the Via Dolorosa and is marked by a white arrow labeled LITHOSTROTOS.

This is not a station of the cross but is of interest because of the ruins underneath the church. The convent was built by the converted French Jew Alphonse Ratisbonne who was active in disseminating Christianity and establishing monasteries and Christian societies. It was completed in 1869.

There is an admission charge to enter and you are provided with a short brochure. Follow the corridor and you will descend to a large pool built into bedrock. This has been identified as the Strouthian Pool, a reservoir supplying the Antonia Fortress and that also formed part of the moat for the fortress. It was covered over during the building of Hadrian's city Aelia Captolina and a large stone plaza was built on top of the vault. The stone pavement is part of the Roman pavement from Hadrian's city. It has been identified in the past with the Lithostrotos, the location where Jesus is believed to have been taken after his trial. However, this is unlikely since this pavement post-dates the period of Jesus. It was also not the location of the Antonius fortress. To exit the building follow the signs and this will lead you back onto the Via Dolorosa.

Pass under the first arch on the Via Dolorosa. This was part of a three-part triumphal arch, the Ecce Homo Arch ⑮, built by Hadrian to commemorate his victory over the Jews. Other parts of the arch can be seen inside the Sisters of Zion Convent by entering the first entrance on your right after the arch. The chapel of the convent can also be viewed from this location, although not entered from here.

The phrase "Ecce Homo" means *"This is the man"* in Greek and according to the New Testament this phrase was said by Pontius Pilate when he displayed Jesus bound and crowned with thorns to the Jerusalem crowd. At one time it was believed that this arch was part of the Herodian Antonia Fortress where his trial took place. However, we now know that this arch was built by Hadrian after the time of Jesus when he built his city of Aelia Capitalino.

At the end of this section of the Via Dolorosa turn left onto El-Wad Rd. Note the irregular Roman pavement stones ⑯ on your left as you turn.

These pavement stones are Roman, although the road you are walking on is not. The Roman road is below ground level and these pavement stones were used to build the Eastern Cardo, which, like the more familiar Central Cardo also started from the Damascus Gate. The stones were raised several meters to their present location.

Shortly beyond the corner you will see Station III ⑰ on your left, next to two ancient columns. Christian tradition holds that this is where Jesus fell under the weight of the cross. There is a relief here indicating this event and also a small Armenian chapel. Immediately after this is Station IV ⑱ where Jesus' mother broke through the crowds to reach him. The relief above the entrance shows the heads of Jesus and his mother almost touching.

Continue on the Via Dolorosa and take the first turn on your right for its continuation. At the corner, notice the circular disc on the left indicating station V ⑲ where it is believed that legionnaires forced a passer-by, Simon of Cyrene, to carry Jesus' cross as he was no longer physically able to bear it. Simon assisted Jesus the entire way to his crucifixion. On either side of the lintel to the chapel is a carved Jerusalem Cross. There is also a depression on the right side of the outside wall of the chapel where, according to tradition, Jesus placed his hand to support himself. You can do the same!

Continue on this road. Shortly after passing under four arches is Station VI ⑳. It can be identified by its wooden door. This is where a woman named Veronica wiped Jesus' face. There is a Greek Orthodox chapel here built over a former Byzantine monastery.

The Via Dolorosa meets Khan al-Zait St./Beit Habad St. and Station VII ㉑ is immediately opposite you. Christian tradition holds that this is where Jesus again fell from exhaustion. This is also where the gate of the city led to Golgotha. The stone fragment here was probably part of the Roman Central Cardo that followed the path of what is now Khan al-Zait St.

To visit Station VIII ㉒, turn right onto the continuation of the Via Dolorosa on El Khanqa St. [If you wish to miss this station, just continue along Khan al-Zait St.]. Sixteen steps up El Khanqa St., a cross and the Greek words NIKA on the stone wall identify this station. These letters mean "Jesus Christ Conquers" and they commemorate where Jesus told the women of Jerusalem not to mourn for him. The Greek monastery here blocks access to the Church of the Holy Sepulcher. Therefore, turn back to Khan al-Zait St. and turn right at this street.

Continue along Khan al-Zait St. and turn right onto Suq Ed-Dubbagha/Shuk Ha-Tsabaim St. to visit the Alexander Nevsky Church ㉓, which is at the corner of Khan al-Zait St. and Suq Ed-Dubbagha. This church is an imposing building with pink margins around its windows, and is of interest because of its interior decor and below ground ruins. The entrance is on Suq Ed-Dubbagha.

The church is owned by the Holy Places Department of the Orthodox Palestine Society and it honors the memory of Alexander Nevsky, a medieval Russian military commander. He was the patron saint of Czar Alexander III who founded this society. Entering the church and viewing the pictures on the walls brings you into an era of Russian history before the Russian Revolution. There is a prayer service held here every Thursday for the Czar. There is an admission fee and you can borrow some printed information sheets in English.

Descend the stairs on your right and go through an arch at the bottom of the stairs. This arch was most likely another of Hadrian's triumphal arches that he built around the city's main forum and close to the temple to the goddess Venus (see the picture on page 67). This is where Constantine would later build his Church of the Holy Sepulcher. The Alexander Nevsky Church considers the thick walls adjacent to the arch to be a Second Temple wall containing the gate through which Jesus was taken to Golgotha. However, there is little evidence to support this and there are other possibilities. Continue further and you are standing where the Roman Central Cardo used to be. The two black columns would have been close to the entrance of the Church of the Holy Sepulcher.

After exiting the Alexander Nevsky Church, there are two possible routes for returning to Jaffa Gate:

1. **Via the Church of the Holy Sepulcher:** On exiting the Alexander Nevsky Church turn right and after crossing the square you will see a small archway that leads into the forecourt of the Church of the Holy Sepulcher **㉔**. Information regarding the interior of Church of the Holy Sepulcher is not provided here but can be obtained from many other sources. Upon leaving the Church of the Holy Sepulcher, exit the court onto St. Helena St. At the end of this street, turn left onto Christian Quarter St. At its end, turn right onto David St. and this will take you through the shuk back to Jaffa Gate.

2. **The most direct route back to the Jaffa Gate:** Turn left upon exiting the church and take the second right onto Khan al-Zait St/Beit Habad St. to go through the Three Markets. On reaching a four-way intersection, turn right onto David St. This road will lead you through the shuk to Jaffa Gate.

Hours the Churches are Open:

Monastery of St. Anne: Monday to Saturday 8 am–12 pm and 2 pm–5 pm (6 pm in the summer).

Churches of the Condemnation and Imposition of the Cross: 8 am–12 pm and 1 pm–5 pm (until 6 pm April to September).

Sisters of Zion Convent: Monday to Saturday 8:30 am–12:30 pm and 2 pm–5 pm.

Alexander Nevsky Church: Monday to Saturday 9 am–1 pm and 3 pm–5 pm.

Church of the Holy Sepulcher: Opens at 5 am and closes at 9 pm April-September, except on Sunday when it closes at 8 pm and 7 pm October-March. There can be a wait to enter if there are a lot of people.

7 Mount Zion Via The Southern Rampart of The Old City Wall

C an German Benedictines, Italian Franciscans, French Assumptionists, Armenians and Orthodox Jews live harmoniously together as close neighbors? On Mount Zion they are succeeding, proving that it is possible for different faiths to live together in the Middle East. This walk visits a number of sites on Mount Zion, including the Tomb of David, the Last Supper Room, and the Dormition Abbey, and approaches Mount Zion via the southern rampart of the Old City wall. You can also walk further along the rampart to almost the Western Wall plaza and then walk back to the Zion Gate. If you want to skip the rampart part of the walk, go directly to Mount Zion from the Jaffa Gate via Armenian Patriach Rd.

OVERVIEWS

MOUNT ZION AND ITS CHRISTIAN TRADITION

Christianity's connection with Mount Zion dates from almost two thousand years ago.

It is impossible to identify the place of Jesus' Last Supper from the New Testament, but Christian tradition holds that Jesus celebrated his last supper together with his disciples on Mount Zion on the first night of Passover. During the meal he told his disciples that the wine and bread they were eating would symbolize his flesh and

blood. Christian tradition says that he reappeared to his disciples on Mount Zion on the Feast of Pentecost, seven weeks after being crucified.

When the Byzantine Empire adopted Christianity and made Jerusalem their holy city, a large church was built on Mount Zion in the 5th century called the Church of Holy Zion (Hagia Sion Church). An upper room of this church was set aside as the chamber of the Last Supper, or in Latin "the

TIME: A few hours to half a day, depending on the sites you are visiting

TYPE OF WALK: Circular

DIFFICULTY: There are a lot of steps to reach the rampart, but this is otherwise an easy walk.

STARTING POINT:
The ticket office for the rampart, which is the second store on the left as you enter into the Old City by the Jaffa Gate. There is a WC by the entrance to the northern rampart.

ADMISSION DETAILS:
There is an admission charge. A ticket is valid for two days for the northern and southern ramparts. The ramparts are open from Saturday to Thursday 9 am—4 pm during the winter and from 9 am—5 pm during the summer. They are closed on Friday.

DRIVING DIRECTIONS AND PARKING: Enter "Jaffa Gate" into Waze, and click on "שער יפו ירושלים." The closest parking is at Karta Parking. Enter "חניון קרתה" into Waze. The parking lot is a short distance from the Jaffa Gate.

PUBLIC TRANSPORT:
Many buses stop just a few minutes from the Jaffa Gate. The nearest light rail stop is City Hall, which is a seven minute walk away.

75

Cenaculum" (the Supper Room). What was here prior to the church being built is unknown, and may have been a Roman building.

The Byzantine church was destroyed by the Persians when they captured the city in 614 CE. The church was not restored until Crusader times when a new church was built in the 12th century on the ruins of the Byzantine one. A gallery was set aside in this church to memorialize the Last Supper in the same location as in the Byzantine church. This Crusader building is still intact and the Last Supper Room is that designated by the Crusaders.

The tradition that the tomb of King David is located here dates from the 10th century, and possibly even earlier (see next article). The Crusaders continued this tradition and included David's tomb as part of their church. Thus, the Last Supper Room and King David's tomb are on different levels of the same church, although there is no direct connection between them. The Crusaders also built a large monastery around the church. After the Crusaders were defeated by the Muslims, some of this area again became ruins.

In the Ottoman period, Suleiman the Magnificent took over this Christian site, and since David is regarded as a prophet in the Koran he built a small mosque within the chamber of the Last Supper. This prayer niche can still be seen. The Ottomans also repaired the Tomb of King David. The Franciscans monks in the church were expelled from Mount Zion.

The Ottomans and the German Kaiser William II were allies. The Kaiser visited Jerusalem towards the end of the 19th century and he was allotted three plots of land to build churches for the Christian denominations in his country.

At this time, the great powers were vying with each other to obtain a foothold in Jerusalem and this was pursued through their religious institutions. One of the buildings built by the Kaiser was the Protestant Church of the Redeemer in the Christian Quarter of the Old City, another was the German Protestant Augusta Victoria on the Mount of Olives, and the third was the Catholic Dormition Abbey on Mount Zion. It was built in 1910 for the German Order of the Benedictines in the same location where part of the Church of Holy Zion once stood. There is a Christian tradition that the site of the Dormition Abbey is where Jesus' mother Mary fell into an eternal sleep after Jesus' crucifixion. She was then buried in Gethsemane.

During the 1948 War of Independence the Old City was captured by the Jordanian Arab League, but Mount Zion remained in Jewish hands. The Muslim family responsible for Mount Zion was expelled. Since Jews were no longer allowed into the Old City, thousands began flocking to Mount Zion since it overlooked the Temple Mount. It was at this time that the Diaspora Yeshiva was allowed to take over buildings for a yeshiva.

Unlike the Old City where people of different religions live in separate Quarters, all the communities here co-exist on one hill. Although there have been challenges in the past, Mount Zion is now a place of calm and mutual respect.

HOW COME THERE IS AN ARMENIAN QUARTER IN THE OLD CITY?

The Armenians belong to the oldest Christian church in Jerusalem, and their church has had a continuous presence in the Old City since the 4th and 5th centuries.

Armenia was the first country to adopt Christianity as a state religion in 301 CE, seventy years before Christianity became the state religion of the Roman Empire. The Armenian Church was also the first to split off from the rest of Christianity in the First Council of Dvin in 506 CE when it rejected the belief in the dual nature of Christ.

Armenian monks from northeast Turkey and Russia began settling in Jerusalem in the 4th century CE when it was ruled by the Byzantines. Armenian churches were built inside and outside the Old City in the 5th century, including St. James Monastery.

Many Armenians living in Jerusalem were killed during the Persian invasion of 614 CE and those who survived decided to live together for protection in what is now the Armenian Quarter in the southwest corner of the Old City. In the 1340's, they were granted permission by the Mamlukes to build a wall around their quarter.

Following the large-scale Ottoman massacre of Armenians in the Ottoman Empire between 1915 to 1917, most Armenians moved to the autonomous republic of Armenia. However, many came to Palestine, and the number of Armenians living in Palestine rose to as high as twenty-thousand, with most of the immigrants living in Jerusalem. This was a major increase, since throughout the four hundred years of Ottoman rule the Armenian population in the Old City had never been more than about six hundred and forty people, and had been as low as one hundred and eighty-nine. However, following their immigration to Palestine, many left for Soviet

Armenia. Thus began the slow decline of Jerusalem's Armenian population, which now numbers about five hundred people.

The Armenians zealously retain their culture. About two-thirds of those living in the monastery are non-ecclesiastic and are descendants of people who moved to Jerusalem during the Ottoman massacre. To live in the monastery they have to abide by its rules, including the closing of its gates by 11 pm. Other Armenians live in the Armenian Quarter but outside the monastery walls and these are families who have lived here for many centuries. The Armenians have always remained politically non-aligned and this is the situation today.

The Armenian population of the Old City is gradually disappearing. The wealthy have moved to other parts of Jerusalem, while those previously living in the monastery have moved to Beirut or the West.

IS KING DAVID REALLY BURIED ON MOUNT ZION?

The tradition that King David is buried on Mount Zion is a late one. Benjamin of Tudela visited Mount Zion in 1173 CE and he mentions that fifteen years earlier the Crusaders found a burial crypt beneath the church they were building and identified it as the burial place of King David. A Muslim historian recorded this tradition even earlier in the 10th century, although it is not clear what he meant by Zion.

Is this tradition compatible with the Bible? According to I Kings 2:10 "David slept with his fathers and was buried in the City of David." A Rabbinic tradition accords with this and relates that the only graves to be found within the city were

The Tower of David from the rampart walk

those of the Davidic kings and the prophetess Huldah. Everyone else was buried outside the city walls. Searches by archaeologists have identified caves within the City of David (see the Weill Excavations on a page 15). However, these caves are not of the grandeur one would expect for a burial sepulcher from First Temple times, and certainly not for royalty. They also contained no material from First Temple times and they may have been storage caves.

It is possible that King David and later Davidic kings were buried outside the City of David, on the current Mount Zion, and as the Upper City became populated during the reigns of the kings of Judah the sepulcher of the kings became surrounded by the population of the Upper City. This location may still have been regarded as part of the City of David by the authors of the Book of Kings.

Another possibility discussed is that David's tomb was by the Jaffa Gate in the location of the Citadel. Josephus relates that the Hasmonean John Hyrcanus and Herod broke into the Davidic royal tombs and found riches there, although he does not mention its location (Antiquities of the Jews 13:249). However, it could have been where the Citadel is now located, since both the Hasmoneans and Herod built fortresses here. A First Temple necropolis has been located in the Citadel area, and it is possible that David and his descendants were buried here, and may even have been moved from another earlier location.

The reality is that we have no idea where King David was buried. The tradition that he is buried on Mount Zion is over a thousand years old, but there is little to support it other than tradition.

THE WALK

After purchasing a ticket for the ramparts, exit the Jaffa Gate ❶ and turn left onto the plaza in front of the Citadel. At the far end of this plaza enter a grey gate marked by the sign "The Southern Ramparts Walk ENTRANCE." After passing through a small office to have your ticket checked, turn right towards the fairly steep staircase to the rampart.

In contrast to the northern rampart, the views of outside the city wall are more impressive than those of inside the wall. In fact, the first part of this walk overlooks undeveloped areas in the Armenian Quarter.

As you begin the rampart walk, the Citadel ❷ is behind you:

For a description of the Citadel and the palace built by Herod along this eastern wall, see pages 21 and 22 in chapter 2.

The ruins of the Citadel

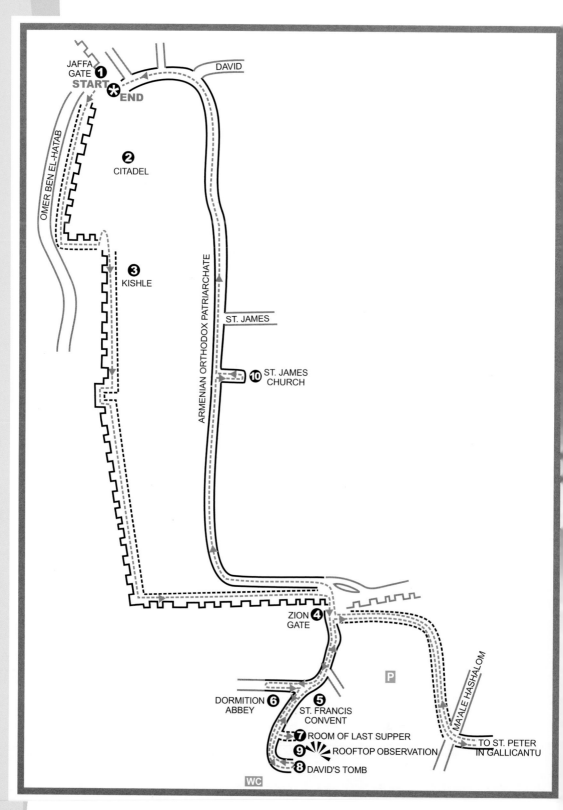

The roof of the "Kishle" ❸ is in front of you.

The Kishle was built by the Egyptian Muhammad Ali and his son as a summer palace in the southernmost part of the moat of the Citadel following their rebellion against the Turks in 1834. It was built on arches so that it could be entered from the Old City at ground level. When the Ottomans regained control of the city they used it as army barracks – hence the name *"kishle"* — which means barracks in Turkish. During the British Mandate it was used as an early detention center for prisoners from the Jewish underground. After the Six Day War, it was taken over by the Israeli police.

As you walk along the rampart, you will see some well-known landmarks outside the Old City, including the high-class neighborhood David's Village, the Mamilla Mall, the King David Hotel further to the left, and beyond this the YMCA building.

From the southwest corner of the city wall, you are overlooking the earliest settlement built outside the city walls, Mishkenot Sha'anamim, constructed in 1860 by Sir Moses Montefiore. He built the windmill to enable the residents of his settlement make a living. To its right is the neighborhood of Yemin Moshe. (For more details about Yemin Moshe see chapter 9 on page 102).

Walk around the corner of the rampart. Take this opportunity to look at the Kidron Valley, the town of Silwan rising up the side of the valley, the Mount of Olives, and the protective wall in the far distance separating Israel from the Palestinian Authority. Descend to the Zion Gate ❹ by the exit marked "Zion Gate Exit." Alternatively, you may wish to continue along the rampart to close to the Western Wall plaza for more wonderful views. You can return to Zion Gate either by going back along the rampart or by taking the road inside the Old City parallel to the rampart. Remember that once you have gone through the green turnstile or taken the Zion Gate exit, you cannot get back on the rampart.

View of the village of Silwan and the Kidron Valley from the rampart walk

In Ottoman times, Zion Gate was at the end of the main north-south market street from the Damascus Gate. Suleiman intended that it be an elaborate gate similar to the Damascus Gate. However, there were time constraints, and decorations for Zion Gate were never completed. The gate was renamed Bab Nabi Da'ud, Gate of the Prophet David, thereby acknowledging that King David was buried on Mount Zion. This name was previously associated with Jaffa Gate.

Bullet holes on the outside of the Zion Gate are a reminder of the fighting that took place here during the War of Independence. The Jewish Quarter of Jerusalem was under siege by the Jordanian Arab Legion, which had taken over the rest of the Old City, and the Jews, who were fighting valiantly, had insufficient food, water and arms. A relief force of the Palmach was sent to help them and it succeeded in capturing the Zion Gate and entering into the Jewish Quarter. However, its commander Uzi Narkiss decided that his force was inadequate and unprepared, and he withdrew to the Zion Gate, although his retained control of Mount Zion. The Jews in the Jewish Quarter surrendered shortly thereafter and were taken as prisoners by the Arab Legion. The Old City remained in Jordanian hands until the Six Day War. By this time Uzi Narkiss was a general of Central Command with seven brigades under his command. At his insistence, his forces captured the Old City, thereby reversing the failure that had haunted him for nineteen years.

After exiting Zion Gate, continue straight ahead onto Mount Zion. At the first fork by the entrance to St. Francis Convent ❺ keep to the right. This will soon take you to another fork. The right fork will take you to the entrance to the Dormition Abbey and the left fork to the room of the Last Supper and King David's tomb.

To visit the Church of the Dormition ❻ take the right-hand fork and soon on your left is a black gridiron gate. The entrance to the church is at the left-hand corner of the building and to the left of the main entrance. Almost immediately on your left after entering the church is a doorway leading down to the crypt where Christian tradition holds that Mary, the mother of Jesus, died. To exit the building, follow the exit signs past the gift shop and cafeteria.

The Dormition Abbey is a German Benedictine abbey. Its circular church with its towers and bell tower are landmarks on the Jerusalem skyline. The abbey was built on the ruins of the Byzantine basilica Hagia Sion. A representation of the Hagia Sion can be seen on the Byzantine Madaba map in the Cardo. According to Christian tradition, this is where Mary the mother of Jesus died. The site for this abbey was allocated to Kaiser Wilhem II when he visited Jerusalem in 1898 to dedicate the Protestant Church of the Redeemer in the Old City. The abbey was constructed by Theoder Sandel, who lived in the German Colony. It was dedicated in 1910.

After exiting the church, turn right onto the alley and head back to the fork in the road. Take the left-hand fork towards the Last Supper Room and David's Tomb. One can visit the Last Supper Room, the rooftop Observation Area, and David's Tomb sequentially, or just visit David's Tomb and the rooftop Observation Area.

Visiting the Last Supper Room and the rooftop Observation Area:

The entrance to the Room of the Last Supper ❼ is on your left. Climb up the stairs. The architecture in this room is one of the best-preserved examples of Crusader

architecture in the country. In the Ottoman period, Suleiman the Magnificent forbade Christians from entering the building and made the Last Supper Room into a mosque. This explains the Islamic prayer niche pointing towards Mecca that covers the Crusader window.

Follow the exit sign from the Room of the Last Supper and descend to the courtyard. At this point, it is worth going up to the rooftop Observation Area ❾ from the courtyard. The three flights of stairs are on your right. For details about this observation area see below.

Return to the ground level courtyard. To visit King David's tomb, turn right and then right again and go through the small wrought iron gate. The entrance to the tomb is immediately on your left and is indicated by a sign קבר דוד, King David's Tomb ❽.

Visiting King David's Tomb and the rooftop Observation Area:

If you are only visiting King David's Tomb ❽, continue to the end of the road. Take the first turn on your left through the small wrought iron gate. The entrance to the tomb is immediately on your left indicated by a sign קבר דוד, King David's Tomb." The tomb is the headstone of a burial chamber. There is a separate prayer area for men and women.

To continue to the rooftop Observation Area ❾, take the steps on the left just beyond the passageway to David's Tomb. From the courtyard you can see additional flights of steps to the rooftop.

The Jewish Quarter surrendered to the Jordanians during the War of Independence, but Jewish fighters did not withdraw from Mount Zion and it has been part of the Jewish state since the War of Independence. Neither the Temple Mount nor the Western wall could be visited by Jews and this rooftop became a popular place to view the Temple Mount. From this observation point you can see the Dome of the Rock on the Temple Mount and beyond this the Mount of Olives. The dome and minaret on this roof are part of the mosque that was erected in the building. The dome is directly above the Last Supper Room, which in turn is directly above David's Tomb. The small room on the roof is called the President's Room. Prior to Jerusalem's reunification during the Six Day War, it was used by Yitzhak ben-Zvi, the second president of Israel, as a room for study.

Visiting the Church of St. Peter in Gallicantu:

You may wish to visit the Church of St. Peter in Gallicantu. Take the road just in front of Zion Gate towards the main road and cross Ma'ale Hashalom St. The entrance to the church grounds is directly opposite and is indicated by a brown sign. Go down the road to its end. There is a ticket office here; there is a charge to enter the church. Outside the church and close to the ticket office is a balcony that provides a splendid view of the surrounding area. It has helpful signs indicating the places you are viewing. There is also a model of Jerusalem from Byzantine times in the church grounds.

The Church of St. Peter in Gallicantu was built in 1931 by the Assumptionist Fathers, a 19th century French order, on the ruins of a Crusader church. According to the New

Testament, Peter was one of the disciples of Jesus who thrice denied knowing Jesus but then regretted doing this. This had been prophesized by Jesus who had said to him, "*Before the rooster crows twice, you yourself will disown me three times...*"

There are three levels to the church. The first level is the church itself, below this the chapel, and in the lowest level there is a series of caves from the Second Temple period. Catholic tradition holds that this site was the location of the palace of the High Priest Caiaphas, in which case Jesus may have been held here in a dungeon.

The Byzantines first erected a church here to commemorate Peter's remorse. This was destroyed by the Muslims, and subsequently rebuilt by the Crusaders in 1102 CE and called St. Peter in Gallicantu. It subsequently fell into ruin after the defeat of the Crusaders and was not rebuilt until 1931. Gallicantu means "cock's crow" in Latin, and appropriately there is a golden rooster on the roof of the church. An ancient staircase on the north side of the church leads down towards the Kidron Valley, and Jesus may have been led down this path to Gethsemane when he was arrested.

Returning to the Jaffa Gate:

Return to Zion Gate and make your way back to the Jaffa Gate via Armenian Patriach Rd. On the way, it is worth turning into the Armenian Monastery to look at the outside of St. James Church ❿. Take the first entrance on your right just before the second arch. The church will probably be closed. You are also not permitted to go further into the monastery.

The church is named after two Christian saints who died for their faith, the brother of Jesus and the apostle James the Greater. The wooden boards and iron sheets outside the church were used to summon people to prayer, as the Ottoman authorities forbade the ringing of church bells.

> ### *Nearby Places of Interest*
> *Tower of David Museum and The Sound and Light Night Spectacular –* see page 29.

8 Nachla'ot and Mahane Yehuda Market ("The Shuk")

TIME: About 2.5 hours

DISTANCE: Just over 5 km

TYPE OF WALK: Circular

DIFFICULTY: An easy walk on paved roads and alleys. Suitable for strollers and wheelchairs, with some adjustment for steps along the way. In fact, you are likely to meet a lot of strollers on this walk!

The neighborhoods of Nachla'ot were some of the first residential areas to be built outside the Old City walls and they still retain their old-world charm. There was a strong feeling of community in these new estates and many of the people who lived here remember this very fondly. The walk ends at the famous, bustling Mahane Yehuda Market.

**STARTING POINT
AND END:**
The junction of Agripas St. and King George St. between the pizza and falafel stores. The walk ends by the light rail stop for Mahane Yehuda on Jaffa St.

**DRIVING DIRECTIONS
AND PARKING:**
Enter "Mahane Yehuda Market" into Waze and click on "Mahane Yehuda Market Agripas Street." There is an indoor parking lot beneath the Clal Building on Ki'ach St. and an outdoor parking lot opposite the Klal Building on Ki'ach St.

OVERVIEW

HOW WEST JERUSALEM BEGAN

Looking at the few original single-story houses here, it is difficult to imagine that these neighborhoods were once regarded as being superior housing. However, compared to living conditions in the Old City, where almost all the Jews in Jerusalem lived in the late Ottoman period, these neighborhoods were very upscale.

The Jewish Quarter in the Old City had become a difficult place to live in. It was overcrowded, unsanitary and expensive. Visionaries such as Sir Moses Montefiore and the builder Joseph Rivlin saw clearly that Jews needed to build outside the Old City. But how could they persuade people to leave the security of the Old City walls when outside the dangers of bandits and predatory animals existed?

The answer was to offer superior housing in gated communities that functioned almost as mini-fortresses. Connected single-story houses were built around a rectangular courtyard, and entrance to the courtyard was through gates that were locked at night. The center courtyard was an open space that functioned as an extension of people's home. This led to a very communal type of living. The houses were small, with just one or two rooms, but the set-up was spacious compared to what existed in the Old City.

The first gated community to be constructed outside the Old City was Mishkanot Sha'ananim, built in 1857 by Sir Moses Montefiore, not far from the Old City. Other residential areas followed in the late 1800's along Jaffa Rd. which was then the major thoroughfare into the city. These included the early sections of Nachla'ot, Mazkeret Moshe and Ohel Moshe. These estates were built with Montefiore funds and were therefore named after him. In actuality, philanthropists and contracters were creating the "modern" West Jerusalem. (See also the article "Sir Moses Montefiore – Entrepreneur Extraordinaire" on page 96).

"Nachla'ot" means quarters or estates. Additional housing was later built in the area between Agripas St. and Bezalel St. Each area was distinguished from each other on the basis of whether their residents were Ashkenazi or Sephardi, as well as by country of origin. In Nachla'ot, each area of immigrants from different countries of origin, with different customs, has a synagogue that reflects the customs of their country of origin. This is why there is such a high density of synagogues in Nachla'ot. There used to be more, but many closed down as their congregants moved away.

When these neighborhoods were first built there were no municipal taxes to take care of upkeep, since the Jerusalem municipality did not yet exist; residents were responsible for the communal expenses of their own quarter.

Water that collected from winter rainfall was stored in huge cisterns beneath the central square in each area. There was no piped-in water; this was the main water supply. These cisterns have since been covered over, replaced with underground plumbing, but their former location in the center of the streets can often be identified. Neighbors used to sit together in the courtyards, to wash their clothes by hand, hang their laundry, and check their grains, adding to the communal atmosphere.

By the 1930's, these small single-story houses were no longer attractive, and people began moving to larger properties in other parts of Jerusalem. Nachla'ot began to decline as a residential area; a high percentage of the remaining residents were elderly and/or welfare cases. Efforts were made in the early 1990's to revitalize this area by renovating the homes and adding additional stories, but it has taken another thirty years or so for people to appreciate the old-world charm and intimate nature of these neighborhoods.

Nachla'ot is now a trendy place to live in, and as you stroll through these old-world streets and alleys you will see a fascinating mixture of English-speaking olim, yeshiva students, haredim, artists, secular Israelis and visiting tourists.

THE WALK

Walk along Agripas St. from King George, which is here a pedestrian walkway. Opposite the traffic circle turn right and enter through the archway to Harav Haim Elboher Alley. You will soon come to the sixth neighborhood built outside the Old City, Even Yisrael ❶, which was constructed in the late 1870's.

Many of the houses here have a dilapidated look, as they have not undergone the renovations that typify much of Nachla'ot. Nevertheless, few people know about this quarter, and its square is a pleasant oasis of quiet just a short distance from bustling King George St. There are photos and descriptions of some of the original inhabitants of Even Yisrael on the right-hand side of the tiled circle.

Exit Even Yisrael by the alley on the far left (but not the exit to Jaffa St). Turn right onto Mashiya Baruchof St. by the orphanage and look down the first road on your left. The second door on the left of this street is the non-used entrance to the synagogue Achdut Yisrael ❷, the synagogue of former fighters of the Jewish underground movement Lechi (the current entrance is round the back). It is the only synagogue I know of that includes pictures of weapons as part of its interior decoration! It is not open during the week, but is popular on Shabbat.

Retrace your steps back along Mashiya Boruchof St. and head in the direction of Agripas St. Cross Agripas St.and turn right.

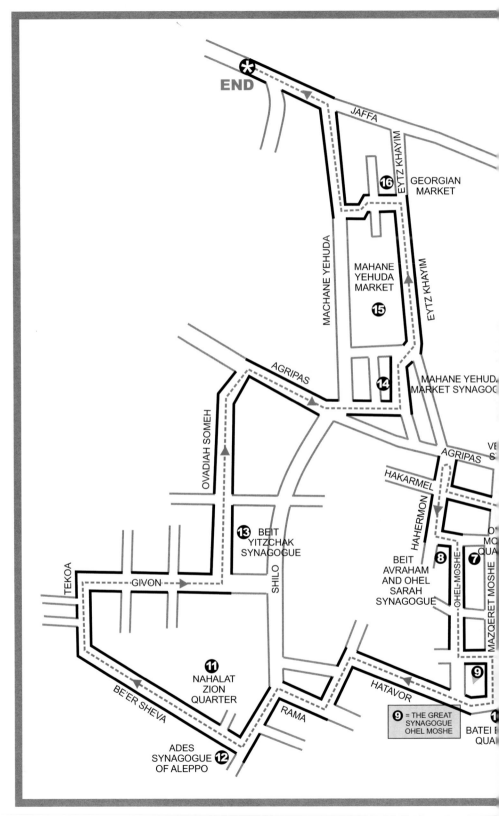

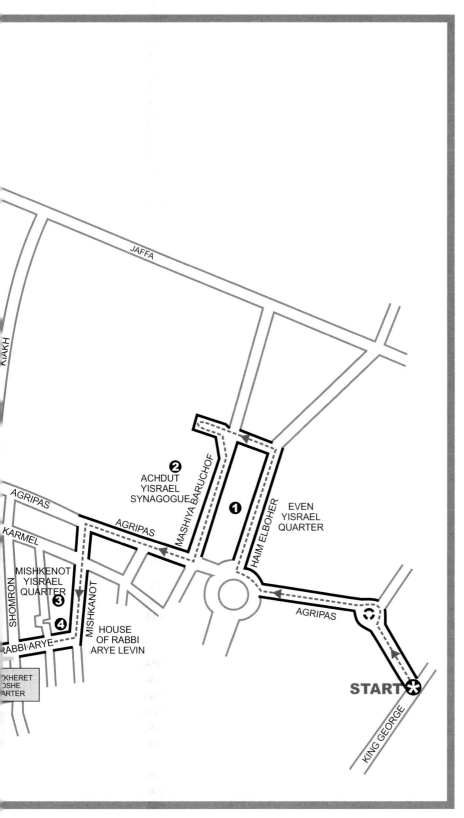

JAFFA

AJAKH

❷
ACHDUT
YISRAEL
SYNAGOGUE

MASHIYA BARUCHOF

❶

HAIM ELBOHER

EVEN
YISRAEL
QUARTER

AGRIPAS

AGRIPAS

KARMEL

❶

MISHKENOT
YISRAEL
QUARTER

SHOMRON

❸

❹

MISHKANOT

HOUSE
OF RABBI
ARYE LEVIN

RABBI·ARYE

AGRIPAS

START ✡

KING GEORGE

KHERET
OSHE
ARTER

89

Take the second left into Mishkanot St. under the brick arch. As you walk along this street you will see on your right the outer walls of the houses of the Mishkenot Yisrael Quarter ❸. This housing estate was erected between the 1870's and 1880's. You can enter into the quarter's courtyard from Yacov Berav St., the first turn on your right.

The name of this quarter Mishkenot Yisrael means "*dwelling places of Israel*" and comes from the Biblical verse "*How goodly are your tents O Jacob, your dwelling places, O Israel*" (Numbers 24:5). The Mishkenot Yisrael Society was established by Joseph Rivlin in 1875. Rivlin not only built the properties but had the difficult job of persuading people to live in a place that was generally regarded as being unsafe. It was originally occupied by religious Ashkenazi Jews. The Mishkenot Yisrael Society needed to be helped financially by the Sir Moses Montefiore Testimonial Fund in order to complete the project.

As you enter into this quarter, look at two elevations on the road in front of you. Beneath them are water cisterns. This is how people got water before they were hooked up to the water mains, each family in the estate receiving an allocation. The cisterns were opened when it rained so that surface water could drain in and then closed afterwards. They are now completely closed over for safety reasons. On the wall opposite the furthest cistern is a communal oven. This was fueled by charcoal, and families used it for cooking before Shabbat began and for keeping their food warm on Shabbat.

Continue along Mishkanot St. and take the next turn on your right into Rabbi Arye St. At the end of this block you will come to the very modest home of the well-known Rabbi Arye Levin ❹ (1885-1969).

Reb Arye was the "*mashgiach*" (supervisor) and teacher at the nearby Talmud Torah (yeshiva) of Etz Haim. His fame came from his numerous good deeds, his humble manner, and his being the 'Rabbi of the Prisoners," the chaplain for prisoners of the Jewish under-ground incarcerated by the British. Each Shabbat he would visit these and other Jewish prisoners to pray with them and teach Torah. He would also transfer messages to them from their families and deliver their replies throughout Jerusalem. This and his other charitable activities very much endeared him to the people of Jerusalem. He and his family lived very humbly and his apartment consisted of no more than a single corridor containing a bed of box crates and a table separated from the kitchen by a partition. After the 1948 War of Independence, he founded Yeshiva Beit Aryeh in his courtyard, and this yeshiva still exists today.

Continue on Rabbi Arye St. past Shomron St. You are now walking past the outer walls of the neighborhood Maskeret Moshe Quarter ❺. After passing the second-hand clothes store, turn right into Shirizli St.

You are now in the courtyard of the Mazkeret Moshe Quarter, which was founded in 1882 by the Sir Moses Montefiore Testimonial Fund. The art gallery, kindergarten, soccer field and community center are later additions to the neighborhood, and from an architectural perspective fit in rather poorly, although they are no doubt appreciated by the residents.

Sir Moses Montefiore retired from the Board of Deputies of British Jewry on his 90th birthday. As a parting gift his friends established in his honor the Sir Moses Montefiore Testimonial Fund. Its aim was to assist something very dear to Montefiore's heart – the development of Jewish settlement in Palestine. Its first activity was to help the Mishkenot Yisrael Society complete that quarter. It also bought for them an adjacent plot of land to develop the Mazkeret Moshe Quarter that would bear Montefiore's name in perpetuity.

The exterior of Rabbi Arye Levine's home. There are numerous stories about Reb Aryeh, each more inspiring than the next

It was an Ashkenazi neighborhood and when built was regarded as super-modern. This is no longer very evident, but initially the houses were only single-story, the additional stories being added later. Like the other neighborhoods in this area, this quarter was an independent entity and money was collected for maintenance and other amenities of the estate. It was not until 1905 that these functions were taken over by the Jerusalem municipality.

Continue to the end of Shirizli St. and then turn left onto HaKarmel St. Almost immediately you will see an alley on your right leading to Agripas St. Turn down this alley. Above the archway facing Agripas St. is a testimonial to Sir Moses Montefiore. Now turn back to HaKarmel St.and turn right to pass the colorful facade of the Sephardi synagogue Hesed VeRachamim ❻.

What is a Sephardi synagogue doing in an Ashkenazi neighborhood you may ask? This building was formerly a pub and was bought by a Sephardi Jew to provide a place to pray in for Sephardi Jews who were working in the area. Like many Sephardi synagogues it has very rich decors both inside and out. The facade is fairly recent and shows a lamp, the Torah, the symbols of the Twelve Tribes, and the words of the poem from Proverbs 31: "*A woman of valor who can find?*"

Continue past Mazkeret Moshe St. and head towards the courtyard of the third neighborhood to be built in Nachla'ot, the Ohel Moshe Quarter ❼.

Jerusalem's Sephardi community also requested help from the Sir Moses Montefiore Testimonial Fund to establish a Sephardi neighborhood in this area, and they were provided with a plot of land and a loan. The project was completed in 1887 and a plaque commemorating this event was placed above the gate to the estate on Agripas St.

On the outer walls of some of the houses are photos and descriptions of the families who once lived here, including that of Yitzhak Navon who was the fifth president of the State of Israel from 1978 to 1983. He was a Sephardi, born in this quarter, and was the first president of Israel born in this country. Previous presidents were born in Russia. As well as being a politician and an academic, he was also an accomplished author, and his well-known play "Bustan Sephardi" (Sephardi Orchard) is about reminiscences of his childhood in Ohel Moshe during the 1930's.

Turn right onto HaHermon St. to view the Moses Montefiore plaque on top of the archway facing Agripas St.

Turn back along HaHermon St., crossing HaKarmel St., and passing the Beit Avraham and Ohel Sarah Synagogue ❽ on the right. This synagogue was founded by Jews from Greece and contains ritual objects from Greek Jewish communities destroyed in the Holocaust. Continue past a quiet garden on the left, and walk over the covered cisterns.

Take the second left, and then first right onto Ohel Moshe St. One intersection before the end of the street, turn left onto the continuation of Rabbi Arye St. You will pass the Great Synagogue Ohel Moshe ❾ named after Moses Montefiore. This was completed in 1887 and for some years was the only Sephardi synagogue outside the Old City.

Turn right on Mazkeret Moshe St. and continue until the end of this street. In front of you is the Batei Brodie Quarter ❿ built in 1903. You may wish to peep into its private courtyard.

This quarter contains a different type of building project than what we have seen up to now. It is one of seven haredi neighborhoods built after those financed with Montefiore's funds. They were financed from outside Israel, and were more spacious than the earlier quarters. This particular quarter was financed by a wealthy Jew from Warsaw, Rav Yaakov Yosef Brodie. He had no children and he financed this project to eternalize his name. He stipulated in its charter that the houses be used only for poor Torah scholars from the Perushim (non-Hasidic) community. This type of singularity was the rule in those days, and was important because of the financial and social support it provided people.

Turn right on Hatavor St. At the end of the street, turn left onto Ezra Refael St. At the end of this street turn right onto Rama St., and then take the first left onto Shilo St.

Turn into the first street on your right, which is Be'er Sheva St. You are now in the beautiful Nahalat Zion Quarter ⑪. Immediately on your left is the famous Ades Synagogue of Aleppo ⑫.

This neighborhood was founded in 1891 by Abraham Antebi, director of the Alliance Israelite Universelle in Jerusalem. It contained low-income housing, and families paid for their home in installments. Things have changed! Most of the homes in this square have been renovated and are far from being low income.

The Ades Synagogue was built in 1901. This neighborhood had a very diverse population, which included a large number of Syrian Jews from Aleppo. They provided the initiative for the synagogue, and the wealthy Ades family from Aleppo provided the funding.

Many visitors visit this synagogue because of its beautiful interior décor. It contains a mural of the Twelve Tribes of Israel painted at the beginning of the 20th century by Ya'akov Stark, a teacher at the then newly established Bezalel Art Institute. However, to enter the synagogue, you will need to come at prayer time or to have made a prior arrangement.

Walk through this beautiful neighborhood with its trees, shrubs and flowers in the central courtyard and gardens. Continue on the right side of the road to the very end of Be'er Sheba St. and follow Tekoa St. as it curves to the right. Turn right opposite the Keter Torah Synagogue onto Givon St. and walk up the series of steps.

Take the third street on the left onto Rechov Ovadiah Someh. You are now in the Neve Shalom neighborhood founded by Iranian Jews in 1896. Look at #11, which is the Beit Yitzchak Synagogue ⑬. This Kurdish synagogue was founded in 1894. If it is open for services, take a look inside to view its decorations. Or look through the windows.

Continue straight ahead until you come to Agripas St. Turn right on this street. You will soon see the famous Mahane Yehuda Market ("the shuk") ⑮ on the other side of the road.

This market was initially for the residents of Nachla'ot, and it has been evolving ever since. Arabs would come here to sell their produce. By the 1920's, the place had become so unsanitary that the British ordered the vendors to leave. However, a loan was arranged and a more acceptable market was developed.

It is now a magnetic place. By day, it is full of vendors selling a variety of local and exotic fruits and vegetables, herbs and spices, fresh-baked bread, clothes, jewelry, household supplies and much more. There are restaurants, cafes, bars, many shoppers, and lots of tourists. Come the evening and its character changes completely. It comes to life again, but this time the bars, restaurants, cafes and musical performances take over. In contrast to many other big cities throughout the world, and even cities in Israel, the atmosphere here is casual, authentic and very friendly.

Cross Agripas St. and take the first left onto Mahane Yehuda St., the main thoroughfare of the uncovered part of the Mahane Yehuda Market. Follow your interests, but if you would like some direction, do the following:

Immediately, take the turn on your right into the covered part of the market. Then take the second turn on the left. Just past some restaurants is the Mahane Yehuda Market Synagogue **⑭** on the right. The times of prayer are noted outside.

At the end of this street turn right and then left onto Etz Hayim St. This is the main thoroughfare of the covered part of the market.

Just before the end of this street, turn left into an alley between two vegetable/fruit stalls. You are now in the Georgian Market **⑯**, so-called because the stalls are owned by people formerly from Georgia. Follow the alley to the left and then take the first right and you will be back on Mahane Yehuda St.

Turn right and you will soon reach Jaffa St. The light rail stop for Mahane Yehuda is close by to the left.

Nearby Places of Interest:

The Gush Katif Museum at 5 Sha'arei Tsedek St. is not far from the Shuk. It has several rooms with photos and two fifteen to twenty minute movies in Hebrew. The main movie has English subtitles. The other has Hebrew subtitles. By the end of your visit you will appreciate the Jewish connection to ancient Gaza, what Israel gave up when it withdrew from the Gaza Strip ($60 million of agricultural exports and 10% of Israel's agricultural production), what the people of Gush Katif gave up when Israel withdrew, and how those who refused to go were forcibly evacuated in October 2005. Open Sunday to Thursday 10 am–5 pm, and Friday 10 am–1 pm. There is an admission charge. Children under age 8 are free. Their phone number is: (02) 625-5456.

9 Yemin Moshe to Nahalat Shivah

This interesting walk begins at Yemin Moshe and visits the first three Jewish residential areas built outside the Old City walls – Mishkenot Sha'ananim, Mahaneh Yisrael, and Nahalat Shivah, the latter being in the center of town. It can also be shortened to a circular walk through Yemin Moshe and Mishkenot Sha'ananim. Yemin Moshe is a very beautiful residential area with picturesque streets, attractive gardens, and impressive views of the Old City and Mount Zion.

TIME: About 2.5 hours

DISTANCE: 5.5 km

TYPE OF WALK: One direction

DIFFICULTY:
An easy walk on paved roads.

STARTING POINT:
Intersection of Keren Hayesod St.,
King David St. and Jabotinsky
St. There are WC's in the adjacent
Bloomfield Park by the water
fountain.

PUBLIC TRANSPORT:
Public transport is advised since
this is not a circular walk. Enter
"Yemin Moshe" into Moovit.

**DRIVING DIRECTIONS
AND PARKING:**
Enter "Montefiore Windmill" into
Waze and click on "Montefiore
Windmill, Sderot Blumfield,
Jerusalem." There is metered street
parking by the windmill.

SIR MOSES MONTEFIORE – ENTREPRENEUR EXTRAORDINAIRE

Montefiore's windmill stands out on the Jerusalem landscape as a testimony to the many projects carried out in Palestine by this special person, Sir Moses Montefiore. In actuality, this particular project was not very successful, even though it was well intentioned. There was insufficient wind, replacement parts were expensive and had to be imported from Europe, and after a few decades it was rendered obsolete by newer diesel technology brought to Jerusalem by a miller in the nearby German Colony. Nevertheless, his other projects were innovative and monumental. All met the needs of the time, although sometimes it took people a while to realize that this was the case.

Moses Montefiore (1784-1885) made his initial fortune as a stockbroker in London. He retired at age forty to devote his life to philanthropy, charitable deeds, and providing assistance to the Jewish people. He not only gave away his own money but was entrusted by others for their charitable contributions, and this made him even more successful as a philanthropist.

His effectiveness for Jewish causes was aided by a number of factors. He had developed a reputation for philanthropy by being active in prominent non-Jewish causes. He had connections with the English aristocracy, including Queen Victoria of England who lived close to him in Ramsgate and who believed that the Jewish people had an important role to play in world history. He was also a business partner and brother-in-law of Lord Nathan Rothschild of the famous Rothschild banking family, who was also involved in projects in Palestine. Like Montefiore, he had a very hands-on approach to his projects and undoubtedly they compared notes. Montefiore visited Palestine seven times between 1827 and 1875. He was much affected by his first visit in 1827 and decided that from then he would lead a strictly religious life.

Montefiore took upon himself the role of ambassador-at-large for the Jewish people and visited countries where they were in distress. His activities and talent were widely recognized. In 1846 Queen Victoria knighted him for his work for the Jewish people. He was President of the Board of Deputies of British Jews for thirty-nine years, the longest time a person had ever held this position. He was elected Sheriff of London in 1837.

One cannot discuss the development of Jerusalem in the 1800's without mentioning the central role of Montefiore, and his name is connected to a number of early residential neighborhoods in the city. The Ottoman Empire had been ruling Palestine for about four hundred years, but they had little interest in developing Jerusalem and it remained a backwater of their empire. The Jews in Jerusalem lived only in the Old City, since its walls provided protection. The city was locked at night. However, living conditions were extremely difficult. Jews could not buy properties in the city and they were dependent on landlords who had no incentive to improve their rental properties. There was severe overcrowding, no leisure space, and the water supply from water cisterns was often polluted, leading to disease. Sewage and debris collected in the streets. It was clear to visionaries such as Montefiore that the Jews had to develop residential areas outside the Old City. However, non-Muslims were not permitted to purchase land and it was dangerous to live outside the city walls.

The Crimean War (1853 to 1856) changed this situation. The Turks won this war against Russia with the assistance of the European powers, and one of the conditions of this help was that non-Muslims would be permitted to purchase land in Palestine. This enabled Montefiore to buy a large plot of land just outside the city walls to build Mishkenot Sha'ananim, albeit at a very inflated price. This land would also be used later for building Yemin Moshe. (This change in Ottoman policy also permitted the Russians to purchase land for the Russian Compound at about the same time and the German Templars to buy land for the German Colony).

The settlement of Mishkenot Sha'ananims — which means "peaceful habitation" — was Montefiore's first effort to persuade Jews to live outside the Old City. It was completed in 1860. The 1.5 rooms provided to each family were more spacious than in the Old City. There was also leisure space outside the home and running water. However, he had no takers, despite his apartments being rent-free. People were concerned about their safety and also about losing their "kollel" funding from charitable organizations. Montefiore upped the offer by providing a stipend. A few people signed on, but returned to the Old City at night to sleep.

A cholera epidemic in 1865 in the Old City, in which about a third of the population died, provided the impetus for people to look seriously at his apartments. The running water in his apartments was clean and there was no risk of disease. People began realizing that Mishkenot Sha'ananim was not as hazardous a place to live in as they had assumed. With the increased demand, a second building was added.

The success of this project provided the impetus for the development of other residential areas in Jerusalem. Mishkenot Sha'ananim can therefore be considered the first stage in the development of modern West Jerusalem.

CONTINUED
NEXT PAGE
BOTTOM RIGHT

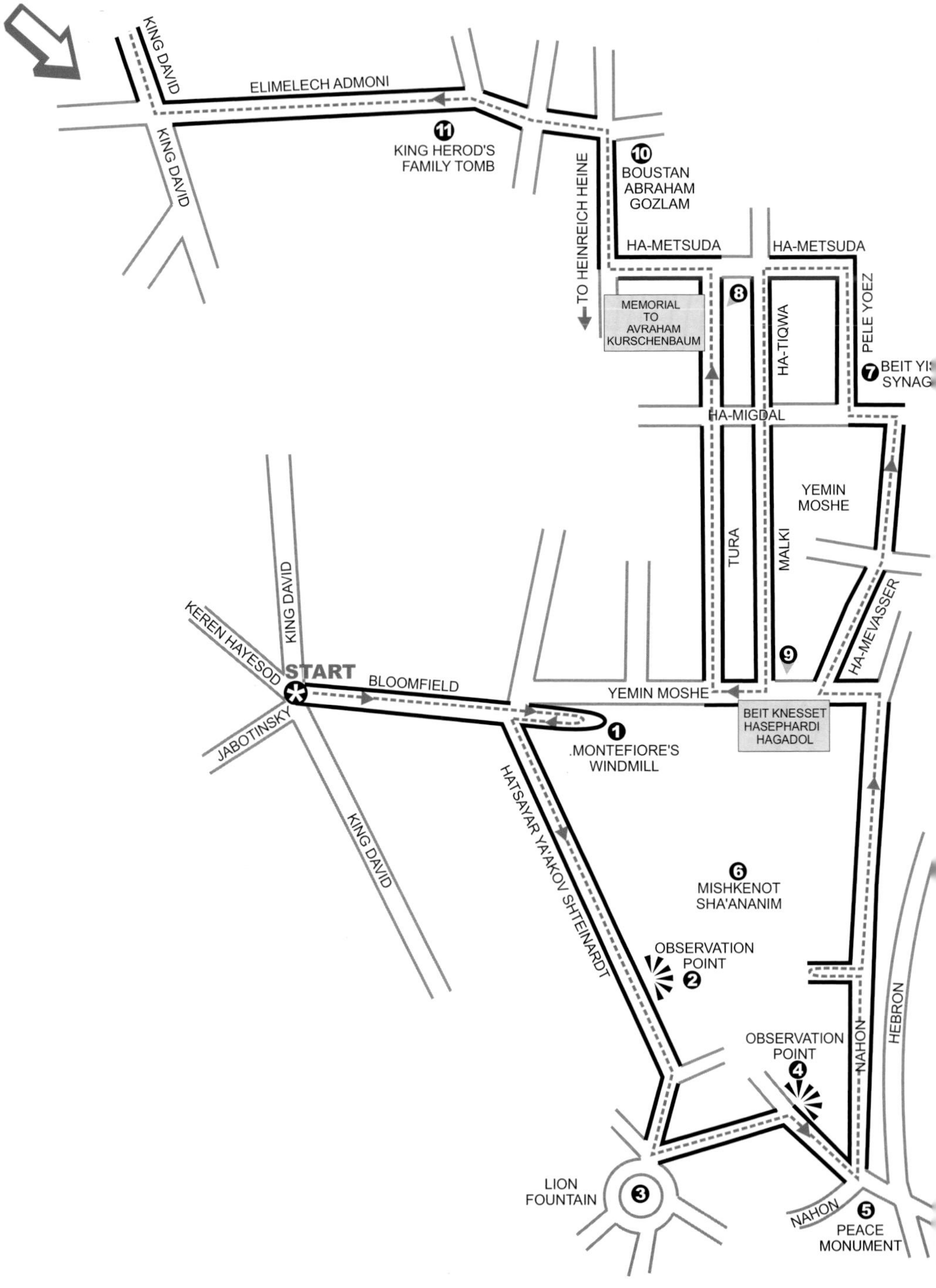

KING DAVID

ELIMELECH ADMONI

KING DAVID

11 KING HEROD'S
FAMILY TOMB

TO HEINREICH HEINE

10 BOUSTAN
ABRAHAM
GOZLAM

HA-METSUDA

HA-METSUDA

MEMORIAL
TO
AVRAHAM
KURSCHENBAUM

8

HA-TIQWA

PELE YOEZ

7 BEIT YI
SYNAG

HA-MIGDAL

YEMIN
MOSHE

TURA

MALKI

HA-MEVASSER

KEREN HAYESOD

KING DAVID

START

BLOOMFIELD

YEMIN MOSHE

9

BEIT KNESSET
HASEPHARDI
HAGADOL

JABOTINSKY

KING DAVID

HATSAYAR YA'AKOV SHTEINARDT

1 MONTEFIORE'S
WINDMILL

6
MISHKENOT
SHA'ANANIM

2 OBSERVATION
POINT

OBSERVATION
POINT
4

NAHON

HEBRON

LION
FOUNTAIN

3

NAHON

5
PEACE
MONUMENT

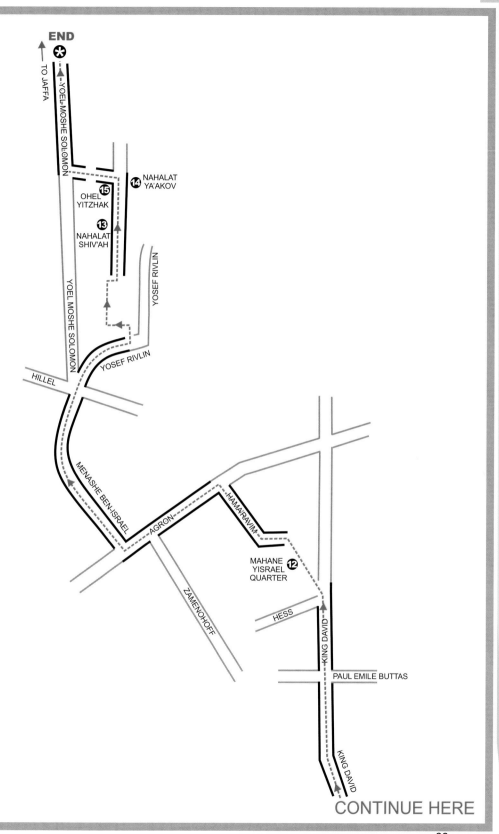

END

TO JAFFA

YOEL MOSHE SOLOMON

14 NAHALAT YA'AKOV

15
OHEL YITZHAK

13
NAHALAT SHIV'AH

YOSEF RIVLIN

YOEL MOSHE SOLOMON

HILLEL

YOSEF RIVLIN

MENASHE BEN-ISRAEL

AGRON

HAMARAVIM

ZAMENOHOFF

MAHANE YISRAEL QUARTER **12**

HESS

KING DAVID

PAUL EMILE BUTTAS

KING DAVID

CONTINUE HERE

From the starting point at the intersection of Keren Hayesod St., King David St. and Jabotinsky St. walk down Bloomfield Avenue. Cross Heinrich Heine St. and go to the windmill plaza to view Montefiore's windmill ❶ and carriage. The building immediately below the observation area is one of the two buildings of Mishkenot Sha'ananim.

The windmill was built by Moses Montefiore to provide work for people living in his new settlement and to cut down the cost of flour for the people of Jerusalem. After nineteen years of use it broke down and was not repaired as a diesel-powered flour mill was now in operation in the German Colony. The mill in front of you is renovated, including new milling machinery. The original was damaged during the War of Independence. The renovations were based on photographs of the original and were completed in 2012.

A reconstruction of Montefiore's carriage is on display next to the windmill. This is how he traveled around the world helping the Jewish people. The carriage added to his aura and effectiveness. His original carriage here was severely damaged in a fire, but was reconstructed in 1990. Note the word Jerusalem on his coat of arms.

Exit the area of the windmill and turn left down the hill along Hatsayar Ya'akov Shteinardt St. in the direction of the Lion Fountain. There are a few observation plazas along the way. The best viewing is from a small observation plaza ❷ on the left that has a wooden platform and benches, a telescope, a plaque clearly identifying points of interest, and a recording in Hebrew, English and Arabic describing Yemin Moshe and the Old City.

Note the sign that identifies the valley below you as the Valley of Ben Hinnom. This was used for child sacrifice to Molech during First Temple times. The word "*guy*" means a valley in Hebrew and what once occurred here helps explain the derivation of the word Gehinnom, Hebrew for hell, and Gehenna in Christian and Islamic sources. This valley joins with the Kidron Valley beyond your view. On your left is the south-west corner of the Old City wall. Ahead of you is Mount Zion and the prominent Dormition Abbey. Below you in the distance is the village of Silwan, a predominantly Arab area with a few Jewish residents. Beyond this is the separation barrier that divides territory under the jurisdiction of the Palestinian Authority from Israel. On the right is the village of Abu Tor, a mixed Jewish and Arab neighborhood. You can also see the roof of the Begin Center, and behind this the St. Andrew's Scottish Church that was built by the British during the Mandate.

Where the road curves to the left to the Adenauer Conference Center, keep straight ahead on the sidewalk. Take the path on the left just before the Lion's Fountain ❸ and this will take you through a pleasant park to another observation area ❹. Continue down the steps to Nahon St.

At the beginning of Bnai Brith Bridge and before it crosses Hebron St. you will come to the Peace Monument ❺ made by Yigal Tamarkin. The verse in Hebrew and Arabic on the statue is the well-known verse from Isaiah 2:4 that speaks of turning war implements into farming equipment: "*... and they shall beat their swords into plowshares and their spears into pruning hooks; nation shall not lift the sword against nations, neither shall they learn war anymore.*" Appropriately, the lower part of the monument is made from parts of military vehicles and farming equipment.

This monument was commissioned by Abie Natan (1927-2008), the well-known humanitarian and peace activist. He advocated for peace with Egypt, and following the Six Day War, for peace with the Palestinians. He is famous for his Voice of Peace radio station, which was once broadcast from a ship outside Israeli territorial waters. The monument was erected at the edge of no-mans land and opposite the Jordanian border just a few months before the Six Day War.

Follow Nahon St. to the left and in a few minutes you will come to an archway on the left with wooden doors, which is a front entrance to Mishkenot Sha'ananim ❻. Go through the archway and walk up the steps. Peer over the metal gate for a view of the building.

The land for Mishkenot Sha'ananim was purchased by Sir Moses Montefiore, and the project was made possible with money from the estate of Juda Touro, an American Jewish businessman and bachelor from New Orleans. Montefiore was the executor for his will in which $50,000 was earmarked for funding Jewish settlement in Palestine. The metal work is from Ramsgate in the United Kingdom, which is where Montefiore lived, and shows his

hands-on involvement in this project. Each apartment, which is numbered with Hebrew lettering, had 1.5 rooms and an outhouse. At the top of the building is a plaque in Hebrew in the shape of a Magen David honoring its two benefactors, Juda Touro and Moses Montefiore.

Security, actual and perceived, was of paramount importance for this project. Note that the roof has parapets. These were meant to resemble those of the Old City wall and to convey the message that these buildings were as safe as those in the Old City. Even its name, which translates as "peaceful habitation," was intended to convey the impression of security. In addition, the building was surrounded by walls with secured gates, one of which you are currently standing by.

This entire neighborhood was renovated by the city after the Six Day War and Mishkenot Sha'ananim was turned into a cultural center and guesthouse for writers, intellectuals and musicians.

Continue along Nahon St. to the end of the street, and turn left onto Yemin Moshe St. From this point, you will be doing some zigzagging to obtain an appreciation of Yemin Moshe.

Yemin Moshe was established in 1892-1894 by the Montefiore Welfare Fund. The land around Mishkenot Sha'ananim had been previously bought by Montefiore using money from the Judo Touro estate and the project so dear to Montefiore's heart, of settling Jews outside the Old City, was continued after his death. The intention was for this to become a middle-class neighborhood.

However, following the War of Independence, Yemin Moshe became a dangerous place to live in because of sniper fire, as it was close to the armistice line with Jordan. It was populated by new immigrants and the area deteriorated. After the Six Day War and re-unification of the city, Yemin Moshe was redesigned as an upscale neighborhood and artist colony, and the immigrants living there were relocated to Meah Shearim and to Nachla'ot. Compensation was provided, but one cannot but feel sympathy for these people who had, over the years, created a community in very difficult conditions.

Nowadays, this is a beautiful, quiet neighborhood with picturesque buildings and attractive gardens. Some would say that it is too quiet. Many of the homes are vacation homes and the owners live in their home countries for much of the year. The artist colony never materialized.

Go up the steps and take the first right onto Ha-Mevasser St. At the end of this road turn left onto Ha-Migdal St., and then take an immediate right onto Pele Yoez St. On the right, you will see Beit Yisrael Synagogue ❼, the original Ashkenazi synagogue of Yemin Moshe.

This synagogue was dedicated in 1899 and was one of the first synagogues to be built outside the Old City. The building was renovated in 1967 after the Six Day War and is now used by an active "Anglo" congregation.

Ahead is a small, pretty garden. Before this, turn left onto Ha-Metsuda St. There is a white plaque ❽ on the four-storied building on the left memorializing Avraham Michal Kurschenbaum who just before the start of the War of Independence used the single but illegal Bren gun in the community to prevent an Arab horde from attacking Yemin Moshe. He had been assigned to this position by the Haganah. Tragically, a British marksman from the King David Hotel shot him, since Jews were not permitted to have weapons during the Mandate, even in self-defense.

After viewing the plaque, turn around, retrace your steps down one flight of steps, and take the first turning on your right, which is Ha-Tiqwa St. This road has two paths, an upper and lower one. Take the upper path as it is more picturesque. After crossing Ha-Migdal St. this road leads directly into Malki St.

Just before the end of this road you will see an inconspicuous building on your left, the neighborhood's original Sephardi synagogue, the Beit Knesset HaSephardi Hagadol ❾.

Between the War of Independence and the Six Day War this was a thriving synagogue, but when the area was gentrified, the community, which until this time had been living rent-free, could no longer afford to live here. I am told that there are still original inhabitants who come back from other parts of the city to attend Shabbat services.

At the end of Malki St. turn right onto Yemin Moshe St. and go up the steps. Take the first right onto Tura St. Continue on this street until you come to its end at HaMetsuda St. Go down and then up the stairs on the left to a Jerusalem treasure – a quiet, beautiful garden, called the Boustan Abraham Gozlan ❿.

Climb up the path to the top of the garden and then turn right. Continue on this path until you overlook the fountain. With the peaceful sound of running water in the background, you may wish to relax a bit and even explore the garden.

At this point, for a shorter circular walk, you can retrace your steps along the top of the garden and via Heinrich Heine St. return to the windmill plaza and beginning of this walk. Alternatively, continue on the longer walk that will take you into the center of town.

Opposite the fountain, turn left and exit the park onto King David St. between building number 27 and the King David Hotel. Before reaching these buildings, notice on your left some rocky ruins in a depression. This is a Second Temple-era burial cave. Some identy this as King Herod's family's tomb ⓫.

At the end of Elimelech Admoni St., turn right onto King David St. and continue past the King David Hotel on your right and the YMCA building on your left.

Cross over King David St. at the second pedestrian crossing just before Paul Emile Botta St. Then cross Abraham Lincoln St. and Moshe Hess St. and you will soon see an alleyway between the two buildings of the King David Residence. Take the steps down to the former Mahane Yisrael Quarter ⓬.

Mahane Yisrael is the second neighborhood built by Jews outside the Old City walls. It was formed in 1968 by Moroccan Jews from North Africa who felt they were not getting a fair share of Sephardi communal funds. Under the leadership of their young and dynamic leader Rabbi David ben Shimon they decided to leave the Old City and go it alone. They bought land without any philanthropic aid and build their own neighborhood. The success of the Mishkenot Sha'ananim project made people realize that this type of venture could be accomplished and that living outside the city walls was not excessively dangerous.

The neighborhood was small, next to a cemetery, and the houses were not well built, although it was constructed with considerable enthusiasm. At the back of the central courtyard on Hama'ravim St. and Zamenohoff St. you can see a few of the original buildings that were built around the quarter. The rest of the neighborhood has been rebuilt.

The courtyard in front of the Worldwide North Africa Jewish Heritage Center

In front of you is one of the most beautiful courtyards in Jerusalem. It forms the garden patio for the Worldwide North Africa Jewish Heritage Center. This building belonged to Rabbi David ben Shimon and once contained apartments. It was deserted after the War of Independence when this area became a no-man's-land. After the Six Day War, the building was renovated as a cultural center and museum. This entire area was recently beautified, and the house and its grounds, with its fountain and plants, now resemble an aristocratic home from Morocco. Twenty-four Moroccan artisans were brought in specially to produce the mosaics.

> Exit the courtyard by the 3rd alleyway on your left opposite the second water fountain. Turn right when this section of alley comes to an end and continue to Agron St.

> Turn left on Agron St., cross over the road at the pedestrian crossing, and take the first turn on your right onto Menashe ben Israel St. between Independence Park and the Mamluke cemetery. Mamilla Pool, which no longer contains water, is located in the cemetery and was part of the water supply system built by Herod for Jerusalem during Second Temple times. Continue on this road until its intersection with Hillel St.

> At the first four-way intersection cross Hillel St. Take the first left onto Yoel Moshe Salomon St. and within a very short distance you will come to the intersection with Yosef Rivlin St. On the wall of the adjacent wine shop is a plaque describing the formation of the third settlement built by Jews outside the city walls.

Walk a short distance along Yosef Rivlin St. until you come to an open archway on the left with an orange information sign on the wall. This leads past the entrance of the Friends of Zion Museum into the Nahalat Shiva Quarter ⓭.

In the 1860's, seven brave families pooled resources to form the Builders of Jerusalem Society, and they bought land adjacent to the main road into Jerusalem (now Jaffa Rd.) to build the third Jewish neighborhood outside the Old City walls. Many of these families were descendants of disciples of the Vilna Gaon who believed in building up Jerusalem as part of the Divine plan for Redemption. Yosef Rivlin, one of the founders, won the lot to build the first house. When the building was completed, his family did not join him, as they considered it too dangerous. Eventually, however, they and the other families moved into their houses, and by 1875 fifty families were living here. After this project, Rivlin took upon himself to help establish other new neighborhoods in Jerusalem.

Each home had only one story, and over time the families moved on to better housing. Older occupants could not afford to upgrade their homes and the area became dilapidated. The entire area was slated for demolition by the Jerusalem Municipality. However, there was considerable resistance to this among Jerusalem residents, and as you can see, the will of the people prevailed. The facades of many of the buildings were renovated, and it is now a delightful place to walk through.

Walk through the central walkway of this neighborhood until you come to its two synagogues. Nahalat Yaakov ⓮ is on your right. It was inaugurated in 1873 and was the first Ashkenazi synagogue built outside the Old City walls. It is now a Chabad Center. Ohel Yitzhak ⓯ is on your left. It was inaugurated in 1888 and was the first Sephardi synagogue to be built outside the Old City.

Turn left into the alleyway adjoining Ohel Yitzhak Synagogue. You will soon see on your right Tmol Shilshom, the popular kosher café/ restaurant/ bookshop/ centre for cultural events. It is named after "Tmol Shilshom", a book by Nobel Prize laureate, S. Y. Agnon ("Only Yesterday" in English). It is located in one of the quarter's original buildings. Continue ahead on Yehoshua Yellin Alley until you come to Yoel Moshe Salomon St.

Turn right on Yoel Moshe Salomon St. and this will take you past HaMashbir Lazarchan Department Store and Zion Square to Jaffa Rd. This is the end of the walk. The closest stop on the light rail is a few minutes away on your left.

Nearby Places of Interest:

You will pass close to several interesting museums on this walk:

Menachem Begin Heritage Center at 6 S.U. Nahon St. has an experiential multi-media exhibit that takes you on a time journey. Menachem Begin emanates Jewish pride and the story of his life and political activities is quite inspiring. It is open Sunday, Monday, Wednesday and Thursday from 9 am–4:30 pm, Tuesday 9 am–9 pm, and Friday and holidays 9 am–12:30 pm. Tours need to be booked in advance. You can fill in a form online or call (02) 565-2011. The museum commentary can be heard in Hebrew and Engish and other languages. There is an admission fee.

Friends of Zion Museum at 20 Yosef Rivlin Street presents a 3-D virtual tour of the non-Jewish political figures, academics, businessmen and military officials who, through their faith, forged a bond between the Jewish and Christian peoples. The museum is open Sunday to Thursday 9:30-6 pm, Friday 9:30-2 pm, and Saturday 10 am–6 pm. You can book a tour in Hebrew or English on line or at (02) 532-9400. There is an admission fee.

Hebrew Music Museum at 10 Yoel Moshe Salomon St. shows the influence of the diaspora on Jewish music. There are several rooms with displays of various instruments from different parts of the world. You can listen to many of the instruments and watch a historical movie. There are organized tours or you can do a self-guided tour with a computer pad and earphones. Tours and pad explanations are available in English. A highlight of the museum is a reality display of the ancient Temple. The museum is open Sunday to Thursday 9:30 am–8 pm and Friday 9:30 am,1:30 pm. There is an admission charge. Their phone number for booking a tour is: (02) 540-6505.

Museum of Italian Jewish Art at 25 Hillel St. displays impressive Italian Judaica from the Renaissance to the present. One exhibit is an entire Synagogue brought over from the Italian city of Veneto. The museum is closed on Monday, and is open Sunday, Tuesday and Wednesday from 10:30 am–4:30 pm, Thursday 12 pm–7 pm, and Friday 10 am–1 pm. There is an entrance fee. Their phone number is (02) 580-1144. The museum is closed on Shabbat and the synagogue is used by Italian Jews for services.

10 Teddy Kollek – A Great Builder of Jerusalem

A discussion of the development of modern Jerusalem would be incomplete without consideration of the role of Teddy Kollek, the first mayor of reunified Jerusalem. This walk visits three of the many projects his Jerusalem Foundation initiated – the continuing development of Yemin Moshe, Teddy Park, and the Jerusalem Walls National Park. We will also watch a short movie in the Artists Colony about Teddy's achievements.

TIME: 2 hours

DISTANCE: 4 km

TYPE OF WALK: Circular

DIFFICULTY:
An easy walk, mainly on paved roads.

STARTING POINT:
The intersection of Bloomfield Boulevard with Keren Hayesod, King David St. and Jabotinsky St. There are WC's in the adjacent Bloomfield Park by the water fountain.

PUBLIC TRANSPORT:
Many buses pass by the starting point of this walk. Enter "Montefiore Windmill" into Moovit.

DRIVING DIRECTIONS AND PARKING:
Enter "Sderot Bloomfield" into Waze. There are parking meters on Heinrich Heine St.

OVERVIEWS

TEDDY KOLLEK – THE GREAT BUILDER

What do the following personalities have in common – King Solomon, King Hezekiah, King Herod and Teddy Kollek? The answer: All were great builders of Jerusalem. Admittedly, the name Teddy Kollek sounds out of place in this list but in terms of the number of projects he initiated he did more for the physical layout of this city than any of these other historic figures.

Teddy Kollek (1911-2007) was born in a small town in Hungary. He spent his early years in Vienna. Following his aliyah to Israel, he became one of the founding members of Kibbutz Ein Gev, but left the kibbutz to take up administrative positions. He campaigned for election as mayor of Jerusalem in 1965, a position that at that time was of no great importance. To his surprise, he was elected mayor of this small sleepy town. After the Six Day War and reunification of Jerusalem he suddenly found himself mayor of a large, vibrant metropolitan city, a position he held for nearly three decades, until 1993.

Teddy established the Jerusalem Foundation soon after being elected. This foundation initiated numerous building projects, including building two hundred parks and gardens, the redevelopment of Yemin Moshe, the Israel Museum, community and health centers, and much more. As mayor of a city in which the three monotheistic faiths had a stake, Teddy appreciated that it was his job to reach out to all the citizens of his city and to include them in his projects.

Teddy was buried on Mount Herzl in an area usually reserved for national leaders – an indication of how highly he was regarded.

WHAT'S IN A WALL?

The present Old City wall was built by the Ottoman sultan Suleiman the Magnificent between 1535 to 1538, and it is truly a magnificent structure with battlements and 34 watchtowers. Much of its foundations, however, are from previous eras.

When King David conquered Jerusalem from the Jebusites it was a strongly fortified city, and David made no major changes to the original Canaanite walls. However, King Solomon, who reigned between about 970 to 930 BCE, extended the city northwards to encompass the Temple Mount and the intervening Ophel Hill.

During the rule of Hezekiah (715 to 686 BCE), the city expanded onto Jerusalem's "Western Hill" and now included Mount Zion and areas of the present-day Jewish and Armenian Quarters. Much of this expansion was due to immigrants arriving in Jerusalem from the Northern Kingdom after its destruction by the Assyrians. Hezekiah therefore extended the walls of Jerusalem to enclose this "Upper City." This new section of the city wall extended from the City of David, enclosed the Siloam Pool which was outside the southern limits of the City of David, and surrounded Mount Zion. It then followed the current western wall of the Old City, and from about where the Jaffa Gate is today it turned eastward to reach the Temple Mount. Nebuchadnezzar, the King of Babylon, destroyed Jerusalem, its Temple, and its walls, in 586 BCE, with a great devastation (II Kings 25:9-10).

When Nehemiah came to Jerusalem from Babylon in 445 BCE to join the returnees, the population of the city was quite small. Rebuilding the city wall was a priority for him, and the area he enclosed was probably equivalent to that enclosed by King Solomon's walls. A remnant of his wall can be seen in the City of David (see page 12 in chapter 1).

During the Second Temple period, the city expanded again to the Western Hill, and the Hasmoneans built what Josephus calls the "First Wall." This more or less enclosed the same area as Hezekiah's wall and it included Mount Zion. During the rule of King Herod (37 to 4 BCE), a "Second Wall" was added to enclose an area north of the First Wall in what is now the Arab Quarter. This extended to the northwest corner of the Temple Mount. The walls of Jerusalem were destroyed by the Romans during the Great Revolt, including a northern wall that extended to where the Russian Compound is today. Their new city of Aelia Capitolina had no walls around it, a reflection of the security they felt as victors.

The Byzantines built a wall around Jerusalem, but this was destroyed by an earthquake in 1033 CE. It was not until the Muslim Fatimid caliphate that a new wall was built around the city. This city wall did not include Mount Zion or the City of David. Much of the Crusader and Ottoman walls were built on top of the foundations of the Fatimid wall, and therefore these also did not include either Mount Zion or the City of David. Knowledge of the location of the City of David was lost and was only discovered by archaeologists in the modern era.

Hence, the present western wall of Jerusalem from the Jaffa Gate to Mount Zion has been the city wall since the time of Hezekiah. This section of the Turkish wall therefore includes foundations from the First Temple, Hasmonean, Herodian, Byzantine and Muslim periods. In one small section of the wall (which will be viewed on this walk in the Jerusalem Walls National Park), remnants of all these historic periods can be seen together.

THE WALK

Additional information about the windmill, Mishkanot Sha'ananim and Yemin Moshe can be found on the previous walk (page 101 to page 103 in chapter 9)

Go down the hill on Yemin Moshe St. You will pass on your right the windmill ❶, the two turreted buildings of Mishkanot She'ananim and the Touro Restaurant. On your left are the beautiful streets and alleys of Yemin Moshe.

Yemin Moshe was established in 1892-1894 with funds from the Montefiore Testimonial Fund. When Sir Moses Montefiore built Mishkenot Sha'ananim with funds from the Judo Touro estate, he also bought the land around it. This enabled his project of settling Jews outside the Old City to be continued after his death. The intention was that Yemin Moshe would become a middle-class neighborhood. However, following the War of Independence, the Hinnom Valley between the Old City and Yemin Moshe became the armistice line with Jordan and Yemin Moshe became a dangerous place to live in because of sniper fire.

After the Six Day War and the reunification of the city, Yemin Moshe was redesigned as an upscale neighborhood that would include an artists' colony. The artists never materialized. Nevertheless, the immigrants that were living here and in Mishkenot Sha'ananim had to relocate. This was one of the tough and controversial decisions made by Teddy. The residents here had endured a lot living close to the border with Jordan and had formed cohesive communities. However, when the area was upgraded, they could no longer afford to live in their homes. They received some compensation, but the communities separated. There have been no large-scale relocations like this in Jerusalem since that time.

At the end of Yemin Moshe St. turn left through the green metal gate onto S.U. Nathon St. As you walk along, notice

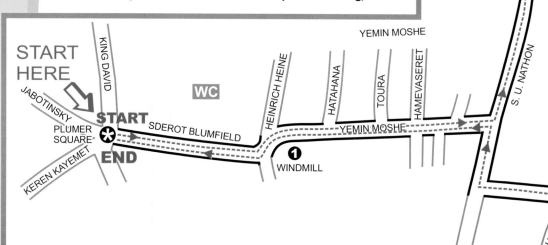

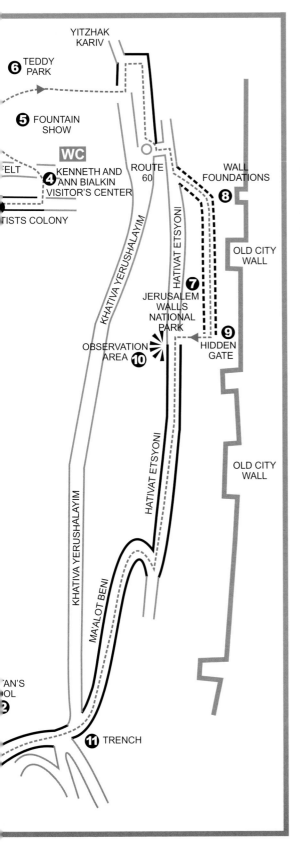

the Sultan's Pool ❷ in the valley below you on your right and the houses of Yemin Moshe on your left.

The Sultan's Pool was built by another great builder of Jerusalem, Herod the Great, to ensure water was available for the palace he built for himself next to the Citadel and adjacent to the western city wall. Water accumulated in the pool from a damming up of the Hinnom Valley. The pool was renovated by the Crusaders in the 12th century — who used it for watering their horses — and again by the Mamluke sultan Barquq. The Ottoman sultan Suleiman the Magnificent enlarged the pool into a reservoir in the 16th century (hence the name of the pool). He also built a public fountain (a *sabil*) on the rim of the pool for the use of travelers coming to Jerusalem from the direction of Bethlehem. To supply this fountain, he diverted water from the Hasmonean-built Lower Aqueduct. This aqueduct skirted the Sultan's Pool (see the essay "Supplying water to thirsty Jerusalem" on page 133). You will see the fountain towards the end of this walk, although it is no longer functional. The pool area is now used as an open-air theatre for concerts.

Exit this road through another green gate and you will come to a small parking lot. Ascend the steps on the far left of the parking lot to Metzuda St. and immediately take the first right onto Pele Yoetz St. You are now in a small, but very pretty garden (Gan Yehudit) containing olive trees.

111

At the next fork, leave the park using the path to the right and exit Yemin Moshe through another green gate. Continue along this path until you reach Dror Elial St. Cross the road, turn right, and after a short distance there are steps on the left leading down to the Artists Colony ❸ in the valley. The soothing sound of Francine's Fountain can be heard as you descend the steps.

On either side of the central lane are impressive high-end art stores selling silver, jewelry, painting, photography and fabric. The stores are not always open. This depends on the season and amount of tourists.

Don't miss the Teddy Kollek movie ❹. About halfway along the building on the left is a glass door with the sign 'push.' The entrance is not very conspicuous. As you enter the walkway, notice the photos of Teddy Kollek on the wall on the left. On the right is a room to watch a 3-D movie about Teddy Kollek. This nine minute movie is quite inspiring and explains how Teddy contributed to making the city what it is today. The corridor and movie room are open from 10 am–5 pm and 10 am–3 pm on Fridays. At these times there is an attendant who will select for you the language in which you wish to hear the movie. There is no charge.

Exit the exhibit room and head towards Teddy Park ❻. This park was established by the Jerusalem Foundation as a tribute to Teddy. Ascend the ramp on the left and you will come to an area with fountain nozzles, the site for Jerusalem's Sound and Light Fountain Show ❺. At fixed times in the evening, synchronized shoots of water come from 256 nozzles accompanied by flashing lights and recorded music by the New Jerusalem Philharmonic. During the day there is a water display only (see Nearby Places of Interest on the next page).

As you exit the park, you will see an old Turkish building. There is nothing special about this building other than that it found itself in this park and no one was prepared to demolish it. You can walk through it if you wish. There are a number of exits from the park to reach Route 60, the main road paralleling the Old City wall.

Cross Route 60 at the pedestrian crossing by Yitzhak Kariv St. and turn right. After a very short distance, turn left at the next intersection towards the wall. Then take the right fork, which is Hativat Etsyoni St. You are now in the Jerusalem Walls National Park ❼ that was established by the Jerusalem Foundation and that partially surrounds the Old City walls.

Take the concrete ramp on your left, which will bring you closer to Suleiman's city wall. Look at the first sign on your left by the far corner of a protruding tower. This sign explains that the foundations ❽ in front of you contain First Temple, Hellenistic, Herodian, Byzantine, early Islamic (Fatimid), Ayyubid and Ottoman components. Each section is identified.

The concrete path becomes a gravel path, and you will soon come to an observation area from where you can view the other side of the Hinnom Valley. There is also a sign to help identify the landmarks.

At the end of the gravel path look for a sign indicating that an entrance way into the city that was close to Herod's palace was covered over by the Turks when they built their city wall. This "Hidden Gate" ❾ was identified by the presence of steps. Go down these ancient steps to another lookout ❿ on Hativat Etsyoni St. There is a recording in English, Hebrew or Arabic, and another sign identifying the various buildings across the valley.

Continue along Hativat Etsyoni St. Opposite the corner of the Old City wall you will see a path called Ma'alot Benny that descends into the Hinnom Valley. Follow this path framed with thyme as it winds down to the Hinnom Valley. Just before the main road, notice a bunker-like structure **⓫** on your left. This is the remains of a tunnel built after the 1948 War of Independence that linked Mount Zion to Yemin Moshe and allowed safe access to Mount Zion. You will recall that Mount Zion remained an Israeli enclave after the War of Independence, with the Old City being in Jordanian hands.

Cross Hebron Rd. and walk on the sidewalk that crosses the valley. The Sultan's Pool will be on your right and a grass-covered park on your left – the Hinnom National Park. Notice the sabil **⓬** on your right built by Sulumein the Magnificent when he renovated the Sultan's Pool.

Ahead of you is a stairway leading to Yemin Moshe. At the fork, turn to the right. Adjacent to the green gate turn left onto Yemin Moshe St. This street will lead you back to your starting point.

Nearby Places of Interest:

***Sound and Light Fountain Show** in Teddy Park. There are only short water shows during the day and it is worth coming back at night to see the full display. The times of the shows during the summer are as follows: Daytime (water display only) 10 am, 12 pm, 2 pm, 4 pm, and 6 pm. Nighttime (water display with lights and music): 8 pm, 9 pm, and 10 pm. There are reduced hours during the winter.*

***Menachem Begin Heritage Museum** at 6 S.U. Nahon St. (see page 106).*

***Tower of David** is by the Jaffa Gate (see page 29).*

***Cable Car Museum** at 17 Hebron Rd. is one of Jerusalem's lesser-known museums. It is in the most northern building of the Zion Hotel although everyone is entitled to visit it. Mount Zion was captured by the Israel Defense Force during Israel's War of Independence but it was dangerous to supply this position because of firing by the Arab Legion. A cable car was therefore set up over the Hinnom Valley and used at night to deliver supplies. The present cable is new, but the cart, which was big enough to transport soldiers, is the original. The museum is open from 9 am–5 pm Sunday to Thursday, and 9 am–1 pm on Friday. Your visit needs to be arranged in advance. Their number is: (02) 568-9569 or (02) 460-9540. There is no admission charge.*

11 Givat Ram – Birds, Roses, The Supreme Court and the Knesset

This circular walk should be fun for all ages. It includes the Jerusalem Bird Observatory, the Rose Garden, the menorah outside the Knesset, the Supreme Court building, and the Biblical displays on the roof of Cinema City, including Noah's ark. Free tours of the Supreme Court building and the Knesset are available in English. After the walk consider visiting one of the nearby museums – the Israel Museum and Shrine of the Book, the Bible Lands Museum, or the Bloomfield Science Museum.

The Ornamental Lake at the Wohl Rose Garden

Consider making this an educational visit for your family. A question for the older kids: What are the functions and inter-relationships between the three branches of the Israeli government – the Knesset, the government administration, and the judiciary? And for the adults: In what ways does the Supreme Court in Israel differ from that of other countries you may be familiar with? A tour in English of the Supreme Court will help you with that one. This free tour takes place only once a day. Plan to be inside the entrance of the Supreme Court before 12 pm (see page 121). Our Background discussion may also be helpful. And to help you complete the topic – there are free tours of the Knesset in English several times a day.

TIME: About one hour of walking, but you may need half a day if including tours, and a complete day if visiting nearby museums.

DISTANCE: 2.25 km

TYPE OF WALK: Circular

DIFFICULTY: An easy walk on paved roads suitable for a wheelchair and stroller.

STARTING POINT: Corner of Sderot Yitchak Rabin and Yoel Zusman St. next to Cinema City.

PUBLIC TRANSPORT: Cinema City is served by many buses. Enter "Cinema City Jerusalem" into Moovit.

DRIVING DIRECTIONS AND PARKING: Enter "Cinema City" into Waze. There is paid underground parking at Cinema City. The entrance to חניון הלאום is from Sderot Yitchak Rabin.

ISRAEL'S SUPREME COURT – A PARADIGM OF JUSTICE OR A JUDICIAL DICTATORSHIP?

In 1949, after the War of Independence, the government of David Ben-Gurion declared that Jerusalem would become the capital of the new State of Israel and announced its intention to move government ministries and institutions to Jerusalem, and specifically to Givat Ram. This hill formerly belonged to the Arab village of Sheikh Badr and was taken over by the Haganah during the War of Independence. It had been used as an assembly point for the officers of the Gadna Youth Battalion and was given the name Givat (Hill of) Ram, Ram being an acronym for the Hebrew words *rikuz mefakdim* (gathering of commanders).

This hill has three ridges. One ridge was designated as a campus for the Hebrew University, another for cultural institutions, such as the Israel Museum, and the third was assigned to the government.

The Torah proclaims the supreme value of justice and that it should be the foundation of a Jewish state: "*Justice, justice shall you pursue, so that you will live and take possession of the land that the Lord your God gives you*" (Deuteronomy 16:20). Understandably, therefore, the practice of justice has been placed on a very high pedestal in Israel. This is reflected in the magnificence and symbolism of its Supreme Court building.

But what paradigm of justice should Israel's Supreme Court practice? Should it be that of the Bible and its accompanying oral traditions as developed by Judaism over thousands of years? Or perhaps it should be the liberal and humanistic traditions developed in Christian Europe over the last two millennia, traditions very much based on human rights? If the latter – how do Zionism and the "Jewishness" of the state fit in? And how does one balance the rights of individuals versus the very real security issues the state confronts on a regular basis?

In Israel there is no consensus on these issues. Israel does not have a secular constitution, although it does have a collection of Basic Laws that serve a similar purpose. The bottom line is that justice in this country is far from being a simple matter!

Israel's Supreme Court functions as the country's highest court of appeals. It also acts as the High Court of Justice (Bet Mishpat Gavoha LeTzedek), more commonly known by its acronym "Bagatz" (בג"ץ). In this role, the Supreme Court handles petitions from citizens and organizations regarding the legality of decisions of State authorities, and even the constitutionality of laws enacted by the Knesset. This very open policy means that the Supreme Court is extremely busy with about ten thousand cases a year compared to about eighty cases a year for the US Supreme Court!

About twenty percent of the court's activities are in the political arena. The Supreme Court has established itself as Israel's most powerful institution, with the ability to override the Knesset, the cabinet, the military, the civil administration for the territories, and the Ministry of Religious Affairs – in fact, this includes just about everybody.

How did this strange situation arise?

In 1992, former Supreme Court justice Aharon Barak put together a constitution for Israel based on two laws passed by the Knesset – "Basic Law: Human Dignity and Liberty" and "Basic Law: Freedom of Occupation."

These two laws were passed by 27% and 19% of Israel's legislature respectively and never mentioned the word "constitution" or the notion of judicial review. However, three years later the Supreme Court held that these two Basic Laws constituted Israel's new "constitution" and that any new Knesset law would be subject to judicial review based on these Basic Laws. In effect, the Supreme Court had accomplished a judicial coup d'etat at the expense of the government.

Moreover, the judges of the Supreme Court are not elected democratically but appointed by a selection committee comprised of two government ministers, two members of the Knesset, three current Supreme Court justices, and two representatives of the Bar Association. Elected officials are therefore a minority of this committee. In effect, the judicial system elects itself, although recently the Government has established more oversight over the election process.

The reality is that this system has some advantages. It can dilute to some extent the stranglehold the ultra-religious can have over the religious life of the State as result of their political power. However, it can also stymie the function of the Knesset. Issues of settlement in the territories and illegal immigration, for example, have become subject to the concept of human rights rather than the will of elected representatives. Depending on the activism of the Court and the direction of the government, it is a system designed for controversy.

Right-wing parties in the government in particular have found it problematic to deal with the Supreme Court in matters related to settlement in Judea and Samaria. To direct the power of the Supreme Court, the Knesset has recently passed a new "Basic law" that emphasizes the "Jewishness" of the state. Judicial disputes regarding land matters in Judea and Samaria have also been transferred from the Supreme Court to lower courts more sympathetic to Jewish settlement. Plus, new (and highly controversial) laws may be brought to the Knesset to curb the ability of the Supreme Court to override Knesset decisions.

So, is the Israeli Supreme Court a judicial dictatorship or a shining light to the nations of the world on matters of justice? One could perhaps say that it is both. Having said this, the decisions of the Supreme Court are highly respected in the country and its dictatorial powers make it the only institution with the ability to dig the country out of political impasses, particularly in matters related to the interaction between religion and the state.

Here are two interesting facts about the judicial system in Israel: Israel does not use a jury system but a court of judges, usually three, and sometimes more. Also, prisoners are not handcuffed during their trial. Why is this so? Jews tend to be very expressive with their hands, and it was thought that handcuffs would limit the ability of prisoners to express themselves!

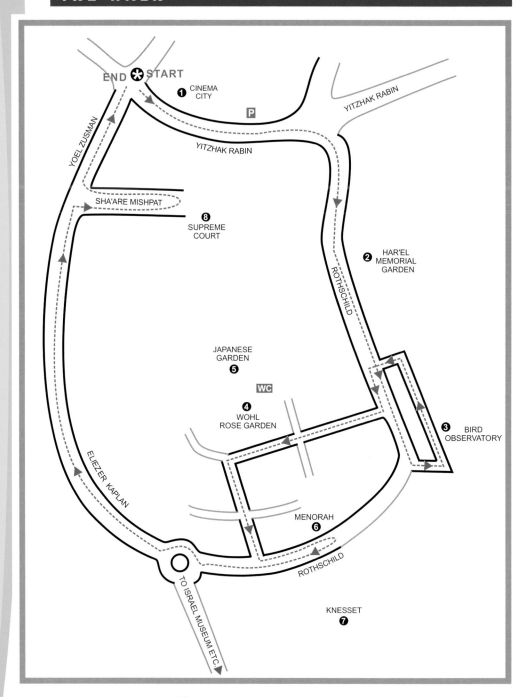

From Cinema City **❶**, cross Sderot Yitzhak Rabin on the pedestrian crossing and turn left. Continue under the bridge and after a few minutes turn right onto James A. De Rothschild St. The back of the Supreme Court building is on your right.

Soon on your left is a memorial garden to the Palmach and Har'el Brigade ❷. The recorded explanation in Hebrew or English is worth listening to.

The Har'el Brigade was one of three IDF (Israel Defense Force) brigades formed from the Palmach after the declaration of the state. Under the command of Yitzhak Rabin it fought tough battles in the Jerusalem corridor and Jerusalem during the War of Independence. About a third of the brigade lost their lives (see also the essay "Israel's War of Independence" on page 200).

Continue along Rothschild St. Just before the barricade, turn into the alley on your left. If you are stopped by a Knesset security guard, tell him you are heading to the Bird Observatory and you will have no problem proceeding. From the alley, take the first turn on the left to the Jerusalem Bird Observatory ❸.

You will soon see two wooden buildings on your right and a visitor center on your left. The wooden buildings overlook a pool and uncultivated land that birds visit. One of the buildings has benches conveniently set up for bird-watching. The Visitor Center is open Sunday to Thursday 9 am–3 pm.

Israel is a land bridge connecting Europe, Asia and Africa. Because of this, a large variety of migratory birds pass through the country twice a year. This bird observatory is an academic project that tags migratory birds entering the observatory. In this way, together with the international community, their flight paths can be determined.

When you have had your fill of bird watching, proceed to the Wohl Rose Garden ❹ by turning right after exiting the bird-watching building and then left up the steps just before the cemetery. Turn left at the top of the stairway onto Rothschild St. and very soon there is a sign to the Wohl Rose Garden on your right. (If you have a mobility problem, retrace your steps back to Rothschild St. and the Wohl Rose Garden is on your left).

Enter the park by the walkway on the left. At the intersection with a map sign continue straight ahead and this will take you to a lovely Ornamental Lake with benches around it.

From this point, there are numerous small gardens that can be explored. My favorite is the Japanese Garden ❺, which is above the lake waterfall. Go up the steps to the right of the pool and behind the brick wall to a grass lawn. Shortly ahead are steps that lead down to the Japanese garden. This secluded spot with its waterfalls and sound of running water is a delightful area for relaxing or picnicking. Continue exploring the gardens. Depending on the season, there are numerous varieties of roses blossoming. The park contains over four hundred species of roses from around the world.

To exit the park, make your way back to the lake, and from here there is a path with steps leading down to the Knesset building. (For wheelchair and stroller users look at the map of the garden which indicates how to avoid the steps. Plus, the final two sets of steps on this path have ramps).

You are now back on Rothschild St. Turn left towards the bronze menorah ❻, which is a short distance on your left. You may meet a security guard as you turn left. State your destination and you will have no problem proceeding.

The menorah by the Knesset building

The menorah was one of the vessels in the Temple and it is now the symbol of the State of Israel. The design of this menorah accords with the relief on the Arch of Titus in Rome that illustrates Second Temple treasures captured by the Romans during the Great Revolt of the Jews.

The initiative for this project came from Lord Edwin Samuel who presented this gift to the Knesset. He was the son of Herbert Samuel, the first British High Commissioner to Palestine. The project was financed by donations from the United Kingdom and constructed by the Anglo-Jewish artist Benno Elkan. Carvings on its branches and stem depict events from the Bible and later Jewish history. These include (from the top left to the right) – Isaiah and his vision of the End of Days, Ezra the Scribe reading the Torah, David and Goliath, Moses during the battle with Amalek, Hillel the Elder teaching all of the Torah on one leg, and Jeremiah bewailing the wickedness of Israel. Above the pedestal and moving upwards you will see Pioneers, Hear O Israel, the Warsaw Ghetto revolt, Ezekiel's vision of the dry bones, two women of the Bible (Rachel weeping for her children and Ruth the Moabite), the tablets of the Covenant, and again Moses during the battle with Amalek. (Note: this is not a complete list of all the illustrations).

Opposite the menorah is the Knesset Building ❼, and this can be visited (see next page for admission details).

Retrace your steps and continue further to the traffic circle on Eliezer Kaplan St.

[This point on Eliezer Kaplan St. is a convenient one for visiting the Israel Museum, Bible Lands Museum and Science Museum, as they are all within a short bus ride and even walking distance from here. Turn left on Eliezer Kaplan St. if walking to one of museums, or to the right for the nearest bus stop.]

To continue on this walk, turn right onto Eliezer Kaplan St. You will pass the Wohl Rose Garden on your right and government buildings on your left, and soon you will come to Sha'are Mishpat St. on your right leading to the Supreme Court ❽. The building is open to the public. You can view it on your own using the brochure provided. However, a guided tour is very helpful to fully appreciate the symbolism of its architecture (see next page for admission details).

Israel's Supreme Court was housed in Jerusalem's Russian Compound from 1948 until 1992. Eight years before the current building was opened in 1992, Dorothy de Rothschild suggested that a permanent home be constructed for the Supreme Court using funds from the Rothschild Foundation. She felt that this would be an appropriate way to commemorate the work her late husband James de Rothschild had done for Israel. He had dreamed of such a project and even set aside funds for it. An architectural competition was held and this was won by a brother and sister architectural team.

The building they designed has three main sections: a square library wing containing a round courtyard with a copper-clad pyramid, a rectangular administrative wing with judges' chambers arrayed around a cloistered courtyard, and a wing containing five courtrooms extending like fingers from a great main hall.

Writing in the New York Times, Paul Goldberg calls this *"Israel's finest public building,"* and writes further: *"There is no clear front door and no simple pattern to the organization. The building cannot be described solely as long, or solely as rounded, or as being arranged around a series of courtyards; though from certain angles, like the elephant described by the blind man, it could be thought to be any one of these."* The building is rich in symbolism. It is also designed to bring together architectural elements from Jerusalem's past.

Exit the Supreme Court and turn right onto Yoel Zusman St. At the corner of Sderot Yitchak Rabin and Yoel Zusman St. is a memorial to Agranet, a former President of the Supreme Court.

Cross the road to Cinema City ❶. The front entrance is straight ahead of you. The mall contains a large selection of stores, kosher cafes and restaurants. If you have kids with you, and perhaps even if you don't, make your way to the roof. A corridor off the central pool is marked "Dynamic Theater/Land of Bible/Visitor Center" and there is an escalator and elevator from here to the roof. The roof is open from 10 am–5 pm and contains very realistic displays of Noah's ark and other Biblical scenes, with the corresponding Torah verses in Hebrew and English.

Further Details about the Knesset and Supreme Court:

The Knesset: The building can be toured from Sunday to Thursday in Hebrew, English and other languages. The tour lasts about an hour and there is no charge. Tours in English are at 8:30 am, 12 pm and 2 pm. There is artwork by Chagall displayed on the way to the Knesset foyer. Be aware of the Knesset dress code – which is enforced. You will not be allowed entrance if you are over fourteen years of age and wearing shorts, ¾ pants, sleeveless shirts, shirts with political slogans, belly shirts, or flip-flops. Allow about half an hour before the tour for the entry process. You will need a passport or Israeli ID to enter.

The Supreme Court can be toured Sunday to Thursday, except on days when special ceremonies are taking place. No advanced reservation is required. There are free guided tours in Hebrew at 11 am and in English at 12 pm. The guided tour takes about an hour and is valuable not only in pointing out the symbolism of the building (pick up an English brochure if you want more on this), but also in explaining how the court functions within Israel's legal system, and how the Supreme Court differs from those of other countries. Time may also be allotted for questions. Their phone number is: (02) 675-9612.

Nearby Places of Interest:

Israel Museum and Shrine of the Book is at 11 Ruppin Boulevard. It is open Sunday, Monday, Wednesday and Thursday from 10 am–5 pm, Tuesday 4 pm–9 pm (in August 10 am–9 pm), Friday and holiday eves 10 am–2 pm, and Saturday and holidays 10 am–5 pm. There is an admission charge which includes an audio guide. Free parking is available but may be limited. Folding chairs and wheelchairs are available. Exhibits are in the categories of Jewish Art and Life, Archaeology, Art, and Family Activities. There is also a model of Jerusalem in Second Temple times, and of course the Shrine of the Book and its Dead Sea scrolls exhibit. An excellent way to appreciate what this museum has to offer is to do a guided tour. They are offered in English and are free with admission: Archaeology at 11 am, Jewish Art and Life at 1:30 pm, the Synagogue Route at 3 pm, and the Shrine of the Book and model of Jerusalem at 3 pm. The museum has a café, and meat and dairy restaurants – all kosher. Their phone number is: (02) 670-8811.

Bible Lands Museum is at 21 Shmuel Stefan Wise St., Museum Row. This museum claims to be the only museum of its kind in the world to bring to life the civilizations of the Ancient Near East from the dawn of civilization to the early Christian era. It is open Sunday, Monday, Tuesday, Thursday 9:30 am–5:30 pm, Wednesday 9:30 am–9:30 pm, Friday, Saturday, holiday eves 10 am–2 pm. It is closed on Jewish holidays. There is an admission charge. Guided tours are free with museum admission (and should be considered for at least the first visit): Sunday in English 10:30 am, and in Hebrew 11:00 am. There is an additional tour on Wednesdays in English at 5:30 pm, Hebrew 6 pm, and on Saturday in Hebrew at 11:30 am. There are also lectures on Wednesday evenings at 7:30 pm that are free with admission. The museum has a café. Their phone number is: (02) 561-1066.

Bloomfield Science Museum at 3 Museum Blvd. is a quality science museum that will keep your family well occupied. Some free parking is available at the Museum's parking lot and there is also paid parking on the street. It is open Monday to Thursday 10 am–6 pm, Friday 10 am–2 pm, and Saturday 10 am–5 pm. Closed on Sundays. Consider an annual subscription to the museum as it provides free entrance to some three hundred participating science museums around the world. Their phone number is: (02) 654-4888.

12 The Haredi Neighborhoods of Zikhron Moshe and Meah Shearim

A bout one-third of Jerusalem's population belongs to the sector known as haredim, often called "ultra-Orthodox Jews." In this walk through the neighborhoods of Zikhron Moshe, Geulah and Meah Shearim you will see the people who live here and view the outside of some important Hasidic centers. The main commercial arteries for Jerusalem's haredi community also provide plenty of opportunities for shopping.

TIME: 1.5 hours

DISTANCE: 4 km

TYPE OF WALK: Circular

DIFFICULTY: An easy walk.

STARTING POINT: Corner of Jaffa St. and Strauss St.

PUBLIC TRANSPORT: The start of the walk is close to the light rail stop "Jaffa Center" and bus stops on Strauss St. and King George St.

OVERVIEW

WHAT DISTINGUISHES HAREDIM FROM OTHER RELIGIOUS JEWS?

What characterizes a haredi Jew is not an easy question to answer, as the term is loosely applied to individuals and groups encompassing a wide spectrum of beliefs, customs and lifestyles. Nevertheless, most of those identifying themselves as haredi share the common characteristic of disengaging in varying degree from the wider secular society around them.

The word "haredi" is derived from a Hebrew word meaning "to tremble," and implies a constant awareness and awe of God (see Isaiah 66:5). Jews of other religious orientations might protest that they too fear God, and indeed at one time the term haredi was used as a synonym for all Orthodox Jews. Nevertheless, members of the contemporary haredi community use this term to indicate that they take on more religious strictures than other religious Jews.

The haredi lifestyle is primarily, though not exclusively, a European/Ashkenazi phenomenon. Haredim can be divided into two major sub-groups - Hasidim and non-Hasidim. Hasidim follow the teachings of Rabbi Yisrael Baal Shem Tov (1700-1760), a charismatic leader who initiated a Jewish spiritual revival movement in the Western Ukraine that spread rapidly throughout Eastern Europe. The movement popularized many of the ideas of Lurianic Kabbalah. Its theology is based on a concept known as "panentheism," the notion that all of existence is suffused with divinity and that God's Presence can be perceived within all nature. (This is different from "pantheism," a doctrine that equates nature with divinity and which is deemed heretical by Orthodox Judaism).

As Hasidism became a mass movement, many of its adherents were unable to handle such profound immanence of God and they gathered around pious leaders who became intermediaries in helping them achieve closeness to God. These leaders lived in various cities and were known as "*Rebbes*." With time, most of these leadership positions became dynastic, and the customs of the sect reflected the practices, customs and perspectives of the Rebbe.

Most of the Hasidic communities of Europe were wiped out during the Holocaust, but some rebbes were able to escape, and they reconstituted their Hasidic sects with remarkable success in Israel and other countries.

Non-Hasidim, often known as *Perushim* or *Misnagdim*, arrived in Palestine from Lithuania in the late 1800's. They were followers of the Gaon of Vilna (1720-1797) and believed that Jewish immigration to the Holy Land would hasten the coming of the final Redemption. Since they were the first religious European Jews to settle in Palestine in significant numbers, their customs would have a significant influence on the Ashkenazi Orthodox Jews who came after them. When they first arrived in Palestine they lived in the Old City, but many later moved to Meah Shearim and other neighborhoods that were being built outside the Old City walls. The Perushim were initially Zionistic, and it was not until between the First and Second World Wars when haredi Hungarian immigrants came to Palestine that they adopted a more non-compromising attitude to Zionism.

The haredim of Jerusalem, many of whom live north of Jaffa Road, can usually be identified by their clothing and appearance. Some aspects of their attire are similar to that of other Orthodox Jews, while other aspects specifically identify them as haredi.

The women and girls dress extremely modestly, wearing long dresses with long sleeves, high necklines and stockings so that their entire body except for their head and hands are covered. Married women cover their hair with a wig or scarf.

Men usually wear suits or full-length frocks. They have fringes (*tzitzit*) on their four-cornered garments as specified in the Torah (Numbers 15:37-39). They also wear a head covering (a *kippah*), which is often covered with a hat, which demonstrates their awareness of God. These *kippot* (plural of *kippah*) are usually made from black fabric rather than the knitted style favored by members of the national-religious community. Some haredim, particularly among the Hasidim, have long side locks (*peyot*), a practice based on the Biblical injunction against shaving one's sideburns (Leviticus 19:26). Those who belong to Hasidic groups dress in an attire similar to that worn by Polish nobles in previous centuries, including married men wearing fur hats (called *streimels*) on the Sabbath and holidays. Some haredim speak Yiddish among themselves instead of Hebrew, to keep themselves apart from the general Israeli society, and also because they regard Hebrew as a holy tongue that should not be used for secular purposes.

The disengagement of many haredim from normative Israeli life, in contrast to the engagement of religious Zionists, reflects a major philosophical disagreement regarding the theological significance of the return of millions of Jews to Israel from exile and the restoration of Jewish sovereignty. Many religious Zionists view these developments as signs of redemption, whereas many haredim reject this idea. In its early days, the Zionist movement was led predominantly by secular, and even anti-religious Jews, and haredim could not accept that such an unholy movement could lead to the Messianic redemption foretold by the ancient prophets of Israel. Many haredim also believe that the future Jewish redemption will occur miraculously and not through the normal processes of history. There are even small groups of haredim, such as Satmar Hasidim, who are anti-Zionist. They sympathize with the aims of the Palestinians and are vocal in their desire to see the dissolution of what they perceive as being a secular Jewish state. By contrast, many non-haredi religious Jews believe that perceived ungodliness in Israeli society is not a reason for the religious community to disengage from the Jewish state, but to involve themselves in all its aspects and to infuse it with more holiness.

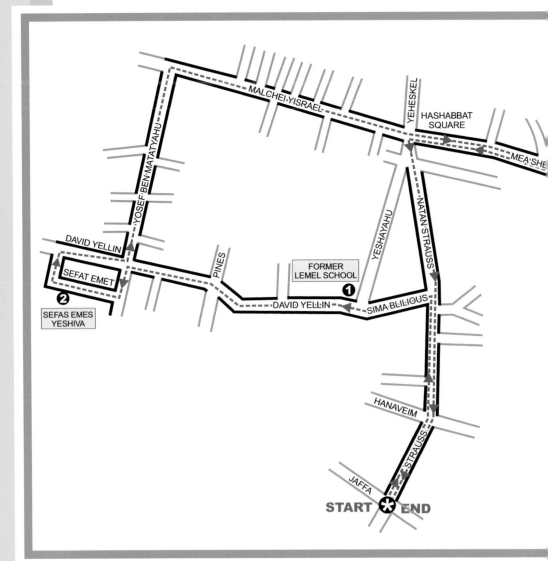

THE WALK

Walk up Nathan Strauss St. Cross Haneviim St. at the old Bikur Cholim Hospital and after this intersection take the second left onto Sima Blilious St. You have now entered a haredi neighborhood with a distinctive old-world charm. At the first major intersection, Sima Blilious St. becomes David Yellin St. This is the southern border of the Zikhron Moshe neighborhood.

Zikhron Moshe was established in 1905 with funds from the Sir Moses Montefiore Testimonial Fund, which was set up by friends of Sir Moses Montefiore in honor of his ninetieth birthday for the purpose of expanding Jewish settlement in Palestine. Zikhron Moshe was one of several Jerusalem neighborhoods promoted by this fund, and like others, such as Yemin Moshe, Mazkeret Moshe, Ohel Moshe and Kiryat Moshe, was named after Montefiore.

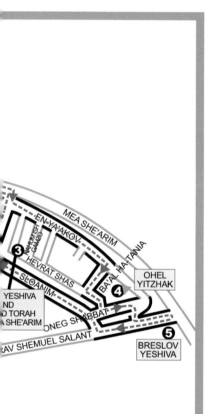

When it was established, Zikhron Moshe was an upscale, modern neighborhood that attracted many educators and liberal thinkers, such as Eliezer ben-Yehuda and David Yellin. Nowadays, the neighborhood is populated mainly by haredim and has many synagogues and yeshivot that cater to their needs. However, evidence of the neighborhood's liberal past is still evident. If you turn right at the intersection of Sima Blilious St. and David Yellin St. onto Yeshayahu St., immediately on your left you will see a building built in 1903 that once housed the Lemel School ❶, one of the first modern Jewish schools in then Palestine. It is a splendid building with a number of impressive touches. Note the Magen David below the upper two windows, the clock with Hebrew letters, and the carving of a palm tree with the Old City in the background above the door. When erected, this was the only building between the main thoroughfares of Jaffa Rd. and Meah Shearim St., and afforded beautiful views of the surrounding hills.

Continue along David Yellin St. until you reach Yosef ben Matityahu St. at the next four-way intersection. Turn left along this walkway, and then take the first right onto Sefat Emet St. Shortly on your left is the Sfas Emes Yeshiva ❷, the main center of the Gerrer Hasidim.

The Gerrer Hasidim are the largest Hasidic dynasty in Israel, with large communities in Ashdod, Bnei Brak and Jerusalem, and smaller groups in other cities. There are also Gerrer communities in the USA, UK and Canada. Gerrer Hasidim can be recognized by their round hats, side locks tucked into their skullcaps, and pants tucked into their socks. This branch of Hasidism originates from Ger or Gur, these being the Yiddish names for the Polish town of Gora Kalworian. The dynasty was founded by Rabbi Yitchak Meir Alter (1799-1866), who was a disciple of the Kotzker Rebbe.

The Sfas Emes Yeshiva of the Gerrer Hassidim on Sefat Emet St.

The Gerrer Hasidim were once the largest Hasidic group in Poland, numbering over 100,000, but they were decimated during the Holocaust. However, Rabbi Avraham Mordechai Alter, the fourth Gerrer Rebbe, managed to escape from Europe and rebuilt his sect in Israel. Today, there are about thirteen thousand Gerrer Hasidic families and about one hundred Gerrer educational institutions throughout the world, a remarkable achievement. Gerrer Hasidim have a less mystical approach to Judaism than other Hasidic groups and place much emphasis on Talmudic learning. Rabbi Yehuda Aryeh Leib Alter, the 3rd Gerrer Rebbe, is known as the Sfas Emes/Sefat Emet after an important book he authored. The street and the yeshiva are named after him and this work.

> Take the next right onto the walkway Yosef Shwartz St., turn right onto David Yellin St., and then left onto Yosef ben Matityahu St.

> Continue along Yosef ben Matityahu St. until it ends, and then turn right on Malchei Israel St. You are now in the Geulah neighborhood and this street is the main commercial artery for the haredim of Geulah and adjacent neighborhoods. This street is always busy with pedestrians, and many of the stores are open until late at night.

> Continue to HaShabbat Square, the first big intersection with traffic lights. Cross this square and continue straight ahead to Meah Shearim St. You are now in the Meah Shearim neighborhood, and this street has many stores catering to the needs of religious Jews.

Meah Shearim was built in 1874 by non-Hasidic religious Jews (Perushim) who followed the practices of the Vilna Gaon. This was the fifth neighborhood built outside the Old City walls. The name Meah Shearim means "one hundred-fold" and comes from a verse in the Torah portion read on the week the settlement was founded: *"Isaac sowed in that land, and in that year he reaped a hundredfold (meah shearim)"* (Genesis 26:12). A building society was set up to purchase the plot of land and resources were pooled and apartments allotted by lottery.

When this neighborhood was first established, living outside the Old City was considered somewhat dangerous. Meah Shearim was therefore built with a single continuous wall that enclosed all the outer dwellings. Gates were locked at night. It was initially a religious neighborhood, but not haredi. By the turn of the century, Meah Shearim had become a desirable place to live in, with modern buildings and attractive parks. However, over time, the neighborhood became more crowded, with houses being built in the courtyards. The character of the neighborhood also changed in the years following the First World War due to a large influx of Hungarian Jews who opposed secularization and Zionism. Today, Meah Shearim is a haredi neighborhood and home to both non-Hasidim as well as Hasidim belonging to various groups, each with their own schools, synagogues, yeshivot and social services.

Turn right at the first vehicular street you come to, Shlomo Zalman Bahran St. Very soon you will turn left onto En Ya'akov, under an arch supporting an apartment and enter the main market street of this neighborhood.

Continue along this street. At the far end of the second street on your right is Nahum Ish Gamzo St., which is just before the fruit and vegetable stores that have awnings. Here you will see the Great Yeshiva and Talmud Torah of Meah Shearim ❸.

This yeshiva was built in 1885. It had strong affiliations with the religious Zionist Mizrachi movement, and their Jerusalem branch was located here during the British Mandate. Things have changed, and the philosophy of the yeshiva is now in line with that of the current residents of the neighborhood.

Continue along En Ya'akov St. Two turns after Nahum Ish Gamzo St. turn right onto Ba'al Ha-Tanya St. At the corner of Baal Ha-Tanya St. and Hevrat Shas St., on the left side of the road, is the Ohel Yitzhak study hall of the Lubavitch or Chabad Hasidim ❹.

Malchei Israel St. in Geula is always busy

This Hasidic group was founded in 1775 by Rabbi Schneur Zalman of Liadi (1745-1812) in the Belorussian village of Lyubavichi. More than most other Hasidic groups, Lubavitch Hasidism involves itself in kabbalistic philosophy, since it was strongly influenced by Rabbi Schneur Zalman and his pioneering book, the Tanya, which contains much kabbalistic thought.

Lubavitch is one of the largest Jewish religious movements in the world due to its vast worldwide outreach program developed under the leadership of the last Lubavitcher Rebbe, Rabbi Menachem Mendel Schneerson (1902-1994), known familiarly as "the Rebbe." Rabbi Schneerson dedicated his life, as do those who have been drawn to his mission, to perfecting the world so as to facilitate the coming of the Messiah. He inherited the mantle of leadership just five years after the Holocaust. He saw this tragedy and mass Jewish assimilation not as reasons for despair but as reasons for hope in the coming of the Messianic age. His faith was so great that he refused to appoint a successor and the Lubavitch Hasidim currently have no Rebbe. Because of the engagement of Lubavitch Hasidism with the general society, this movement has attracted many non-Hasidic supporters throughout the world.

Turn left onto Hevrat Shas St., and at the end of this street turn left again onto Oneg Shabbat St. At its end, take the alley on the right, this being a continuation of En Ya'akov St. At the end of the alley, turn left onto Ha-Rav Shmuel Salant St. At the corner of Ha-Rav Shmuel Salant St. and Meah Shearim St. is the yeshiva of the Breslov (Bratslav) Hasidim ❺.

This branch of Hasidism was founded in the Ukraine by Rebbe Nachman of Breslov (1772-1810), a great grandson of the Baal Shem Tov. His teachings encourage developing an intense joy and sincerity in one's relationship with God and a yearning to return to Him. Worship becomes an emotional experience with singing and dancing. Private individual communication (*hitbodedut*) with God is encouraged. In the past, his ideas were opposed by other branches of Hasidism, and this sect did not develop in Europe as much as other Hasidic groups. Rabbi Nachman did not designate a successor and the Breslovers have not had a Rebbe since his death.

Many followers of the movement were murdered by the Communists and Nazis, but those who escaped reconstituted the sect in Israel and other countries. Since the 1970's, Breslov has engaged in outreach efforts, and its mystical and joyous approach to reaching out to God has attracted many followers, including Sephardim and those from secular backgrounds who have been searching for more spirituality in their lives. The Breslov Yeshiva in Meah Shearim was founded in 1953. Rabbi Nachman's chair, which was smuggled out of the Soviet Union by his followers at some risk, occupies a central position in the yeshiva. A subset of this sect devised the mantra of Na Nach Nachma Nachman Meuman, based on a permutation of the Hebrew letters of Rabbi Nachman's name, and these letters can be seen defacing walls throughout Israel.

We will now encircle the Meah Shearim quarter. Turn right on HaRav Shmuel Salant St., first right onto Avraham Mislonim St., and then right onto Shlomo Zalman Bahran St.

Turn left onto the main artery Meah Shearim St. and this will bring you again to HaShabbat Square. Turn left, and then take the left fork at the next intersection onto Nathan Strauss St. to return to the walk's starting point.

13 The Sherover and Haas Promenades and Water Supply System for Second Temple Jerusalem

Nothing surpasses the Sherover and Haas Promenades for views of the Temple Mount, the Old City, and the surrounding hills. Understandably, the observation area on the Haas Promenade has become a popular place for tourist groups. We will also explore the shafts and entrance to the tunnel that burrows under the Armon Hanatziv mountain range and that was part of the water supply system for Jerusalem during the time of the Second Temple. This water supply system continued to function intermittently for about two thousand years.

TIME: About 1.75 hours, and about 2.25 hours if visiting the water tunnel entrance

DISTANCE:
3.75 km, and about 5.75 km if viewing the water tunnel entrance

TYPE OF WALK: Partially circular

DIFFICULTY:
An easy walk along paved paths.

STARTING POINT:
The beginning of the Sherover Promenade, close to Naomi St.

PUBLIC TRANSPORT: Enter "טיילת גבריאל שרובר" into Moovit. After getting off the bus at Hebron Rd. turn onto Naomi St. At the first fork, turn right in the direction of the Segway Tour sign. The Sherover Promenade begins by the end of the sidewalk about one hundred meters from this intersection.

DRIVING DIRECTIONS AND PARKING: Enter "Sherover Promenade" into Waze and click on "טיילת גבריאל שרובר." (Do not click on "Promenade"). There is free parking on the sides of the road close to the beginning of the Sherover Promenade and also parking at YES Planet. A short distance down the road from the starting point is the Jerusalem Forest parking area where Segway Tours start.

Views from the Promenades

The Sherover and Haas Promenades and adjacent Peace Forest were developed after the Six Day War in what was formerly a demilitarized zone separating Israeli West Jerusalem from Jordanian East Jerusalem.

The views from these promenades are some of the most impressive in Jerusalem. As you face the Mount of Olives Ridge from the Sherover Promenade, you can see three towers on top of the ridge. The one furthest to your left is the water tower in the campus of the Hebrew University on Mount Scopus. After the War of Independence, the entire campus became an Israeli-held enclave inside Jordanian territory that was supplied periodically by a convoy through Jordanian East Jerusalem. This tower was built in 1974 when the campus was rebuilt after the Six Day War. The shorter tower to its right is part of the Augusta Victoria Compound, built by the German Kaiser Wilhem II, as a hospital, hostel and church for German pilgrims, after his visit to Jerusalem in 1898. It is named after his wife. It now includes the Augusta Victoria Hospital providing specialty medical care. The peaked tower to the right of this is part of the Russian Church of the Ascension in the A-Tur neighborhood on the Mount of Olives. According to Christian tradition, this is where Jesus ascended to heaven forty days after his resurrection. Below these last two towers and to their right is the expanse of the ancient Jewish cemetery on the Mount of Olives.

To the left of these towers and a bit below them, you can make out the southern **A** and western **B** walls of the Temple Mount. The Al-Aqsa Mosque **C** and Dome of the Rock **D** can be seen on the Temple Mount. The area of the City of David **E** is below the Temple Mount and to the west of the Kidron Valley **F**. Turning to your far right is the mountain ridge of Armon Hanatziv. There is a Jewish tradition that Abraham and Isaac had their first view of Mt. Moriah, what is now the Temple Mount, from this ridge.

When you reach the Haas Promenade you are able to see more of the Old City, including the white dome of the Hurva Synagogue. This was the main synagogue of the Jewish Quarter until the Old City passed into Jordanian hands during the War of Independence. It was destroyed by the Jordanians and not rebuilt until 2010. You can also see the Dormition Abbey on Mount Zion. This Catholic church and monastery is readily identifiable because of its bell tower and four adjacent towers.

SUPPLYING WATER TO THIRSTY JERUSALEM

The City of David and Temple initially obtained their water from the Gihon Spring in the Kidron Valley. During the First Temple period, King Hezekiah diverted this water and brought much of it into the city via an underground tunnel. This was probably adequate for the population at that time. However, as the city expanded during the time of the Second Temple, additional water was needed, especially for the needs of the Temple and for the multitude of pilgrims coming to the city for the religious holidays. In response to this need, in the early part of the first century BCE, the Hasmoneans constructed an aqueduct system for bringing spring water into Jerusalem. It began at the spring En Eitan near Solomon's Pools south of Bethlehem, and

brought water directly to the Temple Mount via a "Lower Aqueduct." The lavish, water-extravagant Roman lifestyle of Herod the Great in Jerusalem and Herodium, as well as that of the Roman governors who followed him, necessitated even more water and further elaboration of this system.

The heart of the complete system was Solomon's Pools, which were three large reservoirs located five kilometers south-west of Bethlehem that descended in a stepwise fashion down a hill. They are presently in territory administered by the Palestinian Authority and cannot be visited by Israelis. We do not know who built these pools. Could it have been King Solomon? A verse in Ecclesiastes (which he wrote) states: "*I made myself pools from*

133

which to water the forest of growing trees" (Ecclesiastes 2:6). The historian Josephus adds to the mystery by writing that Solomon used to enjoy the water of the nearby spring of En Eitan. Alternatively, and probably more likely, is that the lower pool was constructed by the Hasmoneans.

Solomon's Pools are fed by two aqueducts. The shortest, the Biyar Aqueduct, was 4.7 km long, ran more or less parallel to today's route 60, and was probably built by Herod. It conducted water from springs in Wadi Biyar, as well as dammed up water, tunneled through an aquifer and also an aquiclude until it reached the uppermost of Solomon's Pools. An aquiclude is a solid impermeable layer of rock over or under an aquifer built so that water drains into the aqueduct through the tunnel walls. This was a very advanced technique for its time, and this aqueduct is the only example of its kind in Israel.

A second aqueduct that drained into the middle pool of Solomon's Pools originated in a group of springs between Bethlehem and Hebron. It was forty km long, tunneled through the ridges it encountered, and crossed valleys via stone walls or dams. It may have been built by Herod and was rebuilt in the late Roman period.

Three aqueducts issued from Solomon's Pools: the "Lower Aqueduct" to Jerusalem built by the Hasmoneans, which is the aqueduct of most interest to us on this walk; a "Higher Aqueduct" to Jerusalem built at a later period; and a third aqueduct built by Herod to supply water to his palace at Herodium. All these aqueducts delivered water by gravity over a small and very precise gradient. The channels were built on top of buttressed stone walls, were plastered inside to prevent water leakage, and capped with stone slabs. Anyone caught stealing the water or the stone slabs would have been severely punished.

The Lower Aqueduct was some twenty-one km in length. It began at En Eitan, was connected to the lowest of Solomon's Pools by a side branch, tunneled under Bethlehem (this tunnel is now closed), tunneled through the Armon Hanatziv Ridge, continued below the Sherover Promenade, went through the Abu Tor neighborhood of Jerusalem, continued on the western slope of the Hinnom Valley to Mishkenot Sha'ananim, skirted Sultan's Pool, crossed the Hinnom Valley on an arched stone bridge, and went around the slopes of Mount Zion. It then entered into the Old City west of the Dung Gate, passed through today's Jewish Quarter, and delivered water to large cisterns under the Temple Mount via Wilson's Bridge.

To obviate a detour of some 4 km around the Armon HaNatziv ridge, the Hasmoneans dug a four hundred meter long tunnel through the mountain. Six shafts were constructed from the surface of the mountain to assist in its construction and to provide aeration. One can walk through this tall and narrow tunnel, and tours for the general public are offered periodically. Otherwise it is locked. Sorry.

In addition, Herod constructed an Upper Aqueduct for his palaces in the Upper City of Jerusalem. The aqueduct for this started from the upper pool of Solomon's Pools. It followed the watershed line and was therefore at a higher level than the Lower Aqueduct. It ran by Kibbutz Ramat Rachel and continued along Hebron Road to Hezekiah's Pool, a pool (now dry) within the Old City by the Jaffa Gate.

This system functioned intermittently after the destruction of the Second Temple until about a hundred years ago. In the 17th century the Ottomans replaced the open channels with ceramic pipes encased in cement. These were replaced by iron pipes in the early 1900's and the Armon Hanatziv tunnel was deepened to act as a reservoir. The Ottomans also constructed a branch to Sultan's Pool to provide neighborhoods outside the city walls with water. This branch also supplied the fountain by the Sultan's Pool on Hebron Road.

THE WALK

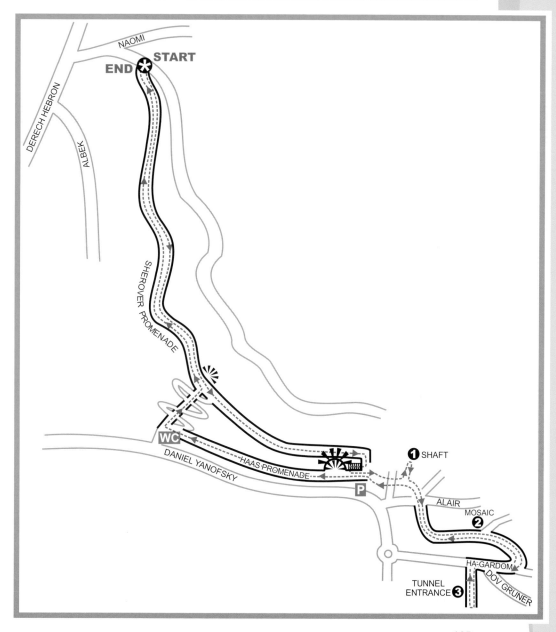

Walk along the Sherover Promenade, first passing the walls of a monastery on your right. There are benches throughout the length of the promenade. There are also observation points, and the views become more impressive and expansive as you continue. Initially, the best views will be of the Armon Hanatziv mountain range, but as you proceed you will see more of the Temple Mount area, and finally West Jerusalem.

The first observation point is within a semi-circular observation area and contains a sign identifying points of interest. The third observation point, which is close to a shaded area with a wooden lattice covering, also has a sign with points of interest. A section of it is missing, but it is still helpful. If you have a stroller or wheelchair you can now use the switchback at this point to ascend to the Haas Promenade, although it is quite steep. Otherwise, continue to the end of the Sherover Promenade.

At the end of the Sherover Promenade, ascend the steps to the Haas Promenade parking lot.

To view one of the six vertical shafts of the Lower Aqueduct, exit the parking lot in front of you by its far-left entrance, and take the sidewalk on the left towards the water fountain. Numbered blue plaques on the road labelled "מסלול האמה החשמונאית" will help you find your way on this second part of the hike.

In front of the water fountain, take the walkway on the left. Immediately in front of you is an enclosed circular area.

You are now viewing the fourth shaft (from south to north) of this part of the aqueduct ❶. It is also the deepest at forty-three meters. It was dug within a hollowed area that had previously functioned as a reservoir, thereby reducing the amount of digging necessary.

To view a second shaft and also for a great view from the other side of the Armon Hanatziv Ridge, follow the blue plaques on the road past the entrance to the UN Headquarters, the administrative center for the United Nations and their peace-keeping forces.

This UN building was originally known as the "Governor's Mansion." It was built during the British Mandate (1918-1948) as a residence for the British High Commissioner of Palestine. It was then known as Armon Hanatziv ("Palace of the High Commissioner"), which also accounts for the current name of this area. With appropriate symbolism, his residence overlooked both East and West Jerusalem. It was built in 1930 in a Middle-Eastern style with courtyards, gardens, and a grand ballroom.

After the 1948 War of Independence, the area surrounding the Governor's Mansion became a demilitarized zone, and the mansion itself and its grounds were used as headquarters for UN observers overseeing the armistice between Israel and Jordan. During the Six Day War, Jordan occupied the building for several hours and began shelling Western Jerusalem, despite entreaties by the Israelis that they not get involved in this conflict. The mansion was quickly captured by the Jerusalem Brigade, which then fought its way to the Old City, thereby reuniting the city of Jerusalem.

Cross the main road (Alair St.) on the crossing. Slightly to its right is a gap in the wall ahead and a footpath indicated by #13 on the blue plaque on the ground. Make your way on this path as it curves to the left towards another shaft for the Lower Aqueduct, this one encircled by a mosaic ❷.

A view of Western Jerusalem, Mount Zion and the Old City wall

This mosaic was built by the Jerusalem Municipality and it illustrates the course of the Lower Aqueduct. It also contains an illustration of an instrument with four arms and plumbs revolving around a central axis that was used during the building of the aqueduct to ensure its slight gradient over the more than twenty km distance. From this side of the ridge you can see the edge of the Judean Desert and its most prominent hill, Herodium.

To view the entrance to the underground tunnel, from the mosaic take the right fork down the slope to Ha-Gardom St. Turn right onto this road and just beyond its intersection with Dov Gruner St., cross on the second crossing to a path going down the hill. There are signposts all the way, including to the entrance to the tunnel ❸. As mentioned, the entrance is locked, but there are periodic tours that walk through the full length of the tunnel.

Return the way you came to go back to the Haas Promenade parking lot. For this circular walk, turn left along the Haas Promenade which runs parallel to Daniel Yanovsky St. Near the beginning of the promenade is a large observation plaza with a sign identifying the places you are viewing. This is an excellent location for appreciating the layout of the area in front of you, as you have a commanding view of East Jerusalem, the Jewish Quarter, Mount Zion, and part of Western Jerusalem.

Continue along the Haas Promenade to its end. Take the steps down to the Sherover Promenade. Turn left on the promenade and this will bring you back to your starting point.

137

Nearby Places of Interest:

YES Planet on 2 Naomi St. is a cinema complex with sixteen cinemas and an IMAX and 4D theater. There are several restaurants. None have kashrut certification as the complex is open on Saturday. It is open from 1 pm Sunday to Friday and 10:30 am on Saturday. There is underground parking. Their phone number is: (02) 531-3424.

Agnon House at 16 Klausner St. in Talpiot was the home of the Nobel prizewinner Shai Agnon, one of the greatest Modern Hebrew writers and the recipient of a Nobel Prize for Hebrew literature. Talpiot was the first garden suburb built in the Jerusalem area and predated Rechavia by a few years. It was modeled on a European style. When it was built, it was outside Jerusalem's city boundary. Agnon's home was built in 1931, and he lived here until his death in 1970. The home has been renovated since. Many of Agnon's best-known books were written here. The house is open Sunday to Thursday 9 am–3 pm during the winter, 9 am–4 pm during the summer, and on Friday 9 am–1 pm. There is an audio guide in English and Hebrew. There is an admission charge. Their phone number is: (02) 671-6498.

The First Station is at 4 David Remez St. If you have not already done so, pay a visit to the First Station. It's a fun place with a market, handicrafts and other displays, stores and restaurants. Check out the program for free concerts. Many of them are of excellent quality. There is also a Kids Area at the northern end of the station with children's activities. Their phone number is: (02) 653-5239.

14 Ein Kerem and Its Artisans Via the Jerusalem Forest

This walk starts from Mount Herzl and approaches Ein Kerem via the Jerusalem Forest and the picturesque Ein Kerem Valley. Ein Kerem is a delightful village nestled within the Judean Mountains. Although within the Jerusalem municipal boundaries, it has its own distinctive charm. The village has attracted a number of artisans and their studios and art galleries can be visited. Ein Kerem is a popular destination for Christians because of its association with John the Baptist.

TIME: 2.5-3 hours

DISTANCE: About 6.5 km

TYPE OF WALK:
One way. Return by bus.

DIFFICULTY: Easy walking. A stroller and wheelchair can be used in Ein Kerem, but not on the forest road to Ein Kerem.

STARTING POINT:
The plaza on Sderot Herzl opposite the Mount Herzl light rail stop overlooking the Ein Kerem Valley.

PUBLIC TRANSPORTATION: Mount Herzl is the last stop on the light rail. [If you decide instead to go directly to Ein Kerem, enter "Ein Kerem" into Moovit. Bus 28 leaves from Mount Herzl and stops at Ein Kerem St. at the bus stop עין כרם/המעיין.

DRIVING DIRECTIONS AND PARKING: Enter "Mount Herzl" into Waze. There is parking outside the Mount Herzl Museum and additional parking at Yad Vashem, although this is a distance to the start of the walk. If skipping the forest part of the walk, enter "Ein Kerem, Jerusalem" into Waze to go directly to Ein Kerem. There is underground parking in Ein Kerem at the corner of Ein Kerem St. and HaMa'ayan St. Enter "Ein Kerem parking, Jerusalem" into Waze.

THE TRADITIONS OF EIN KEREM

There has been settlement in Ein Kerem from ancient times because of its spring. Pottery dating to as far back as the Canaanite period has been found. The village has been identified by scholars as the Israelite settlement of Beth Hakerem. This town is mentioned in the book of Jeremiah: "*Flee for safety, people of Benjamin! Flee from Jerusalem! Sound the trumpet in Tekoa! Raise the signal over Beth Hakerem*" (Jeremiah 6:1) and also in the book of Nehemiah (3:14). Beit Hakerem means "*house of the vineyard,*" and numerous vines on the mountainside terraces during the First and Second Temple periods would have supplied nearby Jerusalem with wine.

Ein Kerem was a Muslim village from the 16th century on. Arabs as well as Jews left Spain after the Christian conquest and a group of Arabs settled here. At that time many of the terraces were replanted with olive trees because of the Muslim restriction on drinking alcohol.

The Arabs of this village were involved in the siege of Jewish West Jerusalem during Israel's War of Independence, and when the Haganah captured the area its Arab inhabitants fled. Israel needed housing at that time for new immigrants, particularly those who had fled Arab countries. The story is told that two trucks of immigrants from Morocco and Iraq were brought to Ein Kerem and were encouraged to take over abandoned Arab properties. However, when they saw the lack of amenities, including the sewage in the streets, and also realized that they were not in Jerusalem, they refused to get off the bus. A nun from the nearby Russian Monastery heard the commotion and told them they were idiots for not wanting to live here, since this was now their country. The occupants of one of the buses did stay and they eventually found that they had chosen a delightful place to live in. Most of the housing here is renovated Arab houses. This is unusual, since old Arab homes were often unsuitable for modern living. However, in this village the effort was made to upgrade them, with very beautiful results. Artisans were encouraged to settle in Ein Kerem in the 1970's.

Christian tradition links Ein Kerem with the birthplace of John the Baptist, and this accounts for the churches and monasteries here. Mary, who was pregnant, had been told by the angel Gabriel that she would give birth to Jesus, and according to the New Testament: "*And Mary arose in those days, and went into the hill country with haste, into a city of Judah*" where her cousin Elizabeth lived (Luke 1:39). Elizabeth was also pregnant and would give birth to John the Baptist.

The identification of Ein Kerem as this "*city of Judah*" was made by Helena, the mother of Constantine the Great. Judea had become depleted of Jews subsequent to the Roman response to the Bar Kochba revolt, and Helena and Constantine aimed to make this land a Christian country – which they succeeded in doing. Helena also identified other places mentioned in the Bible.

The New Testament relates that John's parents, the elderly priest Zechariah and his wife Elizabeth, had been barren for many years. The angel Gabriel appeared to Zechariah while he was offering incense in the Temple and informed him that he would have a son whose name would be John. When Zechariah expressed doubts about this, he was struck dumb. It was not until Zechariah wrote down his son's name on a slate during the circumcision that he recovered his speech. His words of praise on the circumcision of his son were incorporated into the well-known Benedictus prayer, and plaques containing this prayer are located in the courtyard of the Church of John the Baptist.

John became an itinerant ascetic preacher and baptized Jesus. Christian tradition relates that at the time he was baptized a voice from heaven announced that Jesus was the Messiah. It is possible that John was an Essene and he may have stayed for a while in Qumran. There is no evidence that Jesus was a member of this sect, although some ascetic ideas of the Essenes may have been adopted by the early Christians.

John the Baptist was beheaded by Herod Antipas, the son of Herod the Great and the ruler of the Galilee under the Romans, upon the wishes of Herod's step-daughter. John had denounced Herod's rapid marriage to the ex-wife of his brother and the divorcing of his own wife (Matthew 14:1-12, and Mark 6:14-29).

THE WALK

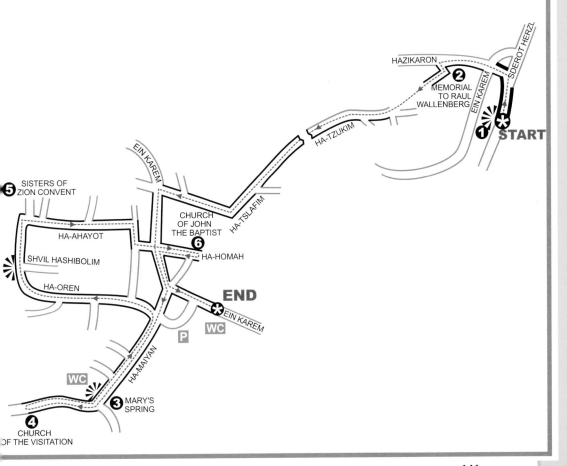

This walk is not intended to provide a tour of all the artisans of Ein Kerem, but only a selection of studios you will pass on this route.

Walk over to the plaza on Sderot Herzl ❶, with its large red sculpture, for a view of the Ein Kerem Valley. The village of Ein Kerem is tucked in the valley below and Hadassah Medical School campus is behind it. The sculpure is called "A Tribute to Jerusalem."

From the plaza, walk to the junction of Ein Kerem St. and Hazikaron St., and turn onto Hazikaron St. in the direction of Yad Vashem. Soon you will come to a yellow-on-brown sign on your left indicating the trail to Ein Kerem. Follow this blue-marked trail down the steps to a memorial to Raoul Wallenberg ❷ erected by Keren Kayemet LeIsrael.

Raoul Wallenberg (1912-1947) was a Swedish diplomat assigned to Budapest during World War II. He saved thousands of Jews in Nazi-occupied Hungary by issuing for them certificates of protection. When the Red Army invaded Hungary, he was arrested during the Siege of Budapest on charges of espionage. He probably died in prison, although the details of his death are still unresolved. Since his presumed death, he has been awarded numerous honors posthumously because of his bravery, and monuments and streets have been dedicated in his name throughout the world.

Follow the steps and path down the hill until you come to a paved road. Turn right on this road, which soon turns into a blue-marked jeep trail.

This section of the forest was burnt by a forest fire in 2014. Since then the debris has been cleared, terraces rebuilt, and trees have been replanted. Nevertheless, it is interesting to compare the forest here with areas not affected by the fire, since it takes time for Mediterrean brush to become established.

The village of Ein Kerem is entered via Hatzukim Lane. When this road ends at a parking area, follow the curve of its continuation Homat Ha-Tslafim to the right and this will take you to Ha-Kastel Square on the main road Derech Ein Kerem.

Turn left on Derech Ein Kerem. Almost immediately on the right side of the road is a group of four studios called the "Workshop" which you might consider visiting. Look also at the structure in the center of the courtyard which was once an olive press. An ancient water cistern is at the edge of the courtyard.

Further along this road at 18 Derech Ein Kerem, on the left-hand side of the road, is the studio of Ruth Havilio who makes hand-painted tiles, ceramic nameplates and handmade jewelry, and this studio can be visited.

Turn right into Ha-Mayan St just before Mala Bistro. It is signposted לרח' המעיין. After passing cafes and restaurants, you will come to Mary's Spring ❸.

According to Luke's Gospel in the New Testament, the pregnant Mary came from Nazareth to this town in Judea to meet her cousin Elizabeth, who was also pregnant with John. Prior to her meeting, she quenched her thirst from this spring. Accordingly, the spring is called the "Spring of Mary" or "Spring of the Virgin." In actuality, the "spring" you see is the end of a thirty meter underground tunnel carved into the rock during Second Temple times that leads to the aquifer. This was once one of the fullest springs in the Judean mountains. The mosque arising from the building reminds us that Ein Kerem was an Arab village prior to Israel's War of Independence. The spring was recently renovated by Baron Edmond de Rothschild and there is a stone block nearby recording this. There are notices not to drink from the water as the aquifer is likely polluted.

On the opposite side of the road to the spring is an observation plaza with a splendid view of the lush valley below.

From here you may wish to walk up the hill on Madregot Ha-Bikur to the Church of the Visitation ❹. Details of this church are described below o the next page.

Retrace your steps along Ha-Ma'ayan St. and take the third named street on your left from the observation area, Ha-'Oren St. Just before its intersection with Derekh Ha-Ahayot is the studio of Yitzhak Greenfield whose paintings are inspired by Jerusalem landscapes, Hebrew letters and Jewish mysticism. His work has been exhibited in Israel and the USA.

Continue along Ha-'Oren St. until you come to a parking area opposite Shvil HaShibolim. From here, there is a beautiful view of the opposite side of the valley. Notice the spire of the Church of the Visitation, and higher up the golden domes of the Russian Monastery of Ein Kerem.

At the end of Ha-'Oren St. is the Sisters of Zion Convent ❺. For details regarding this convent see on the next page.

143

Turn right onto Derekh Ha-Ahayot. When it comes to a T-junction, follow the road as it curves to the right, and then take the first left onto Schvil Ha-Homah. This will lead you back to the main road, Derech Ein Kerem.

To visit the Church of St. John the Baptist ❻, cross Derech Ein Kerem and continue on the continuation of Shvil Ha-Homa. The church is soon on your left. Details about this church are described below. A bit further up the road at 16 Schvil Ha-Homa is the studio of Adina Solomonovich with displays of her ceramic plates, bowls and jewelry.

The easiest way back to Mount Herzl is by bus. Return to Derech Ein Kerem and turn left towards the underground parking lot. The bus stop is on the right just past the parking lot and park. To get to the light rail, take bus 28 and alight at either Sderot Herzl or the next stop Yofe Nof.

Churches in Ein Kerem:

Church of the Visitation: This Franciscan church commemorates the visit of Mary to the summer home of Zechariah and Elizabeth. The current church is built on the site of Byzantine and Crusader churches. On the west side of the courtyard is a collection of inscriptions in many languages of the "Magnificat," a hymn that Mary sang when she met Elizabeth (Luke 1:46-55). There are beautiful frescoes throughout the church. The New Testament relates that around the year 4 BCE, Herod the Great was told that a king of the Jews had been born in Bethlehem and he ordered that all male children less than two years of age living near Bethlehem be put to death. Elizabeth heard the Roman soldiers coming and grabbed her son. An angel opened a rock for her and she was able to hide her son until the soldiers had gone. Leading from the church is a passage to an ancient cistern, and within a niche is a rock where tradition holds that Elizabeth hid her child. The church is open every day 8 am–12.00 pm and 2:30 pm–6 pm, and until 5 pm from October to March.

Sisters of Zion Convent: This international community of Catholic nuns was founded by the two Ratisbonne brothers from France who were born Jewish to a prominent banking family and converted to Christianity. Their initial emphasis was on converting Jews to Christianity, but the mission of the convent is now to foster understanding and ties between Christians and Jews. Alfonse Ratisbonne purchased this land in 1860. The building was initially an orphanage and his private home, and is now a guesthouse for people of all faiths. The brothers also built the Convent of the Sisters of Zion on the Via Dolorosa in Jerusalem. The grounds behind the church and guesthouse are open for visitors Monday to Friday, from 9 am–12 pm and 2 pm–5 pm.

Church of St. John the Baptist (St. John BaHarim): Christian tradition holds that this Franciscan church is the location where John the Baptist was born in his family's main home. His birthplace was in a cave that can be seen inside the church. Zechariah, the father of John, said the Benedictus prayer on the birth of his son after previously being struck dumb. There are twenty-one ceramic plaques on the walls of the courtyard bearing the Benedictus in the twenty-one languages in which he gave thanks on the circumcision of his son. The present church was erected between 1857-1900, and is on the site of a Crusader church that fell into disrepair when the Crusaders left the country. The Crusader church was built on the site of a former Byzantine church built by Helena, the mother of Constantine. By the side of the main entrance to the church is a building with three window openings with metal grills. If you look through the opening closest to the church, you can see somewhat high in the corner a statue of the goddess Aphrodite revealed by excavations here. The church property was acquired by the Franciscan order in 1674, and with the aid of the Spanish royal family they were able to restore part of the Crusader church. The influence of the Spanish royal family is reflected in the Spanish decorations, such as the pictures and blue and white tiles. Queen Isabella also donated the marble altar in the grotto. The church is open to visitors from 8 am–4.45 pm every day. Their phone number is: (02) 632-3000.

Nearby Places of Interest:

Herzl Museum is on Herzl Boulevard. Visitors are encouraged to become active participants in understanding Herzl's bold aspirations and disappoint-ments during his stormy personal journey. There is a one hour audio-visual presentation on the life of Theodore Herzl. Opening hours are Sunday to Wednesday 8:45 am–6 pm (last tour at 5 pm), Thursday 8:45 am–8 pm (last tour at 7 pm) and Friday 8:45 am–12:15 pm. Tours are available in English. There is an entrance fee. Reservations should be made by calling (02) 632-1515 or by booking on line. Visitors without reservations can enter on a space permitted basis.

Yad Vashem is on Har Hazikaron. It is Israel's largest Holocaust memorial and was built to perpetuate the memory of those who died in the Holocaust. Established in 1953, it is a world center for documentation, research, education and commemoration of the Holocaust. The present building, which opened in 2005, is shaped like a prism entering the mountain. There are nine galleries presenting historical displays of the Holocaust. Entrance to the museum is free. It is open from 9 am–5 pm from Sunday to Wednesday, Thursday 9 am–8 pm, and Friday 9 am–2 pm. It is closed on Shabbat.

Hadassah Medical Center, Ein Kerem is worth a visit even if you are not sick! The Chagall windows in the hospital Synagogue are deservedly much visited. The Synagogue is open for viewing from 8 am–3 pm from Sunday to Thursday, but is closed for visitors Friday and Shabbat as the Synagogue is in use. The phone number is (02) 667-6271 for more information. The hospital also has a shopping mall in a lower floor of the hospital. There are stores for clothing, telephone supplies and sweets, a bakery, pharmacy, and many rea-sonably priced cafes – all kosher and many mehadrin. Many of the stores are open from fairly early in the morning until late in the evening. Ask for direc-tions once you are in the hospital, otherwise you are unlikely to find it.

15 Pioneers of Modern Jerusalem – Eliezer Ben-Yehuda, Rav Abraham Isaac Kook and Dr. Abraham Ticho

The appearance of a cosmopolitan, intellectual and Zionistic neighborhood outside the Old City walls was an important stage in the early development of modern Jerusalem. This walk views the homes of three influential Zionist figures who lived and set the tone for this new neighborhood, now in the center of Jerusalem – the first Ashkenazi Chief Rabbi of Palestine Rabbi Abraham Isaac Kook ("Rav Kook"), the linguist Eliezer Ben-Yehuda, and the ophthalmologist Dr. Abraham Ticho. Both Rav Kook and Eliezer Ben-Yehuda would have a profound influence on this country that continues to this day.

OVERVIEWS

ELIEZER BEN-YEHUDA – THE STUBBORN LINGUIST

The notion that Hebrew could be used in contemporary literature, and even become a spoken language, was not new. However, it was Eliezer Ben-Yehuda (1858-1922) who vigorously promoted the idea of reviving Hebrew and turning it once again into the language of a people. Historian Cecil Roth is quoted as saying: *"Before Ben-Yehuda, Jews could speak Hebrew; after him they did."*

Eliezer Ben-Yehuda, born Eliezer Yitzhak Perlman, received a traditional Jewish education in Poland studying Bible, Mishnah and Talmud. His parents intended for him to become a Rabbi. However, while still In Poland he was exposed to secular literature, and he traveled to Paris to study medicine at the Sorbonne. At age 23, he immigrated to Ottoman Palestine and settled in Jerusalem where he worked initially as a school teacher at the Alliance Israelite Universelle School.

As part of his efforts to popularize Hebrew, he edited several Hebrew-language newspapers. He spoke only Hebrew at home and raised his son entirely in Hebrew, making him the first native speaker of modern Hebrew. This was a significant challenge for the family, since he was the only one in the country doing this. Plus, words for many things did not exist. The word *"zeh"* (this/that) was probably used a lot in the home! When a word did not exist, he created it using Semitic roots. Many of the thousands of words he invented caught on, and many did not.

The entrance to Beit HaRav, the former home of Rav Abraham Isaac Kook. This is now a museum about his life and accomplishments

TIME: About 1.75 hours

DISTANCE: 2 km

TYPE OF WALK: Circular

DIFFICULTY: Easy walk.

STARTING POINT:
The corner of Jaffa St. and Ha-Rav Kook St.

PUBLIC TRANSPORT:
The light-rail stop Jaffa City Center is close to the starting point, as are bus stops on King George St. and Strauss St.

PARKING:
חניון העמודים on Ha-Rav Agan St.

He was the author of the first Modern Hebrew dictionary, and was a major figure in the establishment of the Committee of the Hebrew Language, later to become the Academy of the Hebrew Language. The work this institution does is vital to this day in monitoring the development of the language and devising new words. He was also responsible for persuading the British High Commissioner to make Hebrew one of the three official languages of the British Mandate along with English and Arabic.

His personal life was not an easy one. His first wife Devora died of tuberculosis, and shortly thereafter three of his children died from diphtheria. Following Devorah's wish, he married her younger sister Paula Beila, who took the name Hemdah. Hemdah assisted her husband with much of his work, both during his lifetime and after. She rented rooms in the adjoining house, for example, to print his newspapers.

Ben-Yehuda's efforts were not well received by the ultra-orthodox establishment. They objected to his use of the holy Hebrew language for secular purposes and made their objections known in various ways, including throwing stones at his home. Nevertheless, his strong personality was undeterred. The fact that Hebrew is the language of the Israeli people today is a testament to his greatness and perseverance.

RABBI ABRAHAM ISAAC KOOK ("RAV KOOK") - THE MESSIANIC VISIONARY

Rav Kook's influence was considerable during his lifetime and it continues to this day. He was the first major religious figure to conceptualize how Judaism could transition from an exile mode into a faith appropriate for an era of Redemption. Rav Kook saw this country not only as a place of refuge for displaced Jews, but as a bastion of holiness. He was a mystic who saw everything about the universe as unified and the world as being on an evolutionary path to greater holiness. All this was based on his unique interpretation of kabbalistic ideas.

Many people were unable to comprehend his profound ideas, but they very much liked his conclusions. These included his view that the non-religious pioneers in Palestine were a part of the Messianic Redemption. To Rav Kook, their lack of religious observance was in error, but this did not make their contribution to redemption less significant. He also believed that secular activities, such as university study, sports and art, could be readily accepted within a religious framework.

He had a cadre of pupils/disciples, and the synagogue in his home became his yeshiva (academy for Torah study). It eventually became Yeshivat Mercaz HaRav, the flagship yeshiva of the Zionist religious movement. His yeshiva was the first in the country in which the language of instruction was Hebrew rather than Yiddish. His philosophy spawned other Zionist yeshivot, the religious Zionist youth movement Bnei Akiva, and eventually the network of Hesder yeshivot that enable Torah learning to be combined with military service.

His approach to messianism very much influenced his son and foremost pupil, Rabbi Tzvi Yehuda Kook. After the Six Day War, Rabbi Tzvi Yehuda Kook adopted the position that the territories of Judea and Samaria were a gift from God to the Jewish people and a stage in the messianic redemptive process. How then could the Jewish people give up this territory and throw God's gift back in His face? This led to the creation of Gush Emunim, a religious Zionist settlement movement, whose aims dovetailed nicely with those of Arik Sharon, then Agriculture Minister, who wished to establish a defensive line of settlements in the mountains of Samaria to protect the densely populated coastal plain.

Rav Kook provided the philosophy that enabled an active engagement of the religious world in the Zionist undertaking, which at that time was predominantly a secular endeavor. His haredi ultra-religious colleagues disagreed with his ideas, although they respected his erudition. Ironically, through political means, the haredi establishment has managed to exert increasing influence over the Chief Rabbinate, the institution that Rav Kook created, and over the position of Ashkenazi Chief Rabbi, a position he first occupied, thereby ensuring that the struggle between national religious and haredi viewpoints that began at the time of Rav Kook would continue to play out in the Israeli political arena until the present day.

OUTSTANDING CITIZENS - DR. ABRAHAM TICHO AND HIS WIFE ANNA

Neither Dr. Abraham Ticho nor his wife have the name recognition of Rav Kook and Ben-Yehuda, but they were very much part of this new neighborhood both in their outlook and in their work.

Dr. Ticho (1883-1960) was born in Moravia, and studied medicine in Prague and ophthalmology in Vienna. He was appointed head of ophthalmology at the Rothschild Hospital, the forerunner of the present Hadassah Hospital, and later opened a private Ophthalmic Hospital on the ground floor of his home, the one you will be visiting, while living on the second floor.

The eye disease trachoma was then endemic in Jerusalem and had become a significant cause of blindness. Dr. Ticho became famous throughout the country as a compassionate physician who gave the same devoted attention to his Jewish and Arab patients. He also instituted preventive measures against trachoma in Jewish and Arab schools. During the Arab riots of 1929, he was stabbed in the back and seriously wounded. This attack elicited widespread condemnation and concern for his well-being from Jew and Arab alike.

Dr. Ticho's wife Anna studied art in Vienna in her youth. She initially assisted her husband in his medical work, but later spent more of her time doing artwork. She painted scenes of Jerusalem and the countryside around the city. She gained increasing recognition in Israel and abroad for her art, and was awarded the prestigious Israel Prize. She died in 1980, twenty years after her husband. She bequeathed their home to the Israel Museum for use as an exhibition and cultural center. During his lifetime Dr. Ticho had a collection of one hundred and fifty 15th to 20th century menorahs that hung from the walls around his desk. Some of these menorahs are exhibited in his home.

Ethiopia St. is a delightful street in the center of Jerusalem where important figures in the early cultural life of modern Jerusalem once lived

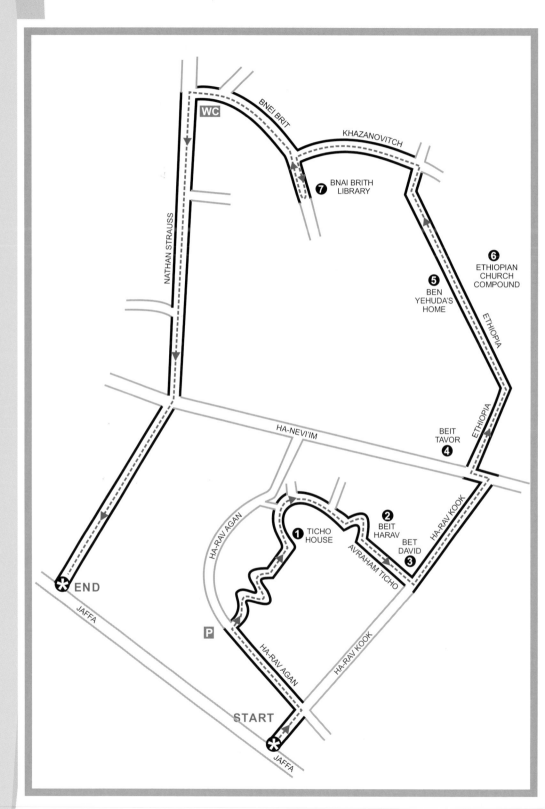

BNEI BRIT

WC

KHAZANOVITCH

NATHAN STRAUSS

7 BNAI BRITH
LIBRARY

6
ETHIOPIAN
CHURCH
COMPOUND

5
BEN
YEHUDA'S
HOME

ETHIOPIA

ETHIOPIA

HA-NEVI'IM

BEIT
TAVOR
4

HA-RAV AGAN

1 TICHO
HOUSE

2
BEIT
HARAV

BET
DAVID
3

AVRAHAM TICHO

HA-RAV KOOK

✳ END

JAFFA

P

HA-RAV AGAN

HA-RAV KOOK

START

✳

JAFFA

Turn into Ha-Rav Kook St. from Jaffa St. Take the first left onto Ha-Rav Agan St. You will soon see a brown sign on your right directing you to the Ticho House. Go up the winding path through the park and enter the garden of Ticho House through the open green gate. Climb up the steps to the main entrance of Ticho House ❶. There is no entrance fee.

This was one of the first homes to be built outside the Old City walls. It was constructed in 1860 by a member of the wealthy Arab Nashashibi family. The garden originally extended to Jaffa St. The house was built in a typical Ottoman style with side rooms off a central area with a vaulted ceiling. The house has since undergone renovations and additions. Dr. Ticho was the home's third owner when he bought it in 1912. You can view a movie in Hebrew about Anna Ticho in one of the rooms, partially narrated by herself. (For more details about Ticho House see page 153).

Leave Ticho House by the main entrance through which you entered and exit the grounds by the gate on your right. Then go up the steps and follow the path around the walls of the grounds of the house. This will lead you directly to Beit HaRav Kook ❷. This building is the former home of Rabbi Abraham Isaac Kook and is now a museum dedicated to his life's work.

Rav Kook took up residence in this house when he was appointed Ashkenazi Chief Rabbi of Jerusalem. Soon after this he was appointed the first Ashkenazi Chief Rabbi of Palestine. This house is part of the Beit David Quarter, the fourth neighborhood erected outside the Old City walls. When first constructed, it was a gated community for poor Ashkenazi Torah scholars and consisted of ten joined initially single-story homes in the form of a square, access to each home being from the central square. It was funded by the philanthropist David Reiss (hence its name Beit David). Rav Kook's home was on a second floor built above the other homes, and a synagogue was added for him. Access to his house was via a specially constructed staircase on the outside of Beit David. The gate to Beit David was locked at night, and it was important to Rav Kook that he was accessible to people at all hours.

His synagogue functioned as a learning center where he studied with his students. This was the origins of the influential yeshiva Mercaz HaRav, which became the central yeshiva of religious Zionism. This eventually moved to a larger building in Jerusalem's Kiryat Moshe neighborhood. His synagogue is still in use as a neighborhood place of worship. (For more details about Beit HaRav Kook see page 153).

After exiting the museum, turn left along Dr. Abraham Ticho St. You will pass by the gate of the Bet David compound ❸, now occupied by a yeshiva, but you can peep through the gates to appreciate the layout of this early, gated neighborhood.

Turn left onto Ha-Rav Kook St. and proceed to the end of the road and its junction with Ha-Nevi'im St. As you walk along Ha-Rav Kook St., you can see the back of Beit David and where Rav Kook had his sukkah.

Cross Ha-Nevi'im St on the pedestrian crossing and almost straight ahead of you is the delightful Ethiopia St. It was once regarded as the most beautiful street in Jerusalem, although it now has lots of competitors. Most of its stately looking homes were built by the Nashashibi family in the late 1800's and early 1900's in a checkerboard fashion, with houses alternately close to or set back from the main road.

Conrad Schick (1822-1901), a German architect and archaeologist, lived in the corner estate (Beit Tavor) ❹, on the left side of the road. He designed important buildings in Jerusalem, as well as the Meah Shearim neighborhood. He also worked for the Palestine Exploration Fund. His house was sold in 1951 to the Swedish Theological Institute, who are its present owners.

By knowing something about the occupants of the homes on this street during the first third of the 20th century, you can appreciate that a new and intellectual stage in the development of Jerusalem was blossoming here. You will soon pass building number 6 on your right, which housed the American School of Oriental Research headed by Professor W.F. Albright. He was a leading figure in the field of Biblical archaeology and received many awards, including the title "*Yakir Yerushalayim*" (Worthy Citizen of Jerusalem). This was the first time this award was presented to a non-Jew. At number 8 lived Professor Boris Schatz, who founded the Bezalel School of Arts and Crafts in Jerusalem. Eliezer Ben-Yehuda and his family lived on the second floor of number 11 ❺. It is not possible to enter his home, but the plaque on the outside wall of his former home is informative.

In building number 10, opposite Ben-Yehuda's home, is the Ethiopian Church Compound ❻ built between 1874 to 1901. The church can be visited.

The connection between Ethiopia and the people of Israel is a long-standing one. From the Bible we learn that the Queen of Sheba visited King Solomon (1 Kings 10:2). According to Ethiopian tradition (although this is not recorded in the Bible or part of Jewish tradition), the Lion of Judah symbol was presented to her during this visit. Her son Menelik I was born from a union with King Solomon, and he became the founder of the Ethiopian royal dynasty. The last emperor of Ethiopia was Haile Selassie. Ethiopia no longer has a monarchy.

Ethiopia accepted Christianity in the 4th century CE. There were Ethiopian Christians in Jerusalem during the Byzantine period, and they continued to have a presence in the Church of the Holy Sepulcher. Despite the rise of Islam, Ethiopia managed to survive as a predominantly Christian country. Ethiopia had a number of properties in Jerusalem, but they had to be given up during the Ottoman period because of their financial difficulties and inability to pay taxes to the Ottoman government. The church on Ethiopia St. dates from 1893 and was built by the royal family. Notice the Lion of Judah symbol above the entrance gate. This was the title of the Solomonic Ethiopian emperors and was also on the Ethiopian flag until 1974.

Continue to the end of Ethiopia St., and this leads into Khazanovitch St. At the corner of Khazanovitch St. and Bnei Brit St. turn left a short distance to view the corner building, the B'nai Brith Library ❼.

This building was built in 1902 and housed the first free public library for Jerusalem's Jewish community. The books were donated by Dr. Yosef Hazanovitch, and the collection, which was called Midrash Abarbanel after the Spanish statesman and scholar Don Isaac Abarbanel, was established on the 400th anniversary of the expulsion of Jews from Spain. The books were subsequently moved to the Hebrew University in 2007 and formed the basis of Israel's National Library located in a newly built building on the Givat Ram campus. The B'nai Brith organization donated money for another library that was set up here in its stead.

Now take Bnei Brit St. in the opposite direction until you come to its intersection with Nathan Strauss St. Turn left on Nathan Strauss St. towards Jaffa St. where this walk ends.

Further details about Ticho House and Beit HaRav Kook:

Ticho House at 10 HaRav Agan is open Sunday to Thursday 12.00 Pm–8.00 PM, Friday and holiday eves 10.00 Am–2.00 PM, and is closed on Shabbat. There are often art exhibits in the house and gardens. The Anna Italian Café is a kosher certified dairy restaurant on the second floor. Their phone number is: (02) 670-8960.

Beit HaRav Kook at 9 Ha-Rav Kook St. is open Sunday to Thursday 9.00 Am–4.00 PM. Friday is by appointment. Admission includes a 20-minute movie about the life of Rav Kook in Hebrew or in English. You may also receive a short personal guided tour from the staff. There are photographs on the walls with explanations in Hebrew. The center also arranges lectures and trips. The facility is not wheelchair accessible. Their phone number is: (02) 623-2560.

Nearby Places of Interest:

Museum of the Underground Prisoners is at 1 Mishol Hagevura St. This building in the Russian Compound was originally a hostel for female Russian pilgrims and was converted into a prison by the British during the Mandate. Not only criminals, but hundreds of resistance fighters from Etzel, Lehi and the Haganah were imprisoned here. It is open 9 am–5 pm Sunday to Thursday. There are tours in Hebrew and English that describe the underground struggle by the Yishuv for establishment of the State. There is also a movie. There is an admission fee. Allow about 1.5 hours for your visit. Their phone number is: (02) 633-3166.

Yad LaKashish is on 14 Shivtei Israel St. With the purchase of a gift at Yad LaKashish, you are not only buying quality and reasonably priced religious and decorative handicraft, but also supporting almost three hundred elderly immigrants who work in the attached workshops. The store is open 9 am–5 pm from May to August and 9 am–4:30 pm from September to April. Products can also be bought from their online store. Free tours of the workshops are encouraged and can be arranged in advance by e-mailing info@lifeline.org.il or calling (02) 628-7829.

Hebrew Music Museum at 10 Yoel Moshe Salomon St. (see page 106).

Friends of Zion Museum at 20 Yosef Rivlin St. (see page 106).

16 The German Colony and Liberty Bell Park

Old Templer homes and quaint streets and alleys are the main attractions in this walk through the German Colony, which starts at the First Station (the old Railway station) and ends at the Liberty Bell Park, with its replica of the Philadelphia Liberty Bell.

The Templer Community Hall at 1 Emek Refaim St. functioned as both a church and community ce

THE GERMAN TEMPLERS IN JERUSALEM – AUSPICIOUS BEGINNINGS AND SAD END

The Templers were a Protestant sect from Southern Germany that espoused a life of simple Christian virtue combined with productive labor. They built a number of communities in Turkish Palestine. They believed that the apocalyptic visions of the prophets of Israel foretold the Second Coming of Jesus and they elected to have a front row seat for when this happened. Templers approved of Jewish settlement, although they believed that the Holy Land would eventually be inherited by the followers of Jesus.

This sect would be of only minor interest today were it not for the fact that they built a very beautiful rural village close to the Old City, in what has now become a very desirable area to live in. They also played a significant role in the development of this country. Jewish immigrants to Palestine from Eastern Europe had little expertise in small industry, while the German Templers possessed this expertise. They also had a very strong work ethic, and developed a well-earned reputation for quality work in building, skilled crafts, road building, the hotel industry, agriculture and commerce.

The first Templer home was built in 1873 at about the same time that the first group of houses in the Mishkenot Yisroel Quarter in Nachla'ot was being built. There is no comparison between them. The Templers came to this country with money and their two-storied homes had spacious living accommodation. Houses in Nachla'ot were then single-storied, attached, had few rooms, and much family activity was by necessity outside the home in the central square.

The contributions of the Templers to the early development of this country have not been well documented – and may never be. It is a sad story. All the Templer communities in Palestine were expelled from the country by the British Mandate authorities during World War II because of their German origins. Many of their youth (i.e., their third generation) were Nazi sympathizers, and the Jews were also not sad to see them go.

The Templers had their time on the stage of this country and moved on. Most of them returned to Germany or

TIME: About 1.25 hours

DISTANCE: 3.25 km

TYPE OF WALK: Circular

DIFFICULTY: An easy walk on paved roads, suitable for strollers and wheelchairs.

STARTING POINT: David Remez St. by the First Station.

PUBLIC TRANSPORT: Enter "The First Station" into Moovit. Many buses stop opposite the Khan Theater on David Remez St. and also on Karen Kayemet St. close to Liberty Bell Park where the walk ends.

DRIVING DIRECTIONS AND PARKING: Enter "First Station" into Waze and click on "The First Station David Remez Street Jerusalem." There is free parking just beyond the paid parking lot and gas station on Emek Refaim St. There is also parking just beyond the First Station on Hebron Rd. which is free for the first three hours.

155

moved to Australia. After the War of Independence, their properties were taken over by the Israeli government and compensation was eventually paid to them by the State. There are currently no Templer groups in Germany or in Israel.

THE WALK

Visit the inside of the First Station ❶ either now or at the end of the walk.

The idea of a railway line between the Mediterranean and Jerusalem was a vision of the early Zionists, but they lacked the financing to construct it. The contract for a line between Jaffa and Jerusalem was eventually bought by a French company and they cut some corners. They followed the winding Emek Refaim Valley, thereby obviating the need for bridges and tunnels. They also purchased the rails from a company that had gone bankrupt, thereby leaving them with the smallest gauge rails in the world. All this led to a very winding and slow ride. Nevertheless, it was still better than a day and a half journey by mule!

The railway's opening in 1892 was a major step in the development of Jerusalem, and the opening ceremony was attended by many Turkish dignitaries. The railway was eventually nationalized by the Turks due to its military significance, and they enlarged the rail gauge and joined the railway to the Hejaz Railway between Damascus and the Arabian Peninsula. The rail gauge was changed to British standards during the British Mandate.

The outside of the station is the original Turkish façade, although design changes were made during the Mandate. The additional floor was added during the Ottoman period.

Exit the First Station and turn left along David Remez St. You soon pass the Khan Theater ❷ on your right.

Originally a Mamluke building, the Khan opened during the Ottoman period as a lodging place for travelers who were unable to make it to the Old City before nightfall. At that time, there were no residential areas in Jerusalem other than the Old City. It was not quite modern hostel accommodation. Customers slept on the floor and brought their own food. It is now the home of the Jerusalem Theatre Company.

At the next intersection of David Remez St. with King David St. and Emeq Refaim St. turn left along Emeq Refaim St. At the next intersection with Beit Lehem Rd. take the right fork along Emek Refaim St. You are now in the old German Colony. Cross over to the left side of the road.

Emek Refaim St. and Beit Lehem St. were the boundaries of the Templer village, and the point where you are now standing is where these two boundaries met. The community's first buildings were on Emek Refaim St. followed by Beit Lehem St., and subsequently on the streets between them. This entire area has now become a high-end residential area, and you will see quite a bit of construction with a pleasant mixing of the modern and old.

Look at the Templer Community Hall ❸ at 1 Emek Refaim St.

This building (see picture on page 154) was the center of the Templers' life for administrative meetings, social gatherings, lectures and Sunday prayer. Everyone was expected to go to the annual meetings. There was even a fine for not attending without a good excuse! The building has a simple design, although its entrance is more ornate. The bell in the belfry called the Templers to worship on Sunday mornings. The Armenian Church used the building for a while after the Templers left.

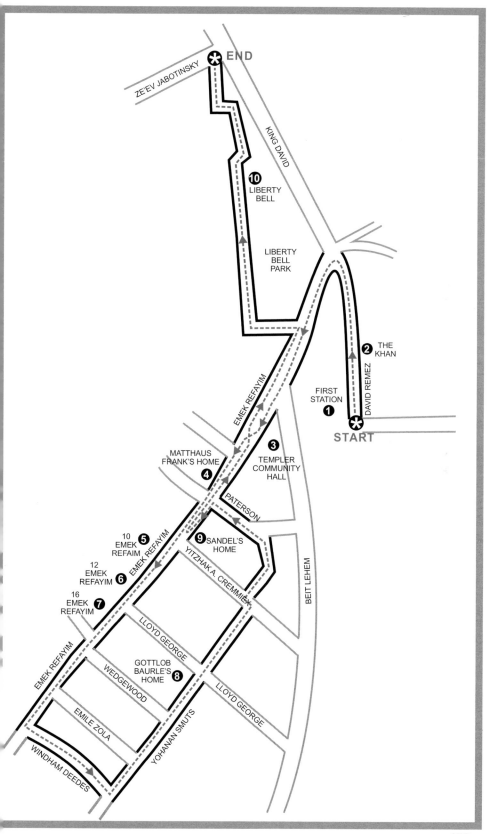

ZE'EV JABOTINSKY

✱ END

KING DAVID

⑩ LIBERTY BELL

LIBERTY BELL PARK

EMEK REFAYIM

❷ THE KHAN

FIRST STATION ❶

DAVID REMEZ

✱ START

MATTHAUS FRANK'S HOME

❸ TEMPLER COMMUNITY HALL

❹

PATERSON

10 ❺ EMEK REFAIM

❾ SANDEL'S HOME

EMEK REFAYIM

12 ❻ EMEK REFAYIM

YITZHAK A. CREMMIEK

BEIT LEHEM

16 ❼ EMEK REFAYIM

LLOYD GEORGE

EMEK REFAYIM

WEDGEWOOD

GOTTLOB BAURLE'S HOME ❽

LLOYD GEORGE

EMILE ZOLA

YOHANAN SMUTS

WINDHAM DEEDES

157

Cross over the road to view the first home of this community at 6 Emek Refaim St. ➍ It was built by Matthaus Frank, a miller, who had a steam–powered mill and bakery on his property. His new technology put the windmill at Mishkenot Sha'ananim out of business.

A common feature of immigrants from Europe in times past (and this was also the case in the USA) was that they built their homes in the style of their home country – in this case southern Germany. Their houses in Germany were made of wood, but since wood was not readily available, they used stone. The features of their early buildings are very characteristic, and once you have seen one you will recognize the others in the neighborhood. They are often two storied and the division between the ground and first floor is marked by protruding stonework. The corners of their buildings have ornate stonework. Windows are arch-like or rectangular, and the original buildings have wooden shutters. Roofs are covered with red tiles. The Templers designed and made these tiles, and they became extremely popular in Jerusalem. They can still be seen in older parts of the city. Low wrought iron railings around the homes made by the local Templer smith are also very typical. Early homes often have a Biblical quotation above the door, usually from the Prophets, with words of encouragement. These quotations doubtless indicate the sentiments of these settlers. Later houses do not necessarily have all these features, but they are still readily recognizable as a Templer home.

On top of the entrance to this house one can just make out the date 1873, the date the house was built, and the words *"Eben Ezer,"* which means *"helping stone."* These words are from Samuel I describing a battle between the Israelites and Philistines at the time of the prophet Samuel. The verse reads: *"The men of Israel ... pursued the Philistines ... Samuel took a stone and set it between Mitzpah and Shen, and named it Eben-Ha'ezer. For up to now,"* he said, *"the Lord has helped us"* (Samuel I 7:12).

This is a typical duplex Templer home with stonework between the two stories, a wooden balcony and wrought iron fence

As you walk along this side of the street, look at other Templer homes. At 10 Emeq Refaim St. ❺, note the German inscription over the lintel that reads: *"The Lord loves the gates of Zion more than all the dwellings of Jacob"* (Psalms 87:2). The owner of this home, which was built in 1874, was an importer of German goods. The duplex at 12 Emek Refaim St. ❻ —built in 1875 — was the home of two sisters and their families. The wooden balcony is original. The Imberger family built the house at 16 Emek Refaim St. ❼ in 1877. The German inscription above the door reads: *"Arise, shine, for your light has come, and the glory of the Lord has shone upon you"* (Isaiah 60:1).

Turn left into the alley Windham Deedes St. to look at a section of the German Colony with later and therefore more modern housing.

[You can also stroll further along Emek Refaim St., with its restaurants and cafes, to the Templer cemetery on the left side of the road where the founder of the Templers, Christopher Hoffman, is buried. Then return to Windham Deedes St.]

Where Windham Deedes St. ends at a park, turn left onto Yohanan Smuts St. There is an interesting corner house at 6 Lloyd George St. ❽ It is one of the grandest Templer homes in the German Colony and was constructed during the British Mandate by the architect Gottlob Baurle.

At the end of Smuts St., turn left onto Yitzhak A. Cremieux St, and then immediately take the first right into the alley Maurycy Gottlieb St. At the end of this alley, turn left onto Paterson St. and this will bring you back to Emek Refaim St.

Turn left to view 9 Emek Refaim St. ❾ on the left-hand side of the street. This was once the home of the Sandels. Above the door is a sculptured lion's head resting on its paws, the symbol of the pharmacy that Theodor Sandel ran in Germany.

Theodor Sandel was a very successful and talented engineer, architect and contractor. He built the Lepers Hospital in Talbieh, the Dormition Abbey on Mount Zion, the Lamel School in Zikhron Moshe, the Shaare Tzedek Hospital on Jaffa Road, the Anglican school on Ha-Nevi'im St, and many other buildings. He was also responsible for construction of the road between Jaffa and Jerusalem.

Retrace your steps and continue along Emek Refaim St. towards the intersection with Beit Lehem Rd. Cross over the road, and after its intersection with Beit Lehem Rd., and between the free and paid parking lots just before the gas station, you will see a brown signpost directing you to Liberty Bell Park. Go down this road and the entrance to the park is immediately on your right. Pass through the gate and head towards the Liberty Bell ❿.

Liberty Bell Park is a park with lots of facilities. There are expanses of green lawn, play areas with swings and slides, some of which are shaded, basketball courts, skateboard areas, and WC's. At the far end of the park is a replica of the Liberty Bell from Philadelphia declaring liberty throughout the land on the Jubilee year. This replica of the original even includes its crack!

Leave the park by continuing up the steps past the bell and this will lead you to the intersection of King David St., Ze'ev Jabotinsky St. and Keren Kayemet St. On the right side, a short distance along Keren Kayemet St., there is a bus stop from where you can catch a bus into the center of town. Alternatively, you may wish to return to the First Station or visit a nearby museum.

Nearby Places of Interest:

First Station at 4 David Remez St. (see page 138).

Nature Museum at 6 Mohliver St. is a small but gem of a museum in the middle of the German Colony, with exhibits on natural history, including dinosaurs, the human body and geology. Older children should find it very worthwhile. Educational activities are also offered. There is a pleasant garden area. The museum is open Sunday 9 am–1 pm, Monday 9 am–6 pm, Tuesday 9 am–1 pm, Wednesday 9 am–6 pm, Thursday 9 am–1 pm, Saturday 10 am–2 pm, and is closed Fridays and holiday eves. There is an admission charge. Their phone number is: (02) 566-4135.

Menachem Begin Heritage Center at 6 S.U. Nahon St. (see page 106).

The Museum for Islamic Art is at 2 Hapalmach St. A room on the ground floor explains about Islam and the different Islamic periods in relation to the exhibits. Children will probably find this museum heavy-going, although there are children's workshops on Saturday and during holidays. The museum is open Monday to Wednesday 10 am–3 pm, Thursday 10 am–7 pm, Friday, Saturday and Jewish religious holidays 10 am–2 pm. It is closed on Sunday. There is an admission charge. Their phone number is: (02) 566-1291.

The Train Theater is in Liberty Bell Park and has regularly scheduled puppet shows and Story Theater for young children. Shows are in Hebrew.

17 The Mei Neftoah (Lifta) Nature Reserve and Arazim Valley Park

Even many Jerusalemites are unaware that there is a beautiful nature reserve, the Mei Neftoah (Lifta) Nature Reserve, less than a fifteen minute walk from the Central Bus Station. It is ideal for a family hike. There is a pool from the spring by the ruins of Lifta deep enough for kids to swim in, and the adjacent Arazim Valley Park in the Arazim Valley has play equipment and picnic benches.

TIME: About 2 hours

DISTANCE: About 4.5 km

TYPE OF HIKE: Walking there and back on the same path

DIFFICULTY: Easy hike along paved roads and footpaths. Walking with a light stroller is difficult, but not impossible, I've seen people do it. But it's easier with a baby backpack.

STARTING POINT: The one-lane paved road immediately before the Paz gas station at the beginning of Ben Gurion Boulevard.

PUBLIC TRANSPORT: Many buses stop outside the Central Bus Station or Binyanei Ha'umah Convention Center. From the Central Bus Station or its light rail stop, walk along Jaffa Rd. in the direction away from Jerusalem. Cross Yirmiyahu St. and take the first turn on your right, Ben Gurion Boulevard. Close to its beginning and just before the Paz gas station, is a single-lane paved road. It's about a seven minute walk from the Central Bus Station.

DRIVING DIRECTIONS AND PARKING: Enter "Lifta" into Waze. The nearest parking is at חניון ליפתה.

The footpath from the pool to Arazim Valley Park passes the ruins of the Arab village of Lifta

The Village of Lifta/ Neftoah – Past and Present

Lifta has been identified with the village of Nephtoah (נפתוח), and its spring is mentioned in the Book of Joshua as delineating the northern border of the tribe of Judah: *"The outcome of the lottery for the tribe of the Children of Judah... The border proceeded directly from the top of the mountain to the spring of Mei Neftoach and broadened to the cities of Mount Ephron"* (Joshua 15:9). It was also the southern border of the tribe of Benjamin (Joshua 18:15). Ruins have been found here dating to the First Temple period. It was inhabited in Roman and Byzantine times, and there was a farmhouse during the Crusader period. It was an Arab village at least from Ottoman times.

The Arab residents of this village were opposed to the Zionist state and there is documentation that they participated in attacks on Jewish communities during the Arab riots of 1929. The village was heavily involved in the siege of West Jerusalem during the War of Independence and militias were ensconced in the village. Some villagers fled when the Jews went on the offensive since they were effectively in a war zone. Reliable information as to whether the remaining villagers abandoned or were forced out of their homes in 1948 is unavailable, but is hardly relevant. They were in a highly strategic location at the entrance to West Jerusalem and were either participants or supportive bystanders in this struggle. As for other Palestinian refugees, they were not permitted to return to their homes after the end of the war.

Abandoned Arab property like this was taken over by the Israel Lands Administration and used for Israeli towns or parks. However, the deserted houses of Lifta still stand. After the war, Jewish immigrants from Yemen and Kurdistan who had been forced from their countries, lived in the buildings, but living conditions were difficult and they had to leave. The buildings were subsequently used as a rehabilitation center and then as a school, but these closed or relocated. The land was slated to be used for apartments, but these plans were stopped by an interesting coalition of archaeologists, architects, and representatives of the descendants of the original Arab residents.

Enter the paved road immediately before the Paz gas station and go past the Magen David Adom station. Continue on this road, which parallels the main road and becomes a surfaced footpath. Take the next turn on the right onto the foot-bridge that crosses Sharei Jerusalem St. The steps or walkway lead to the very bottom of the bridge. Go under the bridge and turn left onto the road ahead.

Take the next turn on the right. When you reach a barrier take the road on the left down the hill. A green sign indicates that this is the entrance to the Mei Neftoah (Lifta) Nature Reserve. At the next barrier take the left fork onto a gravel covered path. This path will take you to the pool. (You will soon see a narrow path on your left which provides a somewhat quicker route to the pool, but it's quite rocky).

The pool is not big enough for adults to swim in, but is fine for kids, although not for toddlers. There are stone steps at one corner of the pool that can be used to get in and out of the water without difficulty. The pool has a smooth bottom and no footware is needed. The water is fairly cold. The tunnel that enters the pool from the source of the spring can be explored.

Now take the steps down the valley on the blue-marked trail. This will lead you past the ruins of Arab houses and then through a lush valley containing non-tended orchards with fig and almond trees.

After jumping over a dry river bed take the right fork. You will soon pass the wreck of a green van.

Just before the bottom of the valley, turn right at the T-junction. This road will lead you to the access road to Arazim Valley Park. This is part of the Jerusalem Park system that extends along the Arazim Valley from Golda Meir Boulevard to Motza Valley, close to Mevaseret Zion. The park contains picnic benches and play areas, many of which are in the shade, climbing equipment, swings, and a mini-cable car.

The way back is the way you came.

Arazim Valley Park

18 A Countryside Hike on the Gazelle Trail in the Ramot Forest

This "countryside hike" is within Jerusalem's municipal boundaries and close to the area of Ramot. The trail is on agricultural land used in First and Second Temple times. Much of it has been forested to create the Ramot Forest. The Biblical Garden and Naftoah Lookout are worth visiting. Mountain gazelle roam in the area and you may luck out and see some. A hike to the Twin Towers Living Memorial in Emeq Arazim should also be considered.

A winepress from First Temple times in the Biblical Garden

Ramot Forest is part of a green belt that was intended to encircle Jerusalem, although a large part of it has since become residential. Much of Ramot Forest was preserved through the efforts of Ramot residents. Ramot is a large residential area built after the Six Day War. This hike starts from Gan Hakipod (Hedgehog Park), a pleasant park in south Ramot that has lawns, playground equipment, a basketball court, and a slide in the shape of a hedgehog. A later part of the hike overlooks Emeq Arazim, which is a section of Nahal Sorek. You can see the ruins of of the Arab village of Lifta and the main northwest entrance to Jerusalem on the other side of the valley.

THE HIKE

There are many intersections on this hike. However, if you follow the signposts and keep to the red-marked trail after passing the event hall Tur Sinai, you should not go wrong. Also, to help you, the main intersections in the map on the next page are numbered and these numbers are referred to in the directions.

To reach the trailhead, walk down the steps to the far right or to the left of the Hedgehog, walk across the lawn towards the left of the small semi-circular paved plaza, and continue down the hill on the steps with green railings. Go past the KKL-JNF sign to a T-junction with a signpost (I1). Turn right onto the blue-marked trail in the direction of "מסלול הצבאים (Gazelle Trail) לשביל התאומים."

At the next junction (I2), the green-marked Gazelle Trail turns to the left and is signposted to "שביל הצבאים." However, before doing this, visit the Biblical Garden by turning right onto the blue-marked trail. You will soon see a grey sign on your left at the beginning of a path indicating that you are entering into the public Biblical Garden (גן תנ״כי קהלתי). There is plenty to discover here.

This Biblical Garden was developed by Ramot resident Ricky Yona with the help of the KKL and local residents, and displays shrubs and trees mentioned in the Bible. It also contains finds from the First Temple period, including winepresses, water cisterns, and a structure that may have been part of a millstone. Green signs by the trees and plants contain relevant Biblical passages. All the notices are in Hebrew.

Walk back to the intersection I2 and continue straight ahead a short distance on the green-marked trail to the next

TIME: About 2.25 hours

DISTANCE: About 5.25 km

TYPE OF HIKE: Circular

DIFFICULTY:
An easy walk on jeep trails, footpaths and paved roads.

STARTING POINT:
Gan HaKipod on the road Mish'ol HaKitron

PUBLIC TRANSPORT:
Gan Kipod is well serviced by public transport. Enter "גן קיפוד" into Moovit and click on "גן קיפוד, Jerusalem." The bus stop for buses 31,32 and 72 is about a nine minute walk away.

DRIVING DIRECTIONS AND PARKING:
Enter "גן הקיפוד" into Waze, and this will lead you to the road משול הכתרון. Park alongside the road.

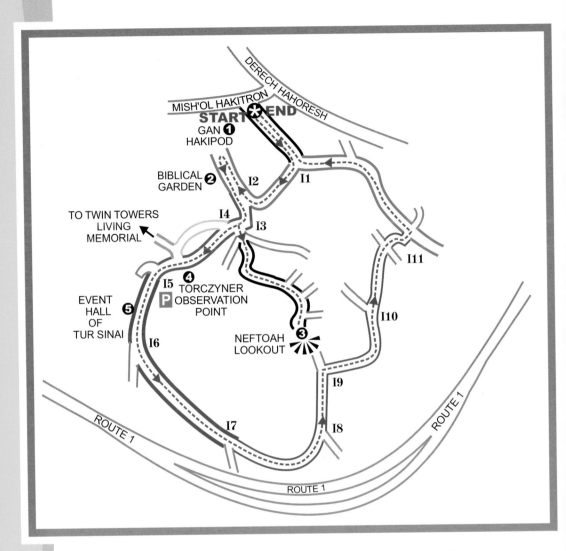

DERECH HAHORESH

MISH'OL HAKITRON

START ✶ **END**

GAN ❶
HAKIPOD

BIBLICAL ❷   I2   I1
GARDEN

TO TWIN TOWERS   I4
LIVING
MEMORIAL ←   I3

                                                    I11

        I5 ❹
        TORCZYNER
EVENT P OBSERVATION
HALL ❺   POINT   I10
OF
TUR SINAI   NEFTOAH ❸
        I6   LOOKOUT

                                    I9

ROUTE 1   I7   I8   ROUTE 1

ROUTE 1

intersection (I3) with a signpost with yellow directions. The Gazelle Trail follows the green markers to the right. However, before turning onto that trail continue straight ahead on the jeep trail sign-posted to the Naftoah Lookout.

As you walk along, you can see to your right the bridge for the new high-speed rail between Jerusalem and Tel Aviv that crosses Emeq Arazim. Also, the buildings of Mevaseret Zion. Behind you and just above the buildings of Ramot is the minaret at Nebi Samuel. Ahead of you on the other side of Emeq Arazim is the Calatrava Bridge, the tallest structure on the skyline, and beneath this the deserted Arab village of Lifta.

The Calatrava Bridge is known in Hebrew as Gesher Hameitarim (the Bridge of Strings). It was built by the well-known Spanish architect and engineer Santiago Calatrava, and its design alludes to King David's harp. It was inaugurated in 2008. It functions as a bridge for the inter-city light-rail and as a pedestrian crossing.

Lifta is mentioned in the Bible as the village of Nephtoah (נפתוח). It was the northern-most point of the territory of Judah and on the border with the tribe of Benjamin (Joshua 15:9 and 18:8). For more information about Lifta and the events of the War of Independence see page 162 in chapter 17.

166

Once you have reached the top of the hill there is no point in going further. Return to the intersection with the signpost (I3) and turn left down the hill in the direction "אנדרטת התאומים" (Twin Towers Memorial) following the green markers. At the next fork (I4), take the left green-marked fork to the Torczyner Observation Point, which is a picnic area with benches.

The Torczyner family planted orchards in Arazim Valley and along the northern slopes of Mitzpeh Naftoah in the 1950's. All that remains of their once thriving agricultural enterprise is the organic farm of Tur Sinai, a fruit orchard, and an events venue that you will pass shortly.

[At this point, from intersection I5, you may wish to hike to the Twin Towers Memorial in Emeq Arazim. It will add about an hour to this hike. After visiting the memorial, return to intersection I5. For further details about the memorial see below].

Just below the parking area, take the red-marked paved road to the left. You will soon pass Tur Sinai on your right.

At the next fork (I6), take the left branch on the red-marked paved road.

At the fork after this (I7), turn left along a red-marked jeep trail signposted in the direction of Ramot.

When the jeep trail comes to a T-junction (I8), take the red-marked footpath on the left up the hill. From here there is a nice view of the ruins of Lifta.

The next turning (I9), which is is on your right, is about half-way up the hill, and just before a rock step on the path. If you are close to the top of the hill, you have gone too far. It is still part of the Gazelle Trail and has occasional red markings.

At the next fork (I10) follow the sign on the pole with the red arrow to the right to "מסלול הצבאים לרמות."

Eventually, close to some houses, the red trail reaches the blue trail. At this T-junction (I11), turn left on this blue-marked jeep trail in the direction of "גן קיפוד."

Follow the blue-signed trail until it ends at a T-junction with a KKL sign post. You are now back at intersection I1 and very close to where you started the hike. Turn right to Gan Hakipod.

Nearby Places of Interest:

Twin Towers Living Memorial is a memorial to the victims of the 9/11 terrorist attack on the Twin Towers in Manhattan in the US. It was established by the KKL-JNF and is located on a hill in the Arazim Valley. The thirty feet bronze statue takes the form of an American flag waving and transforming itself at its tip to a flame. A shard from the ruins of the Twin Towers forms part of the monument's base. The names of the victims are engraved on it and are also on the nearby wall. Below the memorial is the Einot Telem National Park. Directions: From the intersection I5 take the paved road down the hill. This changes to a rough jeep trail. When this comes to a paved road turn right onto a green-marked road. The entrance to the memorial is just after you pass under the railway bridge.

19 The Gorgeous Jerusalem Biblical Zoo

The Tisch Family Zoological Gardens, popularly called the Jerusalem Biblical Zoo, must be one of the prettiest places in Israel. It contains numerous species from around the world, including animals indigenous to Israel, and animals that were once indigenous to Israel, such as the Persian leopard and Nile crocodile. All are displayed in a beautifully landscaped park with a large duck and swan filled lake, green lawns, flowing streams, attractive flowerbeds and interesting paths.

Some Highlights of the Zoo: Look for the Bible Land Wildlife Reserve containing animals mentioned in the Bible, an open African Savanna, three aviaries, and flamingos around the lake. Displays to keep the kids engaged include a children's petting zoo, an area with guides and educational activities, Noah's ark Visitor Center that has movies, a train around the park, and play climbing area. On Fridays, there are activities for kids throughout the day.

There is a coffee shop and food kiosk at the zoo entrance, and a cafeteria at the Noah's Ark Visitor's Center. There are plenty of WC's within the zoo.

PUBLIC TRANSPORT:
Several bus lines go to the zoo. Enter "Jerusalem Biblical Zoo" into Moovit.

DRIVING DIRECTIONS AND PARKING:
Located on Derech Aharon Shulov 1. Enter "Jerusalem Zoo" into Waze. There is free parking outside the zoo.

ADMISSION DETAILS:
Opening hours: Spring: Sunday–Thursday 8 am–5 pm, Saturday 10 am–6 pm. Summer: Sunday–Thursday 9 am–7 pm, Saturday 10 am–6 pm. Fall: Sunday–Thursday 9 am–5 pm, Saturday 10 am–5 pm. Friday and holiday eves all year round 9 am–4:30 pm.

The zoo's brochure lays out three paths for one, two, and three hour walks. The one hour walk includes the children's zoo and play area. The three hour walk includes the Bible Land Wildlife Reserve, African Savannah, and Noah's Ark Visitor Center.

The zoo train has pick-up and drop-off points for a small charge.

Nearby Places of Interest:

The Jerusalem Park is close to the zoo, just across the bridge. It has a large area with elaborate climbing equipment.

The Israel Aquarium is a very short distance from the zoo. It displays aquatic life found predominantly in the Mediterranean and Red Seas. Tickets need to be booked in advance. There are guided tours in the morning, which are also available in English, and self-guided visits from 3 pm–5 pm, on weekends and holidays. There is an admission charge. Their phone number is: (073) 339-9000.

Ein Lavan is a great place for kids for a swim or picnic. It is within walking distance from the zoo and less than ten minutes by car. See chapter 44, "Ein Lavan" on page 142.

Ein Yael Living Museum is open to the public in July and August and on school vacations. There are workshops for pottery, weaving, mosaic making and more. Ein Yael was a Jewish settlement during First Temple times, and also contains ruins of a Roman villa from the 2nd century CE. Its mosaic floor with its pagan representations is very different from the mosaic floors in ancient Jewish buildings. It is open in July: 10 am–4 pm (Friday until 2.00 PM), August: 10 am–6 pm (Friday until 2 pm), Pesach: 10 am–6 pm (Friday until 2 pm) and Succot: 10 am–5 pm. Private tours and workshops can be arranged at other times. There is an admission charge, with an additional fee for festivals. Their phone number is: (02) 645-1866.

20 The Jerusalem Botanical Gardens

Explore colorful paths in the areas of Southern Africa, Australia, Asia, Europe, North America and the Mediterranean, with over six thousand plants and trees from around the globe. The scenic pools, waterfalls, tree walk, and Tropical Conservatory with exotic plants are sure to engage your interest. The numerous multi-colored blossoms after the winter rains are quite inspiring. Most of the paths are paved.

Inside the conservatory

For a detailed tour in Hebrew or English of the Biblical plants and trees located in the Mediterranean area and also a general tour of the geographic areas be sure to pick up a free audio-guide from the ticket office. Many exploratory hours of discovery can be spent in the garden, especially if you follow these tours.

The walking is easy on paved paths that are stroller and wheel-chair friendly. There are WC's close to the ticket office and also in other locations throughout the garden. Free train rides are offered in the summer. The Tropical Conservatory with its exotic and colorful plants should not be missed.

There is a Kafit restaurant just outside the entrance to the gardens. There is also a large plant nursery by the parking lot outside the gardens with a very large selection of plants and trees. It also has a coffee shop.

PUBLIC TRANSPORT:
Enter "Jerusalem Botanical Gardens" into Moovit. There are bus stops within a five to seven minute walk of the gardens.

DRIVING DIRECTIONS AND PARKING:
Enter "Jerusalem Botanical Gardens" into Waze. There is a large free parking area outside the gardens.

OPENING HOURS:
The Park is open during the summer Sunday to Thursday 9 am—7 pm, Friday until 5 pm, Saturday and holidays until 6 pm. In the winter Sunday to Thursday 9 am—5 pm, Friday until 3 pm, and Saturday and holidays until 5 pm. There is an admission charge. Their phone number is: (02) 679-4012

Nearby Places of Interest

Gazelle Valley Park is a natural reserve with ponds, streams, walking trails and bike paths. It contains a herd of Mountain Gazelle that once lived on the slopes of Beit Hakerem, Malha and Emek Rephaim, but who were trapped by construction of Begin Highway. Enter "Gazelle Valley" into Waze and "עמק הצבאים" into Moovit.

AN
INTRODUCTION
TO THE
JUDEAN MOUNTAINS

Hiking in the Judean Mountains at elevations as high as eight hundred to one thousand meters above sea level, it is difficult to imagine that this was once the floor of an ancient ocean. We know this because the primary rock in these mountains is limestone, a marine sedimentary rock formed about two hundred million years ago.

These mountains resulted from the ocean floor folding upwards as a result of shifting tectonic plates, leading to the ocean water receding and the creation of a mountain range extending from north of Shechem to the Southern Hebron Hills. A later and different type of tectonic shift, in which two plates drifted away from each other, created the deep valleys of the Jordan Rift that extend along Israel's eastern border – the Hula Valley, Jordan Valley, the Dead Sea basin and the Arava. The Jordan Rift is part of a larger system that extends from southern Turkey to eastern Africa.

In contrast to the eastern slopes of the Judean Mountains that are characterized by steep slopes and a sharp transition between the inhabited areas on the mountains and the adjacent Judean Desert, the descent of the western side of the central mountain range to the Mediterranean Sea is more gradual. Between the two is a transitional area called the "*Shefela*" which means "lowlands" in Hebrew and consists of several smaller mountain ranges 150 to 450 meters in altitude.

The slopes of both sides of the Judean Mountains are dissected by riverbeds, known by the Hebrew term *nahal* or the Arabic *wadi*, through which runoff rainwater flows to the Dead Sea on its eastern side and to the Mediterranean Sea on the west. The wadis on the western side of the central mountain range are less deep than those on the eastern side because erosion has been more gradual.

The limestone rock forming the heights of the Judean Mountains is harder than the chalk prevalent on its lower slopes, and its surface is perforated by cracks and openings that allow water to penetrate. As the rain water seeps deeper beneath the surface it encounters layers of softer rock through which it cannot pass, and this leads to underground accumulations of water called aquifers. If erosion of a wadi is deep enough to expose an aquifer, a spring will appear. Human settlement has concentrated around these springs because of their consistent water supply.

When the Israelites conquered the land of Canaan at the time of Joshua, they were often unable to subdue the Canaanites living in the fertile valleys and were forced to settle in the mountainous areas. To sustain an agricultural existence, they adopted terrace farming. Stone retaining walls were built on mountainside slopes that already had a natural stepped structure due to different rates of erosion of alternating layers of softer and harder limestone. The walls of the terraces helped prevent rainwater runoff and soil erosion, and the soil behind the walls was used for agriculture. Many of these terraces are still in use today and can be seen primarily to the north and south of Jerusalem in Judea and Samaria. The Judean Mountains within the pre-1967 borders of Israel have mostly been forested, including the terraces, creating the beautiful expanses of green surrounding the western approaches to Jerusalem.

See page 4 for a map of the location of the hikes in the Judean Mountains that are west of Jerusalem.

21 Ancient Agriculture in Sataf

Most of the terraces in the Judean Mountains within the Green Line are no longer used for agriculture, and many have been forested by the Jewish National Fund. Sataf is an exception. Its terraces have been restored by the JNF. Grape vines and olive, fig, pomegranate and almond trees have been planted, and hiking trails laid out to create an outdoor "foots-on" museum of ancient agriculture. The views overlooking Nahal Sorek are extremely impressive. Sataf is only a short distance from Jerusalem and is understandably a popular place for hiking.

TIME: About 2.75 hours

DISTANCE: About 5.75 km

TYPE OF HIKE: Circular

DIFFICULTY: Easy hiking. Fom Ein Bikura to the parking lot there is a thirty minute somewhat steep ascent on a rocky path.

STARTING POINT: Upper parking lot in the Sataf Reserve. There is a WC in the adjacent building.

PUBLIC TRANSPORTATION: Bus 183 provides an infrequent service from Binyanei Ha'umah to Misaf Sataf, and from here it is a six minute walk (0.3 mile) to the Sataf upper parking lot. Enter "מסעף סטף" into Moovit.

DRIVING DIRECTIONS AND PARKING: Enter "Sataf" into Waze, click on "Sataf, Tzova" and "סטף -החניה העליונה" will apear. There is plenty of free parking here.

The vegetable gardens and ruins of the Arab village of Sataf

"ANCIENT AGRICULTURE" IN ISRAEL

The term "ancient agriculture" is a relative one, since the type of agriculture used in these mountains for thousands of years is still being used by many Arab villagers throughout Judea and Samaria. A better term, therefore, might be non-modern agriculture.

There are three components to this type of agriculture: 1. Trees and shrubs adapted to the Mediterrranean climate are grown on mountainside terraces; 2. Vegetables are grown below springs of water; and 3. Wheat and other grains are grown in the valleys. The first two components are on display in Sataf.

When the Israelites came to Canaan at the time of Joshua, the best agricultural land in the valleys and coastal plain was being used by the Canaanites and other tribes, and the Israelites were unable to completely dislodge them. They therefore settled in the mountains and their agriculture was on the mountainside terraces.

To build terraces is not as difficult as it might seem. Much of the ridging on the mountainsides is natural and is due to different rates of erosion of the underlying limestone. Therefore the farmer only needed to gather loose rocks to build walls behind which soil could accumulate. Earth from the valleys may also have been added for topsoil. Trees and shrubs able to survive the long rain-free summer, such as vines and olive, fig, pomegranate and almond trees, were planted on these terraces.

This type of agriculture is often called "Ba'al agriculture," and you will be walking on the "Baal trail."

Why this name?

Ba'al was a Canaanite god believed to control storms, agriculture and fertility. In Hebrew this name means master or lord and can refer to the Jewish God. Thus, early Israelites who used this term were covering both bases!

This hike overlooks the deep Nahal Sorek. The word "*Sorek*" means "special vine," and this area was once an important grape growing area. In Israelite, Roman and Byzantine times, these terraces would have been replete with grape vines. However, when the Muslims took over the country, the vines were uprooted and replaced with olive trees because of the Muslim restriction on drinking alcohol.

The springs in this area also permitted vegetables to be grown throughout the year. The erosion that created Nahal Sorek brought an aquifer close to the surface and there are many springs along the valley. There are two springs in Sataf – Ein Sataf and Ein Bikura. Homes were usually built above the spring so as not to waste good agricultural land, and vegetable gardens were planted below the spring. Water was brought to the vegetable gardens by channels. Look carefully and you will see the aqueducts that still bring spring water to the vegetables grown in this demonstration vegetable garden.

Irrigation has changed the way that agriculture is done in Israel, and irrigating terraces is not usually economical. But thanks to the Jewish National Fund, we can see close up how agriculture was practiced in this area for thousands of years.

THE OLIVE TREE - AN UNIQUELY ADAPTED MEDITERRANEAN TREE

Which city receives more rain every year – Jerusalem or London?

The answer may surprise you, but the average annual rainfall in London is about the same as in Jerusalem, even though London is not usually considered to be a particularly dry city. How can this be? The answer is that rainfall in Israel occurs in strong downpours for seven to eight months of the year while its summers are without rain, giving the impression that Israel is a very dry country. A consequence of this rainfall pattern is that only bushes and trees able to survive the long and dry summers are able to flourish in this country.

The olive tree is one of the "seven species" mentioned in the Bible (Deuteronomy 8:8), some of which are uniquely adapted to survive the dry summers of the Mediterranean Basin. The success of the olive tree is due to its deep rooting system and its ability to use water with a high salt content. In addition, the upper surface of the olive leaf is green and the lower surface is silvery and felt-like, and this aspect of its lower surface reduces water loss. The leaves of the olive tree also turn in sunlight, thereby exposing the lighter-green undersurface of the leaf and giving the tree a glittering appearance in the sun. Like other plants, the olive tree benefits from summer dew. Hot summer air holds more moisture than winter air, and dew condenses on surfaces as the temperature cools at night.

The olive tree thrives well on the calcareous soil of the limestone slopes and crags of Judea and Samaria. It is also a very hardy plant and is often able to survive drought, disease and fire. This is because it produces shoots from the base of the main trunk, and these can develop into new trunks if the main trunk is damaged. In this way, an olive tree can survive hundreds of years. Nowadays, most Jewish olive groves are irrigated to increase the quality and yield of olives, but this is not the case for Arab olive groves and was not the case in the past.

Unripe olives are green and at the beginning of the rainy season they ripen to a black/brown/purple color and become juicier. In Biblical times, olives were harvested by beating the tree. The Torah instructs that some of the produce from these beaten branches be left for the poor (Deuteronomy 24:20). However, such beating can damage the branches and subsequent yield of the tree. In Mishnaic times olives were harvested by picking them.

Olive oil was obtained by crushing the olive and its pit by a stone mill. The pit also contains oil and was included in the crushing. The crushed pieces were then placed in a hanging sack from which the oil dripped out, and in this way olive oil from the "first press" was obtained.

Olive oil burns clearly, without smoke, and was used for cooking and lighting. This was important in ancient Israel since many people were literate, and this property of olive oil enabled reading and writing to continue when the agricultural day was over.

Olives are now one of the most extensively grown fruits globally. Spain is the biggest producer of olive oil in the world. Israel also has an olive oil industry, although it is not as competitive price-wise as Spanish olive oil.

Olive oil is an important ingredient of the Mediterranean diet and is an extremely healthy food because of its high content of anti-oxidant polyphenols that protect against "oxidative stress." Oxidative stress is the basis of many diseases, including heart disease. Raw olives also have a high content of polyphenols, as do olive leaves.

THE HIKE

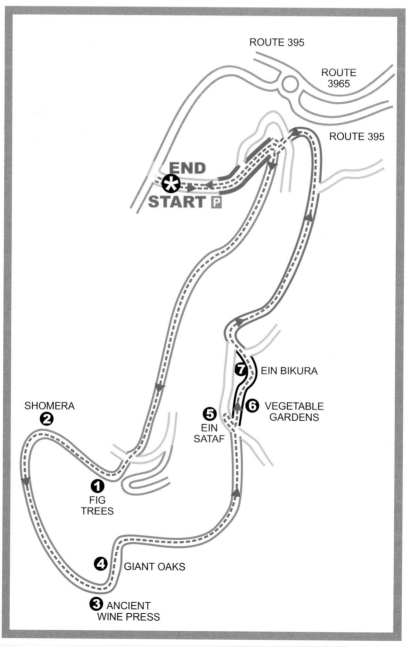

Before starting this hike, walk over to the observation area adjacent to the parking lot overlooking Nahal Sorek to orientate yourself. Its entrance has green railings.

Nahal Sorek is a deep valley that begins close to Ramallah and winds its way for about seventy km to the coast. Opposite you, on a lower hill on the other side of the valley is the moshav Even Sapir, founded by immigrants from Kurdistan. At the bottom of this hill and surrounded by a brick enclosure is the Franciscan Monastery of St. John in the Wilderness. This monastery commemorates John the Baptist living in the wilderness as an orphaned child and young adult. Originally, there was a Crusader church and convent here, although the present buildings date from the 1920's. At the top of the adjacent hill are the houses of the moshav Aminadav and to the left those of Orah. Both were built by Yemenite Jews. On your far left, you can see the campus of Hadassah Medical Center.

Take the paved road that passes some run-down buildings and you will soon see on your right a sign with three green pointers. Follow the green trail down the steps. At the three-way intersection, turn right onto the blue-marked "שביל הבעל" (the Ba'al Path).

After about twenty to thirty minutes, you will come to a picnic area with picnic benches, barbecue stands, and drinking water. Take the steps down to the paved road.

The continuation of the blue trail is on the other side of the road, a bit to your right. To continue, cross the road and go down the steps.

This path soon touches the shoulder of a paved road. Before following the sign pointing you in the direction of the continuation of the blue-marked trail, walk over to the terrace above this to a large wooden sign.

This sign informs you that following Biblical law you may help yourself to any produce that you pick on the terraces, although you are not permitted to take anything away. It also points out the relevant Biblical verse: "*When you come into the vineyard of your fellow, you may eat grapes as is your desire, to your fill, but you may not put into your vessel*" (Deuteronomy 23:25).

Does this mean that the Bible permits any hungry hiker to help him or herself to produce from anyone's field? The answer is that one cannot interpret Torah verses such as this without the help of the Jewish oral tradition. The Talmud explains that this law refers to workers harvesting crops who have the Torah's permission to eat the owner's crops as long as the plant is still attached to the ground (Bava Metzia 87a and b). Otherwise, going into anyone's field and helping oneself to the produce is theft. Nevertheless, you have the permission of Keren Kayemet to take a more lenient approach to the fruit growing here and to eat as much as you like!

Follow the blue-marked trail and you will pass through a terrace with fig trees ❶. In the terrace below are vines, and there are olive trees on the far side of the valley opposite you.

181

You will soon come to a sign pointing to a "shomera" (guard's hut) ❷. It is possible to walk up to it, but it can be seen just as well walking along the path (see page 195 for more information about these structures).

The next stop is a large, well-preserved Byzantine wine press ❸ hewed into the bedrock labelled "גת עתיקה."

In the past, grapes were not sent to a winery for fermentation as they are today, as the fermentation process starts very soon after picking. They were therefore fermented close to the farmer's field in vats chiseled into bedrock. The Byzantine mosaic floor here reminds us that extracting juice from the grapes was a gentle process, usually done by foot. Unlike olives, the grape pits were not crushed, as this would impart a bitter taste to the wine.

You will soon come to the ruins of a Byzantine church and some large Kernes Oak trees (אלון מצוי) ❹ close by. This is the most common oak species found in Israel. Unlike the two other oak species seen in this country, this oak is an evergreen. The large size of these trees is unusual for the Judean Mountains. They are usually shrub-like because of felling and grazing by goats. However, the sanctity associated with this area discouraged people from cutting them down.

When the trail ends at a T-junction, turn left onto the green-marked trail that will take you to the Sataf pool ❺. There is a functioning water tap on the way that provides drinking water.

The entrance to the spring of Ein Sataf

Ein Sataf was the spring for the village of Sataf. A notice by the cave entrance describes how it was constructed. You can enter the cave to see the source of the spring at the end of the tunnel, although you will need a flashlight. In front of the cave is a shallow pool that children will enjoy playing in. A small room built into the back wall of the pool is where women may have done their laundry, although its entrance is now closed.

The vegetable gardens ❻ are worth visiting. Retrace your steps on the green-marked trail and just past its junction with the blue trail you will see on your left a sign pointing to "עין-ביכורה." The vegetable gardens are below you as you walk along the terrace.

At first glance, these vegetable gardens look like any vegetable garden you would see in the West. But look closer and you will see that there are aqueducts and that the vegetables are grown on heaped up soil between channels. This is how vegetables were irrigated in ancient times – by controlled flooding of the plants with spring water.

To visit the pool of Ein Bikura ❼, descend on the steps that are just before the overhead vines.

Just beyond Ein Bikura ascend by the steps by the vines to a three-way intersection. Turn right on the green-marked trail in the direction of "צומת סטף." Behind you are the ruins of the village of Sataf.

Ruins have been found in Sataf from as far back as the Chalcolithic period, between four to six thousand years ago. There were also villages here in the Second Temple and

Byzantine periods. The ruins you see are from the Arab village of Sataf, which was abandoned during the 1948 War of Independence. A moshav was started here by North African Jews, but they gave up after a few months because of the difficult conditions here. None of these Arab houses had basic amenities such as electricity and running water.

[If you would like to lengthen this hike a bit, you can make a delightful loop on the red trail on the right just before the three-way intersection. It will add about twenty minutes to your hike. A black-marked trail to Ein Handak joins this path – do not descend into the valley on this black trail as it will take you far from your car. The red trail eventually joins up with the green trail closer to the upper parking lot].

Ascending the green trail on the stone steps and rock, you will pass the Ophir Rest Area on your left. This is a memorial to a young lad who died from an accident.

Cross the paved road (which is actually a red-marked road), and continue up on the green trail to its junction with the blue trail. This is the junction from which you started this hike on the Ba'al Path. There are picnic benches in this area. Continue up the hill on the green trail until you come to the paved road. Turn left on this road to the parking lot.

Nearby Places of Interest:

There are a number of places of interest in Kibbutz Tzubah, which is just a five minute drive from Sataf:

Galita Chocolate Factory: This is located on your left just after entering the kibbutz. The kids will enjoy working with chocolate molds, chocolate creams and dressings to make chocolates that taste great and have a professional appearance. The chocolate is kosher lemehadrin. A video is shown on the origins of chocolate. The cost depends on what you make. The Factory is open 10 am–6 pm and is closed on Shabbat and holidays. Reservations are required. Their phone number is: (02) 534-7650.

Kiftzubah Amusement Park: This amusement park is located within the kibbutz, on your left as you go through the kibbutz entrance. It has bumper cars for little and bigger kids, a "Jungle train," carousels, crazy bumper boats (summer only), a rope course, omega and climbing structures, jumping castles, a playroom with game machines, laser tag and toddler gymboree, and a café for refreshments. It is open every Friday 10 am–4 pm and Saturday 10 am–5 pm. If rain is expected it will be only partially open. During school vacations it is open every day from 10 am–5 pm and Saturday 10 am–4 pm. During July and August it is open every day 10 am–6 pm and sometimes later, and Friday 10 am–5 pm. Their phone number is: (02) 534-7952.

Tzuba Winery is located on the kibbutz. All wines are kosher mehadrin. The vineyards are cultivated by the kibbutz in an area that was historically a major wine-producing area in Biblical times. There is a guided tour of the winery, vineyards and ancient wine press and wine tasting each Friday at 10.00 am. Call (02) 534-7090 to make a reservation.

22 The Schvil Hamaayanot and Yad Kennedy Memorial

The Schvil Hamaayanot is one of the most popular trails in this part of the Judean Mountains – and with good reason. The views throughout the trail are quite spectacular. You will pass several springs on the trail, and this accounts for its name - "Trail of the Springs." Also consider visiting the impressive Yad Kennedy, a monument to former President John F. Kennedy. The starting point of the hike is only a short distance from Hadassah Medical Center-Ein Kerem and is easily reached by Jerusalem's public transport.

THE SPRINGS OF THE JUDEAN MOUNTAINS

"*For the Lord your God is bringing you to a good land, a land with streams of water, of springs and underground water coming forth in valley and mountain*" (Deuteronomy 8:8).

The Judean Mountains are composed of hard limestone, a sedimentary rock containing mainly calcium carbonate formed about two hundred million years ago from the skeletal remains of marine organisms when this area was a vast sea.

During the country's rainy season, surface water seeps through the earth and dissolves the underlying rock through a process known as karst. As the erosion continues, cracks develop, and rainwater seeps through these cracks and forms underground caves. When the surface water encounters a softer layer of rock that cannot be dissolved, such as marl, which is a calcium carbonate-containing rock with variable amounts of clay or silt, water collects inside the caves to form a natural water tank called an aquifer.

The many springs in this area came about because of erosion of the sides of the valley and exposure of the aquifer. The amount of water seen at the surface may have been no more than a few water droplets, or the unexpected growth of a fig tree, but this would have been enough to indicate the proximity of an aquifer. Villagers would then dig a tunnel into the rock towards the aquifer to obtain a greater flow of water. These tunnels were often of considerable length, and would need to be lengthened even further if the aquifer retracted. The pools you see in front of the entrance to the tunnels were small reservoirs used to supply drinking water to livestock and humans. Sometimes, the water would be directed downhill from the pool by aqueducts to irrigate vegetable gardens.

A view of the moshav Even Sapir, Nahal Sorek and the Judean Mountains

TIME: Almost 3 hours

DISTANCE: Almost 8 km

TYPE OF HIKE: Circular

DIFFICULTY:
Easy hike, although the footpath to Yad Kennedy is moderately steep and minimally difficult.

STARTING POINT:
The parking area for the Aminadav Forest on the road to Even Sapir.

DRIVING DIRECTIONS AND PARKING: Enter "יער פדויי השבי אדום" into Waze. Head towards Hadassah Medical Center Ein Kerem. At the four-way intersection at the entrance to the hospital, take the exit to the left in the direction of Tel Aviv. After a short distance, turn left at the first roundabout. Within a few minutes, you will see an asphalt road on the left leading to a gravel road. This is the parking area for the Aminadav Forest.

PUBLIC TRANSPORT:
The bus stop for Hadassah Medical School in Ein Kerem is about one km and a fifteen minute walk from the start of the hike. Enter "Hadassah Ein Kerem" into Moovit. A number of buses go to the hospital. If using the light

continued

rail, alight at its last stop, Mount Herzl, and take a 27 or 27A bus to the hospital. Alight at the first stop within the campus. From the bus stop, walk back towards the four-way intersection at the campus entrance. Take the exit in the direction of Tel Aviv. At the first roundabout turn left in the direction of the signpost to Even Sapir. When the sidewalk ends, walk on the footpath on the right-hand side of the road adjacent to the railing. You will soon see an asphalt road on the left leading to a gravel road and the parking area for the Aminadav Forest.

THE HIKE

On this circular hike you will be walking along two sides of a mountain ridge.

At the beginning of the hike you will be overlooking Nahal Sorek and its tributaries, and then the Emeq Refaim valley on the other side of the mountain ridge. From the Recreation Area, the walk continues to Yad Kennedy, although if you are short on time this part of the hike can be skipped. On your return, you will be hiking along a jeep trail and descending to Ein Tamar via an extremely beautiful wadi. However, if you want to visit the pools again, just go back the way you came.

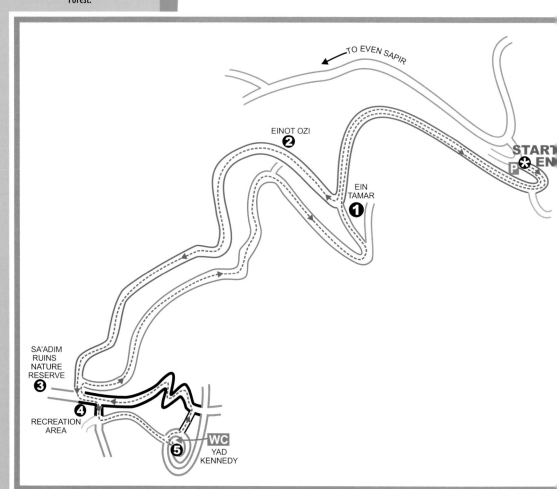

From the parking lot, go up the jeep trail as directed by the green-arrow on the signpost to the "שביל המעיינות" (Shvil Hamaayanot) and "לחר׳ סעדים" (to Sa'adim ruins). There is also a 4 x 4 sign at the beginning of the path. After about 250 meters, make a sharp right by another wooden signpost with the green arrow pointing to the "לחר׳ סעדים" and "שביל המעיינות".

You will pass several dry pools. Ignore them as there are more interesting pools to come. Soon you will reach Ein Tamar ❶. This is a pretty place with a shallow pool, a palm tree, and a shaded picnic bench. The spring is named after Tamar Natan who died at a young age. The pool was built by her friends and other organizations.

Continue on the green-marked trail. Below you is Nahal Sorek and its tributaries and the moshav Even Sapir. Nahal Sorek is a seventy km long, deep valley that starts by Ramallah and winds its way to the coast past Beit Shemesh.

Get your feet wet at Ein Tamar

You will soon come to two other water-filled pools. The second one, Eynot Ozi ❷, is the best one for swimming. Its depth is up to about the level of an adult male's navel. The many pools on this trail indicate that despite its steep slope, this land was once used for agriculture, and indeed, you can see terraces, now forested, on both sides of the trail.

About an hour from the beginning of the hike, you will come to an intersection with a signpost. Go past this, continuing on the green-marked trail a short distance to its intersection with the main road. On the other side of the road is the Recreation Area ❹. This Recreation Area has shaded picnic tables and is a nice place for a picnic. Kids will also enjoy the sheep statues. From here you can also visit the Sa'adim Ruins Nature Reserve ❸ (see the next page).

To Yad Kennedy (optional):

Turn left on the paved road by the Recreation Area. At the end of the Recreation Area ❹, there is a jeep trail on the right. Walk down this path, which is sign-posted to recreation activities, and after about fifty meters you will see a blue marker on a rock on your left. It is easy to miss, so look also for a blue marker on a tree on the other side of the trail opposite to this path. This footpath, which has blue-markers throughout, leads directly to Yad Kennedy ❺.

Exit the footpath onto the paved road by Yad Kennedy and ahead of you is a plaza. There are WC's here. At the far end of the plaza are steps leading directly to the memorial.

An alternative to the footpath is the main road to Yad Kennedy. This is a lot easier but far less challenging. Turn left by the Recreation Area and continue along the paved road until you come to the access road to Yad Kennedy. Take the footpath up to the memorial rather than the road, as it is more direct.

Yad Kennedy is a memorial to John F Kennedy, the 35th President of the United States, who was assassinated in 1963 at the age of 46. This memorial was built three years after his death. It is shaped like the stump of a tree to symbolize his life cut short. The memorial has fifty-one pillars representing the fifty states of the union and Washington DC. The emblems of the states are on the outside of each of the pillars. Inside the memorial is a bronze facial outline of John F. Kennedy, and in the center of the memorial an eternal flame.

The easiest way to leave the memorial is not to go down on the road that encircles the monument, but to take the footpath. Descend one level by the steps and turn right along the paved road for a short distance until you see steps on your left with green railings. This path leads directly to the intersection of the main road with the access road to Yad Kennedy.

Turn left along the paved road in the direction of the recreation area. It is not a busy road, but be careful of traffic as you walk. At the end of the Recreation Area, turn right on the path on which you came towards the Shvil Hamaayanot.

Returning to Ein Tamar:

You can return the way you came, but the following circular route is more interesting. Very soon you will come to an intersection with a blue-signed jeep trail on your right. Turn onto this road. The arrow on the signpost indicates that this is a blue trail, although there are no further blue markings.

About twenty-five minutes from the intersection, you will see a signpost to "שביל המעיינות" and "עין עז." Very shortly after this is a fork. Take the path *to the right* which goes up the hill. After about another ten minutes, you will come to a signpost to "עין תמר." Descend on this path through a gorgeous valley to Ein Tamar.

From Ein Tamar to the parking lot:

From Ein Tamar turn right along the Schvil Ha'mayanot. Follow the green markings to the parking lot.

Nearby Places of Interest:

The Sa'adim Ruins Nature Reserve ❸. *This reserve close to the Recreation Area has been adopted by the staff of Hadassah Hospital. The ruins were called "Khirbet Sa'ida" (the ruins of the happy woman)" in Arabic and are the remains of a Byzantine agricultural farm and Christian monastery. To get there from the Recreation Area, turn left on the main paved road towards its intersection with the Schvil Hamayaanot and continue a short distance on this road. The entrance to the reserve is on your right.*

Hadassah Medical Center Mall and Chagall windows – see page 145.

23 The Springs of Emeq Refaim

This scenic circular hike overlooking the Emek Refaim valley begins by the entrance to the spring Ein Lavan, which is close to the Biblical Zoo. We will visit the spring Mayan Itimar, and then climb up the bank of the valley on a slightly challenging footpath. The hike finishes at the pools of Ein Lavan.

The lower pool at Ein Lavan

TIME: 2.5 hours, but leave extra time for swimming

DISTANCE: 7.25 km

TYPE OF HIKE: Circular

DIFFICULTY: An easy hike on paved roads and jeep trails. From Ein Itamar there is some minimally difficult rock climbing.

STARTING POINT: By the steps to the spring of Ein Lavan

DRIVING DIRECTIONS AND PARKING: Enter "Ein Lavan" into Waze. Drive through the parking lot of the Biblical Zoo and continue past the new Aquarium on the one-lane road. The entrance to Ein Lavan is where the paved road ends. There is parking on the side of the road.

PUBLIC TRANSPORT:
There are two ways to get to Ein Lavan. The first way is quicker, while the second is more scenic:

I. FROM THE JERUSALEM BIBLICAL ZOO: Enter "Jerusalem Biblical Zoo" into Moovit. There are also buses to

continued

the "אקווריום." From the zoo, walk through the parking lot and past the Aquarium — about a fifteen minute walk.

2. FROM ORA INTERSECTION (TZOMET ORA):

Take the bus to Tzomet Ora. Enter "צומת אורה" into Moovit. Just beyond the first roundabout after Tzomet Ora on the Mesho'a Ora Road (in the direction away from Hadassah Medical Center and Route 369) is a brown sign on the road indicating "White Valley." This leads to a paved road with a pedestrian and cyclist sign. The paved path soon turns into a jeep road. You will pass an ancient wine fermentation area and mikvah on your right (they often went together when producing wine for religious purposes). A mosaic sign "עין לבן" points down the valley. There are many interconnected paths in this area, but follow the jeep trail marked with a blue or Shvil Yisrael-marker and you will not go wrong. After some distance, you will see the Ein Lavan park below you. Look out for the footpath on your left, indicated by a Schvil Yisrael-marking that leads to Ein Lavan. When the footpath comes to a paved road with railings follow it to the right, and very soon you will see steps leading into the park.

OVERVIEW

WHY IS THE "GREEN LINE" GREEN?

The hills on the side of the Emeq Refaim valley you are walking on are wooded and verdant, while on the other side they are not.

How so?

This hike overlooks the valley of Emeq Refaim. Prior to the Six Day War, the other side of the valley belonged to Jordan and the armistice line was slightly beyond the railway line on the other side of the valley. The armistice lines were known as the "Green Line" because Moshe Dayan, then Chief of Staff, delineated his troop positions at the end of the War of Independence by drawing on a map with a green felt-tip pen. The lines he drew would become the borders of the new State of Israel.

To emphasize their control up to their new borders, the Israelis planted trees right up to the "Green Line." As a result of these forests, the Israeli side of the Green Line began to look very green. This does not mean that the other side of Emeq Refaim, with its terraces, olive trees and minarets, does not have beauty, but its beauty is not as green. Nowadays, most people have forgotten about Dayan's green felt tip-pen but are well aware of the impressive forested hills.

In the past, pine trees were the predominant tree planted by the Jewish National Fund, since these trees grew quickly. However, pine is not indigenous to Israel. Its root system is shallow, which means it can be easily uprooted. Also, pine cones are released at a distance from a tree under the influence of extreme heat and are very combustible, so that a forest fire can spread rapidly. Pine forests are therefore very vulnerable to arson. Because of these factors, the JNF now plants forests with a greater variety of trees, including ones that are indigenous to the country. You can see this feature on this hike in sections of terraces that have been recently planted.

The area beyond the armistice line in Emeq Refaim was captured during the Six Day War, but was subsequently handed over to the Palestinian Authority. They did not forest it and it is therefore not as green.

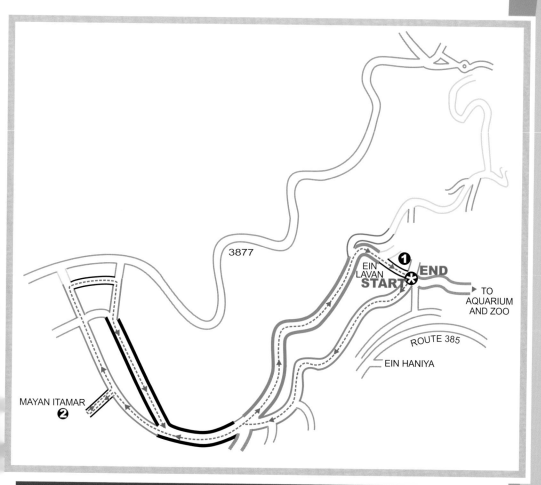

THE HIKE

By the entrance to Ein Lavan, continue on the jeep trail, which has blue and Schvil Yisrael-markings, in the direction away from Jerusalem.

After about thirty-five minutes of walking, you will come to a fork. Keep to the right on the continuation of the blue-marked trail (and not the jeep trail on the left that goes down towards the valley).

Very shortly, this black-marked trail, which for a short distance is unpaved, becomes paved and forks again. Take the paved right fork (and not the paved black-marked road on the left that goes down towards the valley).

At the point where the paved black-marked road curves sharply to the right, take the jeep trail on your left in the direction of Mayan Itamar. As you proceed along, you will see that it has white, blue and orange Schvill Yisrael markings.

Soon you will come to a fork. Turn to the left and after about a minute you will see the pool of Mayan Itamar on your right. [You may note that many hikers continue along this very scenic path. You may wish to do this, but you will get further from your car and further from this circular route.]

This pool is named after Itamar Doron who was murdered in this area. It is a small pool, but the running water is cool and clear and provides a wonderfully refreshing dip, especially on a hot day. Its depth is to a bit below the waist level of an adult. The pool is not difficult to enter or exit.

From Mayan Itamar, head back to the intersection. At this stage, you can return the way you came. More worthwhile, however, is to take the blue-marked footpath on your left up the hill. This is a delightful trail, although it does involve a bit of easy climbing over rocks. There are pools close to the trail, but they are usually dry.

You are now walking on land that formerly belonged to the Arab village of al-Walaja, and you are close to the ruins of the village. It was captured by the Harel Brigade during the War of Independence. It had been defended by the Egyptian Moslem Brotherhood, the Arab Liberation Army and a local militia. Thousands of villagers fled. After the war, some of the villagers settled on land they owned on the other side of the valley, which was now on the other side of the armistice line. After the Six Day War, the villagers again found themselves under Israeli control. Part of their new village was now included within the Jerusalem city boundaries, although sealed off by the separation barrier. This, and the extension of the Jerusalem Park system, involved them in litigation, which was adjudicated by Israel's Supreme Court. They were unsuccessful in their appeal.

Cross a jeep trail. When you come to a second jeep trail in view of the main road (Route 3877) turn right. This will bring you to a paved road that goes down the hill.

Turn right along this black-marked road. Occasional vehicles use this single-lane road, so walk along it carefully, listening for traffic. This road will lead you to the paved road which you originally walked along close to the turn off to Mayan Itamar. Turn left along this black-marked paved road. Except for a very small section, you will now be hiking on paved roads all the way to Ein Lavan.

At the first fork continue ahead (and not to the right on the paved road down the valley).

Very soon there is another fork. Take the left-hand branch, which is a blue-marked paved road. This road runs parallel to the jeep trail on which you began this hike, but at a level higher. It is blocked to vehicles, so you have the road to yourself.

Pass around the green gate. Soon, at the yellow signpost, take the steps and concrete path to the upper pool of Ein Lavan. This pool is appropriate for young children. A level down is a deeper pool. For more details about the pools at Ein Lavan (see page 292).

Take the steps down to the entrance to Ein Lavan to where you began this hike.

At this point, you may wish to visit the spring of Ein Haniya. It is about a twenty minute walk each way. On the other side of the road from the steps up to Ein Lavan you will see a stepped footpath that goes down the valley. When it reaches the railway track it goes underneath this via a short tunnel. After emerging from the tunnel, turn right. After some distance, this footpath will lead you to Route 385. Cross this road to the pool. (For details about Ein Haniya see page 294).

Nearby Places of Interest:

A visit to the nearby **Jerusalem Biblical Zoo** is highly recommended – see chapter 19 "The Gorgeous Jerusalem Biblical Zoo" on page 168.

The Israel Aquarium is also only a short distance from Ein Lavan – see page 170.

Ein Yael Living Museum. This site contains interesting ruins and has workshops during the summer – see page 170.

TIME: 3 hours

DISTANCE: Just under 8.5 km

TYPE OF HIKE:
Circular

DIFFICULTY: The initial part
of the hike is minimally difficult
because of rocks on the footpath,
but the remainder of the trail is
very easy.

STARTING POINT: Parking
area for the Aminadav Forest on
the road to Even Sapir.

**DRIVING DIRECTIONS
AND PARKING**:
Enter "יער פדווי השבי אדום" into
Waze. Head towards Hadassah
Medical Center at Ein Kerem. At the
four-way intersection at the entrance
to Hadassah take the exit to the
left, Route 396, in the direction of
Tel Aviv. At the first roundabout turn
left on the road to Even Sapir. Within
a few minutes you will see an asphalt
road on the left leading to a gravel
road for the parking area for the
Aminadav Forest.

PUBLIC TRANSPORT:
The bus stop for Hadassah
Medical School in Ein Kerem is
about one km, and about a fifteen
minute walk from the start of the
hike. Enter "Hadassah Ein Kerem"

24 To Ein Kerem Via Ein Hindak and The Ein Kerem National Park

This circular hike to the village of Ein Kerem via the spring of Ein Hindak and Ein Kerem National Park provides spectacular views of the Judean Mountains. The starting point is close to Hadassah Ein Karem and Jerusalem public transport.

continued

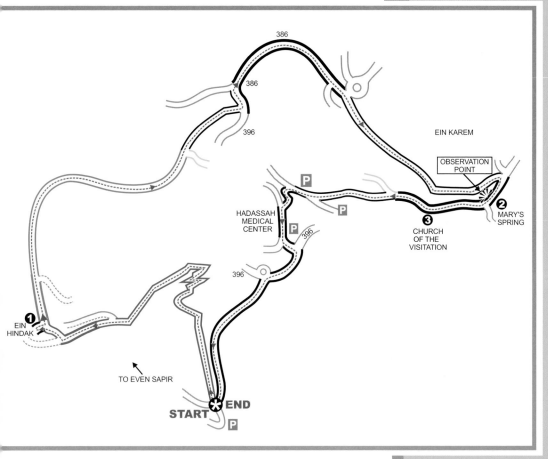

Exit the Aminadav Forest parking area and cross over the main road. On the red brick sidewalk ahead is a green marker indicating the trail. Go down the steps and continue on the footpath. After a few minutes, the green marker will indicate to turn left to descend into the valley. You will soon pass disused terracing and an agricultural watchtower (*shomera*).

Watchtowers such as this have been in use for thousands of years. The prophet Isaiah mentions such a watchtower when castigating the people: *"My beloved had a vineyard in a fertile corner. And he fenced it in, and he cleared it of stones, and he planted it with the choicest vines; and he built a tower in its midst, and also a vat he hewed there; and he hoped to produce grapes, but it produced wild berries"* (Isaiah 5:1-2). Farmers needed to protect their produce, especially close to harvest time, and they may have slept in these structures. They were also used for storing containers and produce.

At the bottom of the valley, you will come to a concrete path. Turn left onto this path following the green marker. After a

into Moovit. A number of buses go to the hospital. If using the light rail, alight at its last stop, Mount Herzl, and take 27 or 27A to the hospital. Alight at the first stop within the campus. From the bus stop, walk back towards the four-way intersection at the campus entrance. Take the exit to Route 396 in the direction of Tel Aviv. At the first roundabout turn left in the direction of the signpost to Even Sapir. When the sidewalk ends, walk on the footpath on the right-hand side of the road adjacent to the railing. You will soon see an asphalt road on the left leading to a gravel road and the parking area for the Aminadav Forest.

few minutes, you will see a green marker on a rock on the left side of the road pointing you to the right and the spring of Ein Hindak ❶.

Ruins of a shomera (watchtower) on the descent to Ein Hindak

This spring is at least two thousand years old. The name Ein Hindak comes from the Arabic Ein-al-Khandak, which means the "spring of the canal." There are tunnels and also pools inside the caves in which children used to swim, but for safety reasons it is no longer permissible to enter the caves. There was formerly an Arab village in this area, and from close to the caves you can see an aqueduct system leading to their agricultural land within the valley. To the right of the cave entrance is a walled area with a grate-covered hole from which villagers used to lower their buckets to obtain water directly from the pools.

From the spring, return to the intersection and take the blue-marked "Hadassah Trail." This is initially a paved road, but soon changes to a footpath overlooking the beautiful Nahal Sorek. Towards the end of the footpath, ignore the blue-marked trail that goes up towards Hadassah Hospital, and continue straight ahead until the footpath comes to a gate. In front of you is Route 396.

Carefully turn left onto Route 396. You will now be walking along the shoulders of busy roads for about half a km. Turn right at the T-junction onto Route 386 in the direction of Ein Kerem Intersection (Tzomet Ein Kerem).

Shortly before the roundabout, there is a paved road on the right that leads you through a gorgeous valley in Ein Kerem National Park to Ein Kerem. Where the road splits into two, take the left-hand footpath for pedestrians rather than the right-hand path for cyclists. There are shaded grassy areas along the way that are popular for family picnics.

At the end of the path is a building with WC's. Take the path by the left of the building or climb the stairs to reach an observation area overlooking the valley and Mary's Spring ❷. There are cafes and restaurants on HaMa'ayan St. to your left.

For information about Ein Kerem see the essay on "The Traditions of Ein Kerem" on page 140 and for the spring on page 142.

To return to Hadassah Medical Center, ascend the hill on the road Madregot Habikur that begins by the spring. You will soon pass steps to the Church of the Visitation ❸. For information about this church see page 144. There are great views from the entrance to the church, although you will need to climb up the steps to get there.

Continue along the road Madregot Habikur and just beyond a yellow fire hydrant and opposite the last house on this road take the footpath on the left. It is not sign-posted and is initially on rock face, but it soon becomes more recognizable as a path. If you are walking on a blue-marked trail leading down the valley you have missed the path and gone too far.

This path eventually leads to a parking area for the hospital. Turn right from the parking lot and shortly opposite another parking area is a paved road on your left leading to the hospital. At the first intersection on this path, turn to the right along a path with railings.

At the end of this path, turn left onto the main hospital road and this will lead you back to the entrance to the hospital campus. From here it is a short distance to a bus stop, or a fifteen minute or so walk to your car at the Aminadav Forest parking area. Follow the directions on page 195.

25 Castel National Park

During the War of Independence, Arab forces controlled the only road to Jerusalem, and the Jewish section of the city was under a devastating siege. The Castel National Park brings to life the struggle for this crucial strategic height overlooking the road, by means of its trenches and bunkers, two audio-visual presentations (that can also be viewed in English), and three game areas that enable groups to internalize the values displayed by the Jewish combatants who fought here and that are still operative in the Israel Defense Force (IDF).

199

TIME: 2-3 hours

DISTANCE: About 1 km

TYPE OF WALK: Circular

DIFFICULTY: An easy walk.

HOURS AND ADMISSION:
The park is open Sunday to Thursday and on Saturday 8 am—5 pm in the summer, and until 4 pm in the winter. During the summer, on Friday and holiday eves 8 am—4 pm. In the winter 8 am—3 pm. There is an entrance fee. Their phone number is: (02) 534-2741.

DRIVING DIRECTIONS:
Enter "Castel National Park" into Waze.

PUBLIC TRANSPORT:
The site is easily accessible from Jerusalem by public transport. Enter "Qastel" into Moovit. From the מחלף הראל bus stop it is about a seven minute walk to the Castel, and from the מרכז קליטה/הראל bus stop it is about a four minute walk.

200

The Romans were the first to build a fortress on this hill because of its strategic position overlooking the road to Jerusalem. It was called Castellum. In the 12th century, the Crusaders built a fortress here called Castellum Belvoir, also to guard the road to Jerusalem. This fortress was destroyed by the Kurdish leader Saladin in 1187 when he drove the Crusaders from the Judean Mountains. Until the War of Independence there was an Arab village on the hill called Al-Qastal, and the home of the muhktar of the village was located on top of the Crusader ruins.

Fast forward to the 1948 War of Independence when West Jerusalem was under siege and there was a severe lack of food, water and arms. It was also anticipated that all the neighboring Arab states would attack the Jewish state once independence was declared. Nevertheless, David Ben-Gurion, president of the Jewish Agency Executive, made the bold decision that the soon to be created State of Israel could not exist without its heart – Jerusalem. Amin al-Husseini, the Mufti of Jerusalem, was also in a struggle for this same heart for a Palestinian state. His military campaign was run by his nephew Abd al-Qadir al-Husseini. The Castel occupied a commanding position over the road to Jerusalem and the story of the Castel is about how it changed hands three times before being eventually captured by the Haganah. A crucial event in the capture of the Castel and the crumbling of the Mufti's campaign was the killing of his nephew.

BACKGROUND

ISRAEL'S WAR OF INDEPENDENCE

How did a people almost decimated by the Holocaust manage to found a state against such overwhelming odds during their War of Independence?

A number of factors should be considered. There was the realization among the Jews in Palestine that another genocide had to be prevented at all costs. Many of the Jewish fighters had received military training, some in the British army, while many of the Arabs fighting for Jerusalem were disorganized peasants with arms but no prior military experience. A hefty dose of heavenly help was also no doubt operative.

By 1947, the British had had enough of their Mandate in Palestine. They were in a no-win situation. Both Jews and Arabs wanted independence and were prepared to fight for it. The British therefore handed the problem over to the United Nations, who came up with a Partition Plan. The Jews, who constituted thirty-two percent of Palestine's population, would be allotted about fifty-six percent of the country, although this was mainly non-arable land in the Negev. Within this territory were about a half a million Jews and four hundred thousand Arabs. Forty-two percent of Palestine would be allotted to the Palestinians — an area that contained approximately eight hundred and eighteen thousand Arabs and ten thousand Jews. The Jerusalem region, which included Bethlehem, contained about one hundred thousand Jews and one hundred thousand Arabs and would be administered by the United Nations.

The United Nations Partition Plan was approved by their General Assembly on November 29, 1947. The territory given to the Jews was far from what they wanted but they accepted it. The Arabs rejected any form of partition, and Amin al-Husseini, the former Mufti of Jerusalem, created immediate mayhem in the country. The Palestinians realized they were not powerful enough to drive the Jews out by themselves, but they anticipated that the surrounding Arab nations would come to their aid to prevent the emergence of a Jewish State.

The first phase of this struggle was from November 1947 until the Declaration of Independence in May 1948 and took the form of a civil war characterized by daily attacks against Jews and tit-for-tat Jewish reprisals. The aim of the Arabs, which they failed to achieve, was to cut off the roads to Jewish settlements. During this period, two thousand Jews were killed and four thousand wounded— an average of one hundred deaths and two hundred casualties a week. The British in the main refrained from intervening, although they maintained an arms embargo over the country. In May 1948 they began withdrawing their forces.

In January 1948, a nephew of the Mufti, Abd al-Qadir al-Husseini, arrived from Egypt with a few hundred fighters. His "Army of the Holy War" recruited several hundred Arab volunteers to besiege the one hundred thousand Jews in Jerusalem using their commanding positions from Arab villages overlooking Route 1, the only road to Western Jerusalem.

This siege was highly successful. The Jewish part of Jerusalem was in desperate straits with insufficient food, water and ammunition supplies. Nevertheless, David Ben-Gurion was determined to defend Jerusalem at all costs. In the attempt to break the blockade and bring supplies to the city, many Haganah armored vehicles were destroyed and hundreds of Haganah members killed. These destroyed vehicles have been left on the side of Route 1 as a memorial to this struggle.

During the initial phase of the fighting, the Jews adopted a defensive position aimed at maintaining control of the areas allotted to them under the Partition Plan. However, by April 1948, with the impending British withdrawal and the expected invasion of Arab armies, the Jewish leadership realized they had to go on the offensive. The first offensive operation was Operation Nachshon, which aimed to relieve the blockade of Jerusalem by capturing the Arab villages overlooking the road to Jerusalem. Their first objective was to take control of the Castel. The movie here shows how the heights of the Castel changed hands several times during the fighting, and how the Arab commander, Abd al-Qadir al-Husseini, was killed during this struggle.

Following the success of Operation Nachshon, Operation Harel brought hundreds of supply trucks to Jerusalem. At about the same time, other operations conquered the mixed Jewish-Arab cities of Tiberias, Haifa, Safed, Beisan, Jaffe and Acre, and control over the major roads was secured.

On May 14, 1948, hours before the expiration of the British Mandate (the following day was the Sabbath), Ben-Gurion declared the independence of the State of Israel at a brief ceremony in Tel Aviv. As anticipated, forces from Syria, Iraq, Lebanon, Transjordan and Egypt promptly invaded the country.

Already in 1946, Ben-Gurion had considered the possibility of such an invasion and had procured light and heavy arms, stockpiled in Europe. The intention was to bring them to Israel as soon as the Jews controlled their own borders and the British arms embargo was no longer operative. More arms were obtained during the war and during the truces, especially from Czechoslovakia, and this infusion of armaments and aircraft was to prove crucial to the eventual Israeli victory.

In December 1947, all Israeli men and women aged 17 to 25 years were conscripted, and by April 1948 conscription was extended to all Israeli men under age forty. By the end of the war, the Israelis had a greater force in the field than the Arabs due to general mobilization and immigration into the country.

The only Arab country to achieve any success in this war was Transjordan under the leadership of King Abdullah. His British-trained Arab Legion was a very effective fighting force. The aim of the king was to take over the area designated by the Partition Plan for a Palestinian state, and he was supported in this by the British who wished to maintain their influence in the country. He succeeded in annexing Judea, Samaria and East Jerusalem, including the Old City. The Jewish settlements of Gush Etzion were also conquered. Many of its defenders were massacred when they surrendered and the rest were taken prisoner.

During the war, Abdullah maintained contact with the Jewish State and made no attempt to conquer areas allotted to it. The other Arab armies were poorly organized, had divergent war aims, and their advances were ultimately halted by the fledgling IDF.

The war ended in early 1949. Six thousand, three hundred and seventy-three Israeli soldiers and civilians had died, amounting to approximately one percent of the Jewish state's population. Israel now controlled seventy-eight percent of mandatory Palestine, which was twenty-two percent more than it had been allocated under the Partition Plan.

About seven hundred thousands Arabs fled and became refugees. Four hundred Arab villages lost their population, as did ten Jewish neighborhoods. At the same time, because of Arab hostility, there was an exodus of about eight hundred and fifty thousand Jews from Arab countries, amounting to a de facto exchange of populations. Many of these Jewish refugees had lost their properties and wealth when they fled.

Walk from the parking lot through the picnic area to the buildings ahead, which contain the pay kiosk and a WC.

The first stop is the nearby pagoda area where there is a short introductory movie about the importance of the roads to Jerusalem during the War of Independence, and the values of determination, comradeship and leadership developed by the Palmach and that are still espoused today by the Israel Defense Force. The movie also gives directions through the park. Press the button to the right of the screen to choose whether you want to hear the movie in Hebrew or English.

Climb up the hill on the main pathway, and get into the groove as you prepare to attack the building on top of the hill! The signs along the road will help you. There are also game areas along the way for groups and families to reinforce the core values of determination, comradeship and leadership. Instructions on playing the games are on the reverse side of the signs in Hebrew.

At the first intersection, turn off to the right to the "Feit Lookout" to appreciate the topography of the Castel in relation to Route 1.

Route 1 is just beneath you and quite close, although foliage and buildings obscure its view. However, you can see the continuation of the road to Sha'ar Hagei to the left and to Jerusalem to the right.

Return to the main path, and descend into the nearby trench that encircles the hilltop. Follow the red arrows. Enter the closed

View of Route 1 from the Feit Lookout

bunker, the "Authentication Simulation Bunker." Lights come on as you enter. It consists of two sections. One has multiple-choice questions on the wall (also in English) and the other contains the answers.

When the bunker allows you to exit, climb up to the "Mukhtar's house observation area" on top of the hill. There are splendid views from here.

Return to the path in the area of the bunkers and follow the sign to the "Battle Film." You will enter the bunkers again as you go around the side of the hill to an ancient cistern where the movie is screened. This eleven minute presentation describes the capture of the Castel and the relief of Jerusalem. It can be viewed in Hebrew or English. The control button is to the right by the entrance.

Follow the Exit sign and make your way back to the Feit Lookout. There is a scenic footpath from here leading down the hill to the parking lot.

26 The Unusual Cave Formations in Nahal Halilim

The highlight of this hike in Nahal Halilim is its unusual cave formations. They are called the "Halilim Caves" because the wind blowing through them makes a sound like a flute (*halil* is Hebrew for a flute), and the openings to the caves look like the holes of a flute. Also consider a short walk in the adjoining park in Emek HaArazim where there are picnic benches, board and stepping games.

HIKING THROUGH HISTORY IN NAHAL HALILIM

Nahal Halilim begins in Mevaseret Zion and is a tributary of Nahal Sorek. Nahal Sorek is a deep valley that starts close to Ramallah and separates Mevasaret Zion from Jerusalem's western neighborhoods while winding its way to the Mediterranean Sea.

The modern town of Mevaseret Zion derives its name from a biblical verse describing a harbinger bringing good news to Jerusalem: *"Upon a lofty mountain ascend, O herald of Zion (mevaseret Zion)....."* Isaiah 40:9). Mevaseret Zion straddles both sides of Route 1. It is the wealthiest municipality per capita in the Jerusalem district.

Hiking through this valley you are surrounded by history. There was once a city in the hills above Nahal Halilim known as Motza, which was allotted to the tribe of Benjamin, and this name appears in the book of Joshua (Joshua 18:26). There was also a city located here during First and Second Temple times, continuing into the Byzantine period. This accounts for the burial caves in the valley.

Motza is mentioned in the Mishnah as the place from which giant willow branches were collected for the Temple during the Festival of Succot

(Festival of Tabernacles) (Sukkah 4:5). The branches were piled on the sides of the Altar with their tops bent over it. These willows no doubt grew by the city's agricultural land at the bottom of the valley. Even today there are willow trees growing in the valley close to the start of this hike.

The Roman emperor Vespasian built a colony on the ridge above Nahal Halilim for veterans of the Tenth Legion, the Roman military unit responsible for the conquest and destruction of Jerusalem during the Great Revolt. This is probably why the Talmud refers to this hill as "Colonia" (colony in Latin). This name was preserved by an Arab village that was located on the southern bank of Nahal Halilim until the War of Independence.

The hill on which Mevaseret Zion is located was of considerable strategic importance during the War of Independence as Arab forces had blockaded the main Jaffa-Jerusalem road, thereby preventing supplies from reaching Jerusalem. The eventual capture of the Castel, located a short distance from this valley, was of

TIME: 1.5–2 hours for both directions

DISTANCE: 4.3 km for both directions

TYPE OF HIKE:
There and back on the same path

DIFFICULTY: Mildly steep footpath with some easy rock climbing.

STARTING POINT:
The bottom of Nahal Halilim at the Emek Ha'Arazim parking lot. If using public transport and/or you intend exploring Mevaseret Zion, start at the top of Nahal Halilim.

DRIVING DIRECTIONS AND PARKING:
Enter "Emek HaArazim" into Waze. If starting from the top of Nahal Halilim, enter "Hashalom School, Mevaseret Zion" into Waze for the parking lot outside Hashalom School (66 Hashalom Street, Mevaseret Zion).

PUBLIC TRANSPORT:
Enter "Nahal Halilim" into Moovit. Buses from Binyanei Ha'umah in Jerusalem stop at חצב/רמב״ם. The top of Nahal Halilim is about a five minute walk from here (and you will be hiking down the valley rather than up.)

considerable importance in relieving the siege of Western Jerusalem. A depiction of this struggle can be seen in the Castel National Heritage Park (see chapter 25, page 199).

More contemporary history is also connected to the bottom of the valley. In 1860, Yehoshua Yellin from Jerusalem, together with his brother-in-law Shaul Yehuda, developed the land which Yehoshua's father had purchased from Colonia Arabs in the Motza Valley close to the main Jaffa-Jerusalem road, in which to live and develop agriculture outside the Old City. They were followers of the Vilna Gaon who believed that developing the land would hasten the coming of the Redemption. This was, in fact, the earliest attempt to develop Jewish agriculture in Palestine. To put this period into perspective, it was just a few years after Moses Montefiore built Mishkenot Sha'ananim, the first residential Jewish settlement outside the Old City. In 1871, Yellin and Yehuda built an inn on their land on the ruins of a Byzantine-era building they had discovered, and part of it became a synagogue. In 1894, several families purchased land from Yellin to form the settlement of Motza and Yellin's Kahn was used as their synagogue. The Yellin house and synagogue are only a short distance from the Emek Ha'Arazim parking lot and can be visited (see Nearby Places of Interest on the next page).

Yellin's efforts have not been given much recognition, probably because they had little influence on the direction of the Old Yishuv in the Old City. They also fitted poorly into the narrative of the early secular labor Zionists. However, Theodor Herzl recognized their importance, and he came to Motza in 1898 during his one visit to Palestine. Impressed by the landscape, he planted a cedar tree here — in Hebrew "*erez*" (although contemporary research suggests it was actually a cypress tree). The place became famous because of Herzl, and the guesthouse built at this site was named "Arza" in honor of his tree. After the establishment of the State of Israel, a tradition developed for State presidents to plant trees at this site. The guesthouse and tree plantation are currently in disrepair, but this part of the valley retains the name "Emek Ha'Arazim" in honor of Herzl's "erez" tree.

Yehoshua Yellin's historic home seen from his orchard

THE HIKE

As described here, the caves are visited on your return as you are walking down the valley, although they can just as easily be visited on the way up:

Take the green-marked trail that ascends from the parking lot. After a short distance there is a junction in front of a small patch of green vegetation and benches. Take the right fork and continue upwards. Notice the houses on the ridges above the valley. They are on prime real estate and there has been tension with real estate developers regarding the extent to which they should be allowed to encroach upon this nature reserve.

After about thirty minutes, a trail on your right with a marker indicating points of interest leads to Jewish burial caves from the Second Temple period. Further down from these are remains of winepresses from the Second Temple period and poorly preserved remains of burial caves from First Temple times.

At the top of the valley, turn around and head back. Alternatively, if you wish to visit Mevaseret Zion, the path to the right is the quickest way into town.

After about twenty to twenty-five minutes descending the valley, the path comes to a fork and the path to the right leads to the caves. One can enter the caves, which are long caverns. These caverns were formed by dissolution of the limestone by the slightly acidic rainwater as it penetrated through cracks in the rock. The area outside the caves is a popular place for a snack or picnic.

A short circular hike along Emeq Ha'Arazim

From the parking lot, one can also take a short circular walk along Emek Ha'Arazim to the Telem Spring. It is about a thirty minute walk there and back. Emek Ha'Arazim is a segment of Nahal Sorek and is part of the impressive Jerusalem Park system. Walk along the bicycle path. There are picnic areas and large sculpted stones containing interesting information about the valley. Soon you will come to an area with board and stepping games. After this, a paved path on your left leads to the Telem Spring. This may be dry during the summer. In the early 1900's an oil factory was built close to the spring, and a few families settled here, but the place was abandoned after the 1929 Arab riots and was never rebuilt. Return to your car using the path on the other side of the stream bed for a circular walk.

Nearby Places of Interest:

Yellin House at Motza. This is a few minute's drive from the Emek Ha'Arazim parking lot. The site is run by the Society for Preservation of Israel Heritage Sites and is open Sunday to Thursday by appointment. During the tour you will visit his renovated home and the homes of early settlers in Motza, the synagogue and spring. There is also a short movie about the Yellin family and their pioneering projects. There is an admission charge. Their phone number is: (02) 534-5443.

Castel National Heritage Park is in Mevaseret Zion – see chapter 25 "Castel National Park" on page 199.

27 To Tzuba Spring and the Crusader Ruins of "Belmont"

This very pleasant, scenic hike visits the Tzuba Spring and the ruins of the Crusader fortress of Belmont on Tel Tzuba.

Many Arab villages retain their original Jewish name, a fact which is commonly used to identifying places mentioned in the Bible. Hence, the Arab village of *"Tzubah"* may well be the same village as the *"Tzubah"* mentioned in the book of Samuel where one of David's soldiers lived (2 Samuel 23:36).

During the War of Independence, the Arab village of Tzubah was captured without a struggle by the Palmach's Harel Brigade when the noise of an otherwise largely ineffective Davidka cannon encouraged the Arabs to flee. (The Palmach was the elite fighting force of the Haganah, the underground army of the Jews during the British Mandate). The villagers had previously taken part in the battles against the Palmach for control of the Castel. After the war, veterans of the Palmach formed Kibbutz Tzuba close to the Arab village of Tzubah.

The ruins of the Crusader fortress Belmont

CRUSADES AND CASTLES

The fortress on Tel Tzuba is one of the fifty Crusader fortresses built in the Holy Land and in Syria. There are in fact more Crusader castles here than anywhere else in the world.

What are these European transplants doing here?

In 1095 CE, Pope Urban II urged European Christianity to participate in an expedition to save the Christian holy places in Jerusalem from Islam. Many Christians responded to his call and set out on a series of military campaigns that became known as the "Crusades." This name is derived from a French word meaning "marked with a cross" and it refers to the emblem that the fighters wore on their clothing.

In addition to the Pope's stated purpose of liberating Christian holy places from the Muslims, historians have suggested a number of additional reasons for his initiating the Crusades. The papacy was involved in a struggle for supremacy with the kings of Europe and a successful outcome would boost the Pope's leadership. It would expand the influence of the Catholic Church into eastern Byzantia. There was also insufficient land for all the nobles in Europe, and a Crusade

would redirect the fractiousness of the aristocracy to a holy cause.

To promote his war, the Pope demonized the Muslims. He spoke of unspeakable desecration of the Christian holy sites and claimed that Christians living under Muslim rule had been reduced to a state of slavery by "sword, rapine and flame." This was an exaggeration. Certain Muslim rulers had destroyed major churches, but in general, Christians were permitted to practice their faith in Muslim countries with relative freedom.

For those who participated in this holy venture, the Pope offered forgiveness from all confessed sins, and this was a powerful incentive to peasants and aristocracy alike. In Medieval Europe it was difficult, particularly for the nobles, to live lives fully in accord with Christian ideals, and the prospect of eternal damnation was very frightening.

The first organized Crusade left France in 1096 CE. This First Crusade met with many trials, but eventually succeeded in capturing Jerusalem in the year 1099. Its success was due in no small measure to the religious fervor of the

TIME: About 1.75 hours

DISTANCE: 4 km

TYPE OF WALK: Circular

DIFFICULTY:
An easy hike on paved roads and smooth dirt trails. Encircling the tel is minimally difficult.

STARTING POINT:
Parking lot for the OSG glass factory at the far end of the kibbutz past the hotel.

DRIVING DIRECTIONS AND PARKING:
Enter "Tzova" into Waze. Enter the kibbutz, follow the sign to the kibbutz hotel, and continue past the hotel until you come to parking lots by the factory.

PUBLIC TRANSPORT:
Enter "Tzova" into Moovit. A bus goes directly to the kibbutz from Binyanei Ha'umah in Jerusalem. More frequent buses from Binyanei Ha'umah involve a thirty minute or so walk from the bus stop משלט פלמ"ח. From the kibbutz bus stop, go back towards the kibbutz entrance and take the main road past the hotel to the glass factory – about a 7 to 8 minute walk. There is also a shorter footpath.

Crusaders, as well as Muslim disunity and apathy.

The Crusaders succeeded in establishing a network of Christian states extending along the coast of the Mediterranean for about five hundred miles from the southern part of the Holy Land to as far north as present-day Turkey. The Holy Land was ruled from Jerusalem and was known as the Kingdom of Jerusalem.

The fortress built here was part of a string of fortresses erected in strategic locations along an old Roman road between the port of Jaffa and Jerusalem. This road more or less follows today's Route 1. These fortresses controlled the road and also provided services to pilgrims visiting Jerusalem, functioning as hospitals, monasteries and hostels. The fortress on Tel Tzuba was named "Belmont" ("beautiful mountain"), and was built between 1140 to 1160 at about the same time as the fortress at Ein Hemda and the Emaus fortress at Latrun.

The Crusaders were European volunteers fighting in the Levant for only a limited time, and it became apparent that more professional and permanent forces were needed to maintain control of the Crusader kingdoms set up in the Middle East. This task was taken on by two religious orders, the Hospitallers and Templars that combined the ideals of knighthood and monasticism. Their members took upon themselves the obligations of poverty, charity and discipline, and they remained in the Crusader kingdoms to fight and do good deeds. They were formidable forces.

The Crusaders were able to maintain control of the Kingdom of Jerusalem for just under a hundred years. However, in the latter part of the 12th century, the Kurdish warrior Salah a-Din (known in English as Saladin) established a Sunni Muslim caliphate stretching from the Nile to the Euphrates, and in 1187 he routed the Crusaders in the Battle of Hittin in the Lower Galilee. He then went on to conquer the Kingdom of Jerusalem. This was now depleted of forces as most of its knights had been killed or taken captive at the Battle of Hittin. Belmont was captured and destroyed by Saladin in 1191.

Shortly after this, the Christians responded with the Third Crusade, but were only able to regain control of the coastal areas of the country. They remained in the Levant for about another hundred years until being driven out by the Mamlukes in the early part of the 14th century.

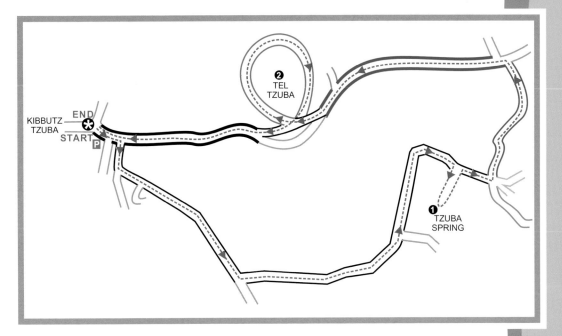

From the intersection by the side of the factory take the paved road to the right by a faded noticeboard and grey gate. (The paved road ahead of you leads uphill directly to the tel and you will be returning on this road). At the next intersection, take the jeep trail on the left through the open grey and red gates. Continue on this scenic trail, ignoring the path down the hill on the right by the cyprus tree.

After about fifteen to twenty minutes (about 1 km), you will see a wooden sign on the right with the word למעין and an arrow on its other side indicating the direction to Ein Tzuba ❶. Just before and after the sign are footpaths to the spring.

Walk down the stone steps to the pool, passing by a small area with picnic benches under a tree. The pool is adjacent to a shade-providing wooden structure with a long stone bench. There is flowing water in the pool even in the summer, but the water is only deep enough to get your feet wet.

On both sides of a noticeboard is a detailed explanation in Hebrew and English about the structure of the spring. Water was led from the aquifer by an underground channel. This was lined by ashlars and covered with a roof supported by arches. The outside pool was probably used mainly for providing water for flocks. An aqueduct also collected water into a large lined underground reservoir. The building of these structures probably happened over many years. Repairs were made during Second Temple times and also during the British Mandate. Entry into the tunnel is no longer permitted.

Return to the jeep trail and turn right. Soon you will come to a rough footpath on your left with green markings. Take this path up the hill.

After passing a parking area, turn left onto the paved road and this will take you to the ruins of Belmont.

The pool of Ein Tzuba

At the very top of the hill, climb up the stone steps to Tel Tzuba ❷. At the fork by a signpost to Tel Tzuba take the path on the left, marked in blue, that encircles the castle ruins. This path will provide you with views in all directions. It is minimally difficult as the path is rocky. Do not take any of the trails down the hill from the tel. If you wish, this part of the hike can be made easier by turning to the right rather than to the left by the signpost and turning back if the going gets difficult for you.

This fortress was built by a Crusader knight, and later purchased by the Crusader Hospitaller order in 1168 and completely rebuilt. It was destroyed by Saladin when he brought the Crusader Kingdom of Jerusalem to an end. However, much of the destruction you see dates from 1834 when the Egyptian rulers of the area shelled rebellious villagers from nearby Abu Gosh who had taken up positions here.

From the path around the tel there are wonderful views in all directions – including of Kibbutz Tzuba, the Arab village of Ein Nakuba, and the Castel. You can also appreciate that Tel Tzuba has a commanding view over Route 1, the former route of the Crusader road to Jerusalem.

From the intersection with the paths around the fortress, walk on the footpath to the paved road. This will lead you down the hill to the parking lot by the glass factory and your car.

Nearby Places of Interest:

Kiftzuba Adventure Park in Kibbutz Tzuba – see page 183.

Galita Chocolate Factory in Kibbutz Tzuba – see page 183.

Tzuba Winery in Kibbutz Tzuba – see page 183.

28 The Spring of Ein Hod and Crusader Castle at Hurvat Beit Itaab

I t is likely that the Crusaders in the Levant did not feel completely secure even in their massive fortresses. At Beit Itaab they constructed a long underground escape tunnel. This scenic hike visits the spring of Ein Hod, the ruins of this Crusader castle, and the exit of their secret tunnel.

TIME: About 2.5 hours

DISTANCE: 5.5 km

TYPE OF HIKE: Circular

DIFFICULTY:
Easy walk along jeep trails and footpaths. The ascent to the crusader ruins is moderately steep.

STARTING POINT:
The parking lot by Bar Bahar. There are WC's here, a cafe, a dairy restaurant, information center, nature exhibits (in Hebrew), and picnic areas. The cafe is open Saturday and has no kashrut supervision.

DRIVING DIRECTIONS AND PARKING:
Enter "Bar Bahar" into Waze and click on Bar Bahar, Bar Giora, Israel. There is a parking lot by Bar Bahar. If it is full, drive along the initially paved road in the direction of the bus parking lot signposted to Nahal Katlav.

PUBLIC TRANSPORT:
Enter "Bar Giora" into Moovit. The moshav is serviced by several buses from Jerusalem and from here it is a short distance to Bar Bahar. In addition, bus 192 from Binyanei Ha'umah in Jerusalem stops at Tzomet Nes Harim, which is about a ten minute walk from Bar Bahar.

n Hod was the spring for the Byzantine, usader and Arab villages that existed here

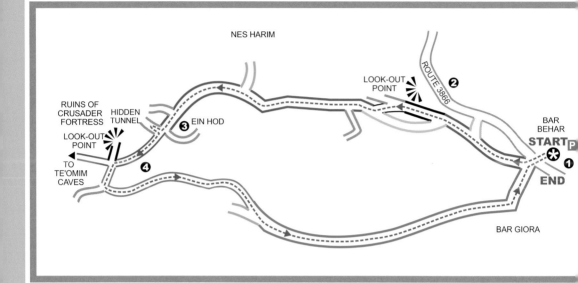

Exit the main entrance of the parking lot by Bar Bahar and turn right on the main road, Route 3866. After a very short distance, take the turn on the left. From this road, turn right onto the jeep trail by the JNF sign for the American Independence Park. Continue along this trail until you come to a cemetery.

Continue on this path by the metal fence and this will take you around the cemetery and a vineyard. At the corner of the vineyard is a signpost. Continue straight ahead on an unmarked trail (and not the red-marked trail to the left).

After passing an overnight camping site, you will come to an observation area with five benches arranged in a semi-circle. From here you can see the ruins of the castle on the hill ahead and appreciate its commanding position.

There is a footpath opposite the benches. Take this delightful path down the hill. Turn right when you come to the red-marked trail.

When you come to a brick wall on your left with a blue national park sign, turn left on the red-marked trail towards the spring of Ein Hod.

This spring is known as Ein Bet It'ab, and in Arabic En Khod, which means "Spring of the Water Trough." It was the spring for the Byzantine, Crusader and Arab villages that were once here. There is an above ground shallow pool. Underground is a reservoir from where a forty meter tunnel leads to the source of the spring. There is a shaft to the underground reservoir adjacent to the pool, although this is now closed off by a metal grid.

Continue on the red-marked trail up the hill and you will soon come to a three-way intersection with the black trail. To visit the exit to the secret tunnel, turn right here onto an unmarked trail and you will soon see stone steps on your left leading to a cave with a green sign outside it warning people not to enter. Ledges within the cave identify the cave as a colobarium (a place for raising doves). Look even closer and you can see an opening at the bottom of the cave beneath the ledges. This is the exit for a steep seventy-five meter underground tunnel built by the Crusaders that leads from inside the castle to the bottom of the hill. The entrance to the tunnel from the castle has collapsed, but it is theoretically possible (although not permitted) to climb up to that point.

Go back to the intersection and continue up the hill on the red-marked trail. At the fork where it meets the blue-marked trail, turn right onto the continuation of the red-marked trail to the ruins of the Crusader castle. The ruins are closed off, but you can ascend to an observation area for a beautiful view of the surrounding Judean Mountains, the Shefela, and to as far as the coastal plain. Beit Shemesh is straight ahead of you and to your right is the moshav Nes Harim.

The ruins of the castle Hurvat Ita'ab and the observation area

This fortress was built by the Frankish Crusader knight Johaness Gothman during the period of the Crusader Kingdom of Jerusalem in the middle of the 1100's. (For more information about the Crusaders, see the article "Crusades and Castles" in the previous chapter 27 on page 209.) He was captured by Islamic forces in 1161, and his wife was forced to sell his landholdings to pay for his bail. The property was taken over by the Church of the Holy Sepulcher. Its days as a Crusader fortress came to an end with the dissolution of the Kingdom of Jerusalem following the defeat of the Crusaders at the Battle of Hittin in the Galilee in 1187.

It has been speculated that this may have been the hiding place for Samson when he *"went down and dwelt in the top of the rock Etam"* when he was hiding from the Philistines (Judges 15:8). Many Arab villages retain the name of Jewish settlements from Biblical times. *Etam* means an eagle's nest in Hebrew, and it was not uncommon for an "m" to change to a "b" (i.e., Etam to Itab).

The Arab village of Bayt Itab was located around the fortress. It was captured by Israeli forces during the War of Independence as part of Operation Nachshon. Its inhabitants fled.

Descend from the observation platform and at the T-junction turn left onto the red trail. At the next intersection at the bottom of the ruins go down the hill on the blue-marked trail.

Continue on this blue-marked trail to the security fence of the moshav Bar Giora, and then to Route 3866. The entrance to Bar Bahar is a very short distance on your right on the other side of the road.

Other options:

1. To extend this hike by an hour or so, after coming down from the observation platform from the Crusader ruins, at the first intersection turn right onto the red-marked trail (instead of continuing to the next intersection to meet the blue-marked trail). Go down the hill until you come to a broad unmarked jeep trail at the very bottom of the hill. Turn left and continue on this trail until you meet the blue trail on the left which comes from the fortress. The road straight ahead continues to Bar Giora as above.

2. Serious hikers may wish to continue on the red-marked trail to the Te'omim Caves. Instead of turning left onto the unmarked jeep trail as the paragraph above, continue on the red-marked Wadi Me'ara trail. This is a popular, mildly difficult hike. However, to do this hike you will need to have a second vehicle waiting for you in the parking lot off Route 3855. The Te'omim Caves were used as a hideout during the Bar Kochba Revolt and remains from this period were found in the caves. You can enter the caves, so bring a flashlight. The caves are closed from November to March to protect the many hibernating bats.

29 The Beautiful Nahal Katlav

For spectacular views, this popular hike from Bar Bahar along the banks of Nahal Katlav and Nahal Sorek to the ruins of the fortress of Khirbet Tura will not disappoint you. The hike is slightly difficult in a few places and is best for those with some hiking experience.

Overlooking Nahal Katlav

TIME: About 4 hours

DISTANCE: About 7.75 km

TYPE OF HIKE: Circular

DIFFICULTY:
Mainly easy hiking along a dirt path, but some parts of the trail are somewhat narrow and adjacent to a steep slope, and one section involves slightly difficult climbing. Walking sticks can be helpful for this hike, if only as a psychological aid. If the path is likely to be wet and slippery, leave the hike for another day.

STARTING POINT:
The parking lot outside the dairy café and restaurant Bar Bahar ❶. The café and restaurant are open on Saturday and do not have kashrut certification. There are WC's by the café.

DRIVING DIRECTIONS AND PARKING:
Enter "Bar Bahar" into Waze and click on "Bar Bahar, Bar Giora, Israel." There is a parking lot by Bar Bahar. If it is full, drive along the initially paved road in the direction of the bus parking lot signposted to Nahal Katlav.

continued

PUBLIC TRANSPORT:
Enter "Bar Giora" into Moovit. The moshav is serviced by several buses from Jerusalem and from here it is a short distance to Bar Bahar. In addition, bus 192 from Binyanei Ha'umah in Jerusalem stops at Tzomet Nes Harim, which is about a 10-minute walk away.

The name Nahal Katlav comes from the Hebrew and Arabic name for a tree common in this wadi that is popularly known as the "Eastern Strawberry Tree" due to its red and succulent berries. They have no resemblance to strawberries. The tree has single or multiple stems, and is readily recognizable by its smooth, reddish-brown bark that annually peels in picturesque scales.

According to local folklore, the name "*katlav*" comes from the words "*katal*," meaning he killed, and "*av*," meaning father. In one version of the legend, a shepherd was in conflict with his son. The quarrel spun out of control and the son grabbed a piece of wood and used it as a club to kill his father. The bloodstained stick turned red and grew into the katlav tree with its reddish bark.

Nahal Katlav is a tributary of Nahal Sorek. Nahal Sorek is one of a number of valleys that, like the fingers of a hand, cut through the Judean Mountains and drain surface runoff water to the Mediterranean Sea. Nahal Sorek begins close to Ramallah and winds its way through the Judean Mountains and Shefela to the coastal plain. In ancient times it was a thoroughfare to Jerusalem and there were agricultural settlements along its path. The Hebrew word sorek means "special vine" and refers to the rich vines that grew along the valley.

THE HIKE

Prior to your hike, you may wish to look at the displays in the JNF information center adjacent to the café. It has maps and information about the flora, fauna and trails in the area, although it is all in Hebrew. There are often personnel in the information center who are happy to provide advice. The restaurant at the back of the cafe has a lookout and sign identifying nearby places.

To reach the trailhead from the parking area, as you face the café, go to the right on an initially paved road in the direction indicated by the signpost to נחל קטלב. At the far corner of a gravel parking lot at the end of the path is another signpost directing you to Nahal Katlav. Go through the gap in the brick fence to the beginning of the black-marked trail.

At the intersection with the red-marked scenic path, continue down the valley on the black-marked trail. After about

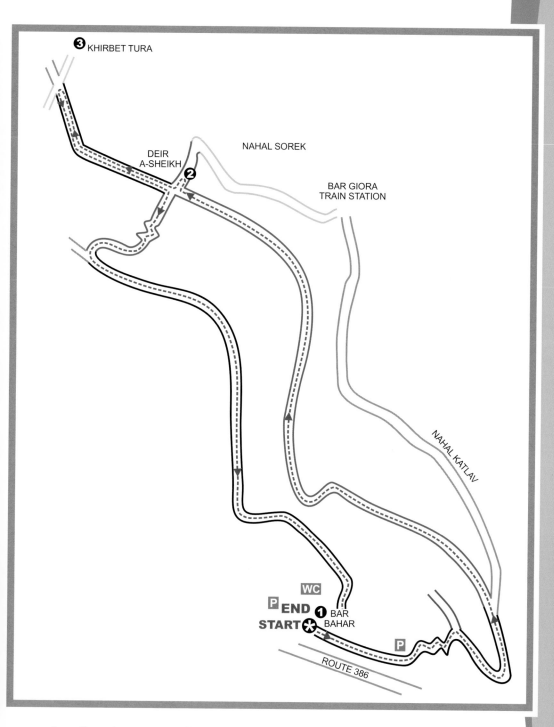

forty-five minutes, you will come to a fork with the blue-marked trail. Take this blue-marked trail along the side of the wadi.

You will eventually come to T-junction with the green trail. To visit the ruins of Deir a-Sheik ❷ turn right on the green trail. It will add about ten minutes to your hike.

Deir a-Sheikh, in Arabic, means the Sheikh's monastery. These ruins contain the tomb of Sheikh Sultan Badr. The tomb has three small halls, the largest of which is a mosque containing his tombstone.

The ruins of Khirbet Tura are on top of the hill

Go back up the green-marked trail and you will soon see a black-marked trail on your right. This easy trail will take you towards the ruins of the fortress of Khirbet Tura ❸.

Stop at the intersection with (another) blue trail to view the hill and ruins of the fortress. There is no particular reason to go any closer than this to the ruins.

You are viewing the ruins of a royal fortress from the Hasmonean period. The original Arabic names of the site, Khirbet Sammunieh and Khirbet Tantura, preserve the ancient name of the fortress "Tur Shimon" or the Mountain of Shimon. The fortress may have been built by Simeon (Shimon), the son of the Hasmonean ruler Mattathias (Matityahu), or by Simeon's son, John Hyrcanus, in memory of his father. Naming fortresses after other rulers, family or friends was common in the Hellenistic and Roman world; there are other examples of this in Israel. The fortress overlooks the Sorek Valley and provided

protection to this approach to Jerusalem. Six large underground cisterns provided water. Tur Shimon was also a fortified settlement during the Bar Kochba revolt and is mentioned in the Jerusalem Talmud (Ta'anit 4:69a). During the Crusader period, a fortress or fortified farmhouse was built on the ruins of the Hasmonean fortress.

Return on the black trail the way you came, to its intersection with the blue-marked trail. Turn right on this trail up the hill. You now have about twenty minutes of slightly difficult climbing ahead of you, although the rock faces have convenient natural footholds.

When you come to a black-marked jeep trail turn left. Easy walking takes you back to the café and your car.

Other options:

1. The hike can be shortened by about forty-five minutes by skipping Deir a-Sheikh and Khirbet Tura and going straight up the green-marked trail.

2. Hike to Bar Giora train station: Instead of going along the side of the valley on the blue trail, continue on the black-marked trail as it descends to the wadi. This trail will take you to the non-operative Bar Giora train station. Here you will meet the green trail, which will take you up to Deir a-Sheikh. Then continue as above. (Note: Water flowing through Nahal Sorek contains treated wastewater. Do not drink or swim in it).

30 Outpost 21 via the Historic Burma Road

This circular hike begins along the historic Burma Road by the edge of the scenic Martyr's Forest and ascends to Outpost 21, a military outpost during the War of Independence. The climb is worth it!

THE BURMA ROAD AND THE SIEGE OF JERUSALEM

During the 1947-1948 War of Independence, West Jerusalem was under siege. By May 1948 the situation had become critical. Supplies of food, water and arms were at rock bottom and there was a very real possibility that Jewish Jerusalem would have to surrender to the Jordanian Arab League.

TIME: About 3 hours

DISTANCE: Almost 9 km

TYPE OF HIKE: Circular

DIFFICULTY:
The hike is minimally difficult in a few places with climbing over bare rock and loose stones, but these are not at all dangerous.

STARTING POINT:
The Burma Road by the Makhal Monument. There are many picnic benches around the monument.

DRIVING DIRECTIONS:
Enter "Monument Makhal" into Waze and click on "אנדרטת מח״ל." From Route 1, turn onto Route 38 towards Beit Shemesh. After a few minutes, on your right and just before the Paz gas station, you will see a brown signpost to the Machal Monument and Burma Road E. Turn onto the underpass to Burma Road E.

PUBLIC TRANSPORTATION:
Buses 415 and 417 from the Jerusalem Central Bus Station stop at the Mesilat Tzion intersection. From here, it is about an eighteen minute walk to the beginning of the trail. Enter "Memorial Monument Makhal" into Moovit.

In January 1948, local Arab forces had taken control of the hills between Sha'ar HaGai and the Castel and convoys carrying supplies along the only road to Jerusalem were suffering heavy losses in their unsuccessful attempts to reach the city. In April 1948, Jewish forces went on the offensive and the Palmach was able to capture these positions during Operation Nachshon (see also the essay "Israel's War of Independence" on page 200). However, a new problem now emerged preventing Jerusalem from receiving supplies.

On May 15, 1948, at the end of their Mandate, the British vacated Latrun monastery and the police fort that dominated this part of the road. The Harel Brigade immediately took control of these hills but was dislodged by the Arab Legion. Despite repeated and very costly attempts, Jewish forces were unable to dislodge the Arab Legion. So desperate was the situation that ill-prepared refugees fresh off the boat were sent into battle.

At this time, a shepherd's footpath known as the "Gazelle Path" was discovered that bypassed the Latrun junction, and a makeshift speedily-erected bypass route was constructed. It was called the Burma Road after the war-time road built by the British to supply Burma from Southwest China during the 2nd Sino-Japanese War. Initially, vehicles had to be pushed part of the way and supplies had to be carried by mule, and even by hand, on the steep sections of the road. By June 10, the steepest section, the Serpentine Path, was open for vehicles, although they had to be dragged up by tractors. The Arab Legion in Latrun was aware of what was happening and shelled the road, but had no direct view of the construction.

The Burma Road was completed on June 14, 1948, and by the end of June nightly convoys were delivering supplies to Jerusalem. The Arabs had previously cut off the water supply to Jerusalem, and water and fuel pipes were therefore also laid alongside the road. For several months this route was the sole means by which supplies were delivered to Jerusalem, even though Latrun remained in Jordanian hands (and continued to be so until the Six Day War).

The Burma Road road began not far from Kibbutz Harel and crossed what is now Route 38. From here, it ascended to the Jerusalem Mountains, joined the road by Bayt Mahsir (now called Beit Meir), passed Saris (now called Shoresh), and then connected with the main Jerusalem road. The part you will be hiking on is the section from Route 38 to Beit Meir.

The commander of this operation was "Mickey" Marcus (1901-1948), who had previously been a US Army colonel and had taken part in many high-level assignments for the US. After V-E Day he was put in charge of providing for the millions of displaced persons in Germany. He was shocked by what he saw and began thinking seriously about Zionism. In 1947, his help was requested by David Ben Gurion, and Mickey volunteered for the then fledgling Israeli army. He designed a command and control structure based on that of the US army. He was the first general of the Israel Defense Force and in May 1948 took command of the Jerusalem front, including construction of the Burma Road. Unfortunately, he was killed in the middle of the night, when he was mistaken for an enemy infiltrator. He did not fully understand Hebrew and was unable to provide the password that would have identified him. Those who shot him did not understand his English. He was buried in West Point cemetery in the USA.

THE HIKE

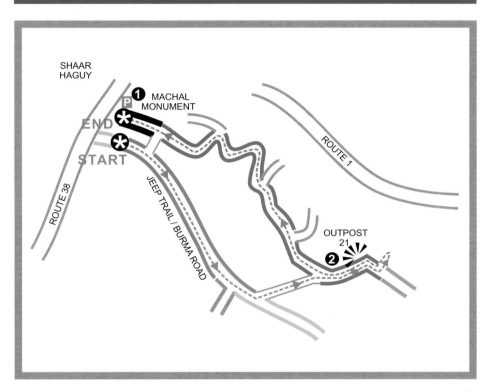

Before starting on the hike, take a few minutes to look at the Machal Memorial ❶ on the far side of the parking lot.

Three thousand and five hundred non-Israeli volunteers came to Israel to fight in the War of Independence and this memorial commemorates those who lost their lives. "Mickey" Marcus, the commander who built the Burma Road, is included in the list on the wall.

Take the red-marked "Jeep Trail," which you drove on as you entered the parking lot and which is part of the Burma Trail, into the Judean Mountains. It ascends along the edge of Martyr's Forest, which was planted in memory of those killed during the Holocaust. A forested deep ravine is to your left and a forested incline is on your right.

After about twenty minutes of hiking, take the blue-marked footpath into the wadi on your left. The beginning of the path is about three hundred meters after the first intersection on your right. It is easy to find as there are blue markings on both sides of the road and there are wooden steps at the beginning of the trail.

After reaching the bottom of the wadi, the path ascends and after some distance meets the green-marked trail, which is also a Schvil Yisrael trail with blue, white and orange markings. Turn right towards Outpost 21 ❷.

225

View of Outpost 21 from the Burma Trail

You will know you have reached Outpost 21 and the top of the mountain when you see two metal signs, one of which is a map of the Burma Road, and the other describes in Hebrew the events that occurred here during the War of Independence. There are wonderful views from here. You can also turn to the left along a short, unmarked trail for a different view, with Route 1 now being directly below you.

The Palmach defended this height from waves of Arab attackers on May 10, 1948 during the War of Independence. Six defenders died and many were wounded. The views from the top of this mountain of the Shefela and Coastal Plain are quite outstanding. You can also appreciate why the Palmach were so anxious to control it.

Turn back the way you came on the green-marked/Schvil Yisrael trail down the mountain. This is a popular trail and you may well meet other hikers, many of them going towards Jerusalem. (You will pass the blue-marked trail, but it is a thin footpath and you are unlikely to turn onto it in error). The trail continues through a forest and leads eventually to the monument and your car. If you need a cold drink or snack, it is a very short distance to the gas station along Route 38 in the direction of Beit Shemesh.

Monument to the volunteers who came from outside Israel and died in Israel's War of Independence

Nearby Places of Interest:

Biblical Museum of Natural History is at 5 Ha-Tzaba St. in Beit Shemesh, but will be moving to new premises. This unique museum is part zoo, part natural history museum and part Torah education center. Included are hands-on encounters with exotic live animals. There is an admission charge. Their e-mail address is office@tevatanachi.org or call (073) 213-1662 to book a tour.

Stalactite Cave Nature Reserve *(Sorek Cave/Avshalom's Caves)*. This is a warm (22°wC), eighty-two meter long cave containing formations in a rich array of shapes and in a variety of mineral-based colors. Some stalactites meet stalagmites to form stone pillars. Some stalactites have been dated to as much as 300,000 years old. There are a lot of steps to the entrance. The cave can be slippery so use shoes with traction, although there are guard rails throughout. Hours from April to September: 8 am–5 pm Sunday to Thursday, Friday and Saturday 8 am–4 pm, and from October to March 8 am–4 pm Sunday to Thursday, Friday and Saturday 8 am–4 pm. Holiday eves 8 am–1 pm. Admission is up to one hour before closing time. There is an admission charge. Their phone number is: (02) 991-1117.

Israel Police Heritage Museum at 9 Virginia St., West Industrial Park, Beit Shemesh. Exhibits illustrate the history of policing through multi-media presentations, holograms, films, reconstructions of crime scenes and more. Open Monday through Thursday excluding holidays 9 am–4 pm. There are tours in Hebrew at 10 am, 1 pm and 2:30 pm. Tours are also available in English, but call ahead. Their phone number is: (02) 578-8268. There is no admission charge.

31 The Hahamisha Forest and Ein Kfira Spring

TIME:
3 hours, and about 4 hours and 15 minutes if visiting Ein Kfira

DISTANCE: Almost 9.5 km, and 12.5 km if visiting Ein Kfira

TYPE OF HIKE: Circular

DIFFICULTY:
An easy hike mainly on paved roads, although the black-marked trail has a gradual but long ascent. The descent to Ein Kfira is minimally difficult with climbing on rocks.

STARTING POINT:
The picnic area by the Red Army Memorial.

DRIVING DIRECTIONS AND PARKING:
Enter "הצבא האדום" into Waze and click on "כניסה ליער ע״ש הצבא האדום". Two brown signs on the main road point to HaHamisha Forest and Mt. HaRuach. Parking is on the sides of the jeep trail.

PUBLIC TRANSPORT:
There is no convenient public transport. The nearest bus stop is at Ma'ale HaHamisha, which is about a 2.4 km walk to the start of the hike. Enter "Maale HaHamisha" into Moovit. Buses

continued

From the HaRuach Mountain range there are wonderful views of the wadis on either side, Nahal Yital and Nahal Kfira, and the Judean Mountains and Shefela. There is also a footpath that will take you to Nahal Kfira and the spring of Ein Kfira. Ahead of you can be seen Tel Kfira, the site of the ancient Gibeonite town of Kfira.

OVERVIEW

JOSHUA AND THE GIBEONITES

There are interesting Biblical connections to the area you are now hiking. Tel Kfira has been identified with the city of Kfira, a city that belonged to the ancient Gibeonites. The surrender of this tribe to the Israelites had major implications for Joshua's rapid conquest of the country.

The book of Joshua relates (chapter 9) that this Canaanite tribe was fearful of the invading Israelites. Their representatives therefore dressed up as travellers who had come from a distance and they approached Joshua to make a peace covenant. The Israelites were fooled and only later did they discover that the Gibeonites lived in the Judean Mountains only a 3-day walk away. The Israelites did not break the peace treaty, but as a result of what the Gibeonites had done, they became water carriers and woodcutters for the Israelites.

There were important strategic implications to this peace treaty. The Gibeonite's main city of Gibeon (located where the Arab village of al-Jib is today) controlled an important intersection – the main north-south highway through the mountain range from Shechem to Hebron and an east-west road crossing the Ayalon Valley and ending at Gilgal in the Jordan Valley. The Gibeonites also possessed other cities that were now effectively neutralized, including Kfira and nearby Kiryat Ye'arim (Joshua 9:17). The latter may have been close to nearby present-day Tel Stone or Abu Gosh. The southern Canaanite cities quickly realized the strategic significance of the Gibeonite capitulation and five of them formed an alliance to attack Gibeon – Jerusalem, Hebron, Yarmus, Lachish and Eglon. The Gibeonites appealed to Joshua for help, and the Israelites made a surprise and successful raid on the alliance (Joshua, chapter 10). The remainder of the alliance army was destroyed in the Valley of Ayalon when the sun and moon stood still. By defeating these five kings in one battle,

Joshua had succeeded in conquering the southern part of Israel without having to besiege their cities individually.

Tel Kfira is now under the jurisdiction of the Palestinian Authority, but archaeological excavations have been carried out and findings include ruins of fortified cities from the Bronze Age to Second Temple times.

THE HIKE

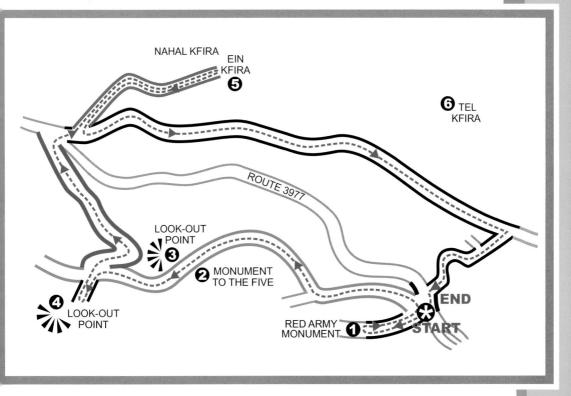

By the first signpost in the picnic area, take the fork in the direction of "הצבא האדום." After a short distance you will come to an unimposing memorial to the Red Army ❶ erected in 1950.

Your first thought could well be – what is this doing here? The monument and this part of the HaRuach Forest were planted in commemoration of the victory of the Red Army over the Nazis during the 2nd World War, a reminder of the high regard that many of the early socialist Zionist pioneers had for communism. The inscription reads: *"This forest was planted by the residents of Israel in honor of the Soviet Army, 1950."* On the Saturday closest to May 9, the day the Red Army was victorious over the Germans, thousands of left-wing supporters of Russia used to gather for celebrations and a picnic. As positive sentiments for communism diminished, so did the number of attendees for this picnic. Nevertheless, for many reasons, friendship with Russia is a priority for the Israeli government. There is another Red Army Victory Monument in the city of Natanya, far more imposing than this one, that was opened by Vladmir Putin in 2012.

After viewing the monument, return to the signpost and take the paved road which is blue-marked in the direction "בית חיל" and "מצפור יתלה." There are two stops to make along this trail. After about 15-20 minutes of walking, you will see on your left a stone memorial ❷ to five young men who were murdered by Arab terrorists in 1937 while working on afforestation and paving roads for the Jewish National Fund. About 40 meters further along, on the right, is an observation area ❸ with excellent views and a sign pointing out what you are viewing. Kiryat Sefer can be seen in the distance and on a clear day you can see all the way to Natanya and Hadera.

As a result of these murders, in 1938, it was decided to establish a new settlement in their memory. It was called Ma'ale HaHamisha (Ascent of the Five) and was started by pioneers then living in Kiryat Anavim. This settlement was one of fifty-seven "tower and stockade" settlements built rapidly in Mandatory Palestine during the Arab Revolt, between 1936 to 1939. They consisted of a tower and sheds for the settlers, surrounded by barbed wire, and were intended to create defensive facts on the ground on Jewish-owned territory. This was the second settlement to be formed in this part of the Judean Mountains. Over time, the lack of good agricultural land forced the kibbutz to develop sources of income other than agriculture. One of their ventures was a hotel. This hotel is still operative, although is no longer under the management of the kibbutz.

During the War of Independence, Ma'ale HaHamisha was attacked twice by the Jordanian Arab Legion, and these attacks were successfully repulsed. The women and children were evacuated and the kibbutz became the command center for the Palmach. Fighters set out from here for actions at the Castel and other places in the Judean Mountains. Some of the fighters slept in part of the hotel. After the War of Independence, Ma'ale HaHamisha found itself close the armistice line between Israel and Jordan. The kibbutz was privatized in 2005.

At the next intersection and signpost, turn left on the paved footpath in the direction of the sign to "נחל יתלה." Overlooking the valley you will come to another observation area ❹. There is a sign here indicating the places you are viewing, as well as a picnic area with picnic benches and play equipment.

Return to the intersection and turn onto the red trail, which is another paved road, in the direction of "חוות עזים." At the end of this road is a memorial to Polish Jewry. Cross over the main road to the parking area and look for a black-marked jeep trail.

To visit Ein Kfira, turn left onto the green-marked trail a short distance from the beginning of the black trail. This footpath descends gradually into the valley. If you are not visiting Ein Kfira, just continue on the black-marked trail.

After about forty-five minutes on the green trail, you will pass the ruins of a Sheik's tomb on your left, some distance from the trail. Shortly after this is a stone wall and just before a solitary palm tree there is a footpath to the right. Take this footpath. The pool of Ein Kafira ❺ is just before the rock face. It is fed by two sources of water, one near the pool and the other higher up. Whether there is water in the pool depends on the season.

Tel Kfira is ahead of you, but this is as far as you need go on the green trail. Turn around and go back to the black-marked trail and then turn left. As you walk along the black-marked trail you will see below you the prominent hill of Tel Kfira ❻ and at its base the Arab village of Katana.

Tel Kfira from the footpath to Ein Kfira

When the trail comes to a T-junction, turn to the right up the hill on the continuation of the black-marked trail. This trail passes the outskirts of Ma'ale HaHamisha and ends on the main road. (Note that this part of the trail winds more than indicated by the map). Turn left and you will soon see the back of the signs to HaHamisa Forest and Mt. HaRuach. Turn down this road to your car.

Nearby Places of Interest

Harel Brigade Monument. *This monument to the Harel Brigade is in the nearby town of Har Hadar. The tower can be climbed and offers great views of the surrounding area, including Nebi Samuel. There are also military vehicles that can be climbed upon and that give new meaning to the words "war games." Directions: Put into Waze "Harel Memorial", and click on "אנדרת חטיבת פלמ''ח הראל." Explanations of the military significance of Har Hadar are all in Hebrew.*

32 Herodium

Herod the Great's palace at Herodium was recognized in its time as the most beautiful palace in the Roman Empire. Even today its ruins emanate its former splendor and the egomania of its owner.

The ruins of the reception hall of Herod's palace and it's northern tower, which is the tower best preserved

TIME: About 1.5 hours

DIFFICULTY: Easy walking, although there are moderate inclines up to the fortress and down the tunnels.

STARTING POINT: The parking lot outside the main office building.

DRIVING DIRECTIONS AND PARKING:
Enter "Herodium" into Waze and click on גן לאומי הרודיון. Park outside the main building.

PUBLIC TRANSPORT: Put "Herodium" into Moovit and click on "גן לאומי הרודיון". Bus 266 departs from Binyanei Ha'umah in Jerusalem several times a day. Bus 166 leaves from Derech Chevron.

SECURITY: Herodium is in area C. The main road to Herodium, Route 356, passes many Arab villages, but it is also the main road to Jewish settlements such as Tekoa and is usually regarded as being safe.

Herodium is open from 8 am–5 pm April to September and 8 am–4 pm October to March. There is an admission charge. There is a shaded area outside the building with benches for picnicking. Cold water is available from a large tank. The only WC on the site is here. Cold drinks and ice cream can be bought at the ticket office.

There is much to be said for seeing this site for the first time with a guide. Tours are available on Friday and Saturday at 12 pm, but only in Hebrew. Nevertheless, by following the signs, using the brochure provided, and reading our mini-essays it is possible to gain much from a visit without a guide.

OVERVIEWS

HEROD THE GREAT

Herod ruled Judea, Samaria and the Galilee from 37 to 4 BCE. Most of his Jewish subjects hated him. Nevertheless, it is possible to see both positive and negative aspects to his reign. Many of these would impact the Jewish people well after his death.

Herod succeeded in bringing prosperity to a favored semi-independent province of Rome. He was genuinely concerned about the welfare and religious freedom of his Jewish subjects, and Judaism was able to flourish under the leadership of sages such as Hillel and Shammai. He rebuilt the Temple, and this magnificent edifice brought knowledge of monotheism to the entire Roman world. This encouraged conversions to Judaism and laid the ground for the proselytizing of the early Christians.

On the other hand, he delivered his country to Rome and destroyed any hope of Jewish independence. He eliminated all members of the Hasmonean dynasty even when they were his own flesh and blood. His appointing high priests diminished the prestige of the priesthood

and encouraged corruption. The large sums of money flowing into his kingdom aggravated social tensions. Attempting to analyze his psychological state also leads in contradictory directions. He was a cruel and vindictive egomaniac. Yet these same attributes enabled him to keep a tight lid on Jewish aspirations for independence, maintain peace throughout his reign, and bring fame and wealth to his kingdom.

He was raised as a Jew in Rome. His father, Antipater, was from a noble family in Idumaea who had converted to Judaism with his family when the Maccabees conquered Idumaea and forcibly converted the population. Herod's mother was Nabatean. Many in his kingdom regarded him as no more than half-Jewish.

The Hasmoneans destroyed their own dynasty, and with it hopes for Jewish independence, when the two sons of Alexander Yannai engaged in a civil war for kingship. This struggle allowed Antipater to take control of Judea by becoming an advisor to one of the brothers, Hyrcanus, and by strongly allying Hyrcanus' kingdom with Rome. Antipater was poisoned, but Herod would follow the devious machinations of his father and his strong pro-Roman policies.

When the Parthians invaded Judea and defeated the legions of Rome, Antigonus, a nephew of Hyrcanus, reopened the previous rift in the family by allying with the Parthians and taking over Jerusalem. Hyrcanus accepted the situation, but Herod, who by now had a governmental role, escaped to Rome and persuaded his childhood friend Mark Anthony to appoint him king of the Jews with the intention of realigning the Jewish kingdom with Rome. The Roman Senate ratified his appointment. Herod then raised an army and spent the next three years fighting Antigonus until he succeeded in conquering Jerusalem. Antigonus was beheaded and his supporters were massacred.

Following the assassination of Julius Caesar, Mark Anthony and Octavian vied for power, and in the Battle of Actium the forces of Mark Anthony were defeated and Mark Anthony committed suicide. Octavian renamed himself Augustus and began the process of changing Rome from a republic to an empire. Herod had been the protégé of Mark Anthony but he ingratiated himself with Augustus who saw the usefulness of such a ruthless person and a close friendship developed between them. This close friendship was advantageous to both during Herod's thirty-four year reign.

Herod maintained his close connections to Rome by adopting the ways of a Roman aristocrat. His palace displayed the best of Roman decor. Guests to Herodium were entertained in its amphitheater and fed with the finest of imported foods and wines.

To satisfy his egomania and curry favor with his subjects, Herod began building on a lavish scale. The best technological building skills of the Roman Empire were brought to his kingdom. For the Jews, he built a tomb over the Cave of Machpela, the site where the Jewish patriarchs and matriarchs were buried, and he rebuilt the Temple. Jews from throughout the Empire flocked to its precincts. Its construction was one of the wonders of the Roman world and Jerusalem became famous as a tourist site, even for non-Jews. For the pagans in his kingdom, he built Sabastia in Samaria and the port of Caesarea.

His personal life was a shamble. He was fond of women and had ten wives. He married Miriam, a granddaughter of Hyrcanus, to provide legitimacy to his rule. However, he was paranoid, perhaps with some justification, of a Hasmonean attempt to return to power. He appointed Miriam's brother, Aristobulus III, as High Priest, but when Aristobulus flaunted his popularity Herod invited him to his winter palace in Jericho and drowned him in a pool. He genuinely loved Miriam, but she was framed as being associated with a palace intrigue and he had her put to death. The two sons he had with Miriam were suspected of treachery and were strangled.

Following his death, no ruler after him was able to replicate his ability to create some form of modus vivendi between Jewish and Roman culture. Not his son Herod Archelaus who reigned after him, but who was fired by Augustus for cruelty and divisiveness. And not the Roman procurators appointed by Rome who lacked the sensitivity to dampen the messianic yearnings of the Jewish people. Within seventy-four years of his death the Jews had revolted against Rome in the Great Revolt of 70 CE. The glorious Temple he had erected was destroyed and the Jerusalem he had helped beautify was burned to the ground.

WHY DID HEROD BUILD HERODIUM?

Unlike his other building projects that were often named after influential friends and relatives, Herod named Herodium after himself. It was a palace that reflected his personality. This was where he could act like a Roman and entertain and impress his Roman friends. And this was where he could conduct matters of state away from the claustrophobic atmosphere of nearby Jerusalem.

But why erect a palace and fortress on the edge of the desert when he already had so many other luxurious palaces? It would seem from the historian Josephus that this location had sentimental associations for Herod. It was here that he had defeated the Parthians when escaping from Jerusalem. It adjoined the border with Idumaea, the birthplace of his father. It was located on the main road to Nabatea, the birthplace of his mother. It was also close to Jerusalem.

Herodium consisted of a fortified palace on top of a mountain, a three hundred seat amphitheater on the side of the mountain, and a "country club" — Lower Herodium, at its base.

The palace was a circular structure surrounded by two parallel walls with four towers that faced the four coordinates of the compass. The eastern tower was the largest and was circular, while the others were semi-circular. Around the outer wall were windows through which circulating air cooled the building.

Guests ascended to the palace from the base of the mountain on two hundred pure white marble steps. Activities of the palace took place within its central enclosure. On its eastern side was an ornamental garden with colonnades, and on its western side a courtyard, bathhouse, living quarters and reception hall. The latter was used for entertaining and dining, all of which were on a lavish scale.

On the northern side of the mountain slope, Herod built a three hundred seat amphitheater, connected to the palace by the marble stairway. At the top of the amphitheater was a theatre box for he and privileged guests, and the walls of the amphitheater were decorated with frescoed paintings specially painted for important guests. This area is now enclosed by glass to preserve its artwork.

At the very bottom of the mountain was Herod's "country club" — Lower Herodium. This was almost a small town and contained a large ornamental pool, gardens and baths, and living accommodation for his numerous staff. Lower Herodium is not usually part of any tour, but its ruins can be clearly seen from the top and northern side of the mountain.

A specially built six km aqueduct brought water from King Solomon's Pools to Lower Herodium. The palace obtained water from four underground cisterns. Three of these were on the side of the mountain and collected rainwater.

A cistern directly below the palace was manually filled by containers, and water was drawn from the cistern for its needs.

As a master schemer, Herod was always one step ahead of the game. He even planned his own funeral years before his death. Two years before he died, by which time he was probably already sick and aware that his time on earth was limited, he built a mausoleum for himself on the side of the hill adjacent to the amphitheater. He also converted the mountain into a monument to himself by covering the palace and amphitheater with earth and rock, making the mountain dome-shaped and even more noticeable from afar.

Herodium may have been covered up, but this was not the end of Herodium as a functional building. It was taken over by Jewish rebels during their Great Revolt against the Romans in 70 CE. They converted Herod's reception hall into a synagogue by erecting pillars and placing benches along its walls, constructed two ritual baths in the courtyard, and dug a tunnel to the cisterns so they could draw water without being seen by the Romans.

Herodium was again occupied by Jews during the Bar Kochba Revolt (132-136 CE), and likely functioned as a second headquarters for Bar Kochba. More tunnels were dug for carrying out surprise attacks against the Romans. To keep the tunnels hidden, the rocks from tunnel making were dumped into the cisterns. Much of this debris has been removed during archaeological excavations and it is now possible to walk through many of these tunnels.

In the Byzantine period, one of the wings of the courtyard was converted

Model of Herod's mausoleum

into a small chapel. Lower Herodium also contains the ruins of a Byzantine farming community.

Today the mountain of Herodium is the tallest mountain in the Judean Desert and can be identified from many kilometers away because of its characteristic shape. It is one of the most impressive archaeological sites in Israel. Herod planned that after his death he would not be forgotten. For better or worse, he succeeded.

Viewing Herodium:

Herodium is an active archaeological site and its presentation is a work in progress. When you visit it, there may well be changes from this description.

View the short movie about Herod in the ticket office building. It can be seen in Hebrew or English and is about Herod's funeral. Although an important aspect of this site, it is a bit like reading the last chapter of a book and skipping everything before it. There is also a model here that provides a useful orientation to the set-up of the palace and amphitheater.

Exit the back door of the building and take the uppermost path towards the palace. You will soon reach a vantage point from which to look down at Lower Herodium. This has a sign identifying the various parts of the ruins.

At the very top of the path is another model of the palace. Looking at the palace ruins below, you should be able to identify the four towers, with the eastern tower being the most intact. Herod probably had his living quarters within this tower.

Model of Herod's palace

Continue on the path around the mountaintop for incredible views from all sides. You are now walking on top of earthen ramparts used by Herod to enlarge the mountain before his death. There are signs to help you identify places you can see in the distance.

Opposite the northern tower you can see parts of Jerusalem, including the Mount of Olives, Ramat Rachel and Har Homa. If you have good eyesight, you can make out Bethlehem, Ma'ale Adumim and Efrat in the distance. From adjacent to the western tower is an excellent view of Tekoa and other nearby Jewish settlements. From the southern tower view the expanse of the Judean Desert and the Dead Sea.

Descend to the enclosure of the palace. Visit the Roman-design bathhouse. Notice also how Herod's large reception hall was converted to a synagogue when it was occupied by Jews during the Great Revolt and Bar Kochba Revolt.

At the foot of the eastern tower are railings leading to the entrance to the tunnel system. The first tunnel you walk through was built during the Great Revolt and allowed Jews to take water from the lower cisterns into the palace without being seen by the Romans. Close to this is a network of tunnels built during the Bar Kochba Revolt for surprise attacks against the Romans.

Upon exiting the tunnels turn left onto the upper path. Herod's tomb can be visited by taking the branch trail to the lower path and then turning right. Go up the stairway. Pass the central stairway that provided access to the amphitheater from the palace and view the model of Herod's tomb. Jewish rebels destroyed his mausoleum and smashed his sarcophagus.

Retrace your steps down the staircase and return to the main building by the lower path.

Nearby Places of Interest:

Sde Bar Farm is close to Herodium. It has a store that sells wine and cheeses manufactured in the farm. There is a restaurant overlooking the Judean Desert that serves hot drinks, salads and cheese plates. The restaurant is open Sunday to Thursday 10 am to 6 pm, and Friday 9 am to 4 pm. It is Kosher Lemehadrin and closed on Shabbat. Their phone number is: (052) 525-5710, email: info@sde-bar.com. There is also a farm and petting zoo that can be visited during the summer, "The Exotic Animal Experience."

33 The Gush Etzion Springs

This popular hike follows a beautiful forest path providing impressive views, visits two or three springs, and explores the ruins of Khirbet Jumjum, a fortified Jewish town from the Second Temple and Talmudic periods.

OVERVIEW

THE LONE OAK IN GUSH ETZION

If the centuries-old oak tree outside Alon Shvut could talk, it would have a lot to tell.

The area known today as Gush Etzion was inhabited by Jews during the Second Temple period and beyond, but until the last century there was no Jewish presence there for over one thousand five hundred years. This began to change in the early twentieth century when two separate attempts were made at resettling the area on land purchased from nearby Arab villages. These fledgling communities were abandoned following the Arab riots of 1929 and 1937.

A third attempt to settle the area was made in 1943 by a group of young pioneers, some of whom were Holocaust survivors. The hills were rocky and barren, the water supply tenuous, the winter weather bitterly cold, and the settlement was isolated. However,

despite the difficulties, the settlers of Kfar Etzion and three other nearby kibbutzim made steady progress and by 1947 there were about four hundred and fifty Jews living in Gush Etzion.

Following the approval of the United Nations Partition Plan on November 29, 1947, the settlers of the Etzion block had some tough decisions to make. The UN decision was widely celebrated by the Jews in Israel because of its historic approval of an independent Jewish state. However, according to the provisions of this plan Gush Etzion was slated to become part of an Arab state. Hostilities broke out a few hours after the vote, and Arab militias began attacking Jewish vehicles on the roads. Travel between Gush Etzion and Jerusalem became extremely dangerous, and supplying the residents and

TIME:
For Hike A about 2.5 to 3 hours, including visiting Khirbet Jumjum. The hike can also be extended for about another hour to visit the spring of Ein Livna (Hike B).

DISTANCES:
Hike A: 6 km
Hike B: 7.5 km

TYPE OF HIKE:
Both hikes are circular

DIFFICULTY:
There is a fairly steep and slightly slippery descent to Ein S'ajman at the beginning of the hike, although this shortcut can be bypassed by continuing along the road. From Khirbet Jumjum there is a moderately steep ascent to Ein Huvela. Otherwise, this is an easy hike. For Hike B, the return incline can be a bit strenuous due to its length.

STARTING POINT:
The parking area at an intersection just before the Gavna catering facility. In front of the parking area are two Keren Kayemet L'Israel pillars and a Gavna sign.

DRIVING DIRECTIONS:
Enter "Gavna, Bat Ayin" into Waze and click on "Gavna Events."

continued

PUBLIC TRANSPORT:
Enter "Kfar Etzion" into Moovit. There are regular buses to Kfar Etzion from outside the Jerusalem Central Bus Station. It is about a fifteen minute walk to the starting point from the entrance of Kfar Etzion. From the roundabout outside Kfar Etzion, take the exit towards Bat Ayin signposted to "Gush Etzion Springs" and "Regional Cemetery." Take the first turn on the right marked "Gush Etzion Springs." Continue along this road until you come to the intersection just before the Gavna catering facility.

SECURITY:
This hike is in Area C, as is the rest of Gush Etzion. However, it is in a Jewish enclave and there are no Arab villages in the immediate vicinity. It is a popular hike with often lots of people around and is usually regarded as being safe.

their defenders with provisions and reinforcements exceedingly difficult.

At this point the settlers could have abandoned their homes and relocated to Jerusalem. However, the decision was made that only the children and mothers would be evacuated while the others would remain to face what would likely be a difficult siege.

After a two day battle on the eve of Israel's declaration of independence, Gush Etzion fell to the Jordanian Legion who were aided by British and Arab irregulars. The defenders of Kfar Etzion surrendered their arms, were told to assemble for a photograph, and were shot. The defenders of the other settlements were taken to Jordan as prisoners of war. In total, one hundred and fifty-one people died defending Gush Etzion, which was then taken over by the Jordanians.

For each of the next nineteen years, the survivors of Gush Etzion would gather together at a site on the mountains outside of Jerusalem from where they could look across the border and just make out the silhouette of the "Lone Oak Tree," a centuries-old oak growing on a hilltop between them and their abandoned homes. This landmark became a symbol of the hope that one day they would return.

Less than two decades later, after Israel's surprising victory in the 1967 Six Day War, they did indeed return. The Jordanians had been warned not to initiate hostilities when war broke out. Nevertheless, the Jordanians attacked and opened another front against Israel. The Israel Defense Force (IDF) had no option but to advance against the Old City, East Jerusalem and the rest of the West Bank.

Israel had no plans to take over Judea and Samaria, but the Jordanian forces retreated and this allowed the IDF to capture these areas with almost no fighting. Following the capture of these historic and strategic areas, there was considerable ambivalence within the Israeli government and among Israelis about what to do with these territories. Nevertheless, a consensus quickly emerged that Gush Etzion would not be relinquished.

With the permission of the government, Kibbutz Kfar Etzion was reestablished several months after the Six Day War. Many of its members were children of fathers killed during the War of Independence. Shortly after this, a town was founded adjacent to the Lone Tree and given the symbolic name Alon Shvut, meaning "Tree of Return."

Today, Gush Etzion is a flourishing suburban area consisting of nineteen small Jewish communities and the large towns of Efrat and Beitar Illit, having a combined population of over eighty thousand residents. There is also a thriving agricultural sector based mainly on fruit trees and vineyards.

THE HIKE

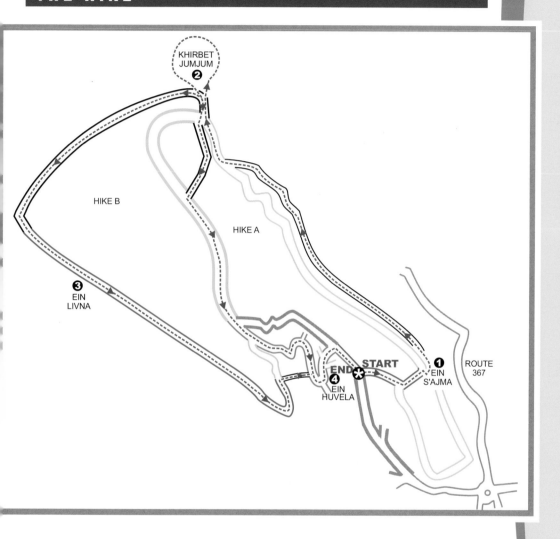

From the parking area, take the blue-marked jeep trail signposted to חורבת גומג'ום עין סג'מה. Soon, on your left, you will see a sign that says "למעין" (To the spring) indicating the path to Ein S'ajma (עין סג'מה) ❶. This footpath is slightly difficult because of its steep incline and slipperiness due to frequent use, but is not dangerous. However, if you wish to bypass this short cut, continue along the jeep trail, turn left at the next intersection, and after about fifteen minutes you will be at the same point as for the short cut.

When the footpath reaches a jeep trail, turn right, and within a few meters, by the end of the railing, are steps leading down to the spring and pool.

This spring is known in Arabic as Ein S'ajma (Arabic for a deer), and is also called "Ein Yitzhak" in memory of Yitzhak Weinstock, a nineteen year old from nearby Alon Shvut who was killed by terrorists in a roadside attack near Ramallah in 1993. The pool is small and 1.8 meters deep. There are a few picnic tables. [A bit further down the hill is a second pool fed from the same spring named "Dubak's Pool" after Yitzhak's father who passed away from an illness in 2007, but this is not part of this hike].

The pool of Ein S'ajma

At the pool turn left onto a footpath marked with a red bicycle symbol painted on a rock. This very beautiful path passes through a pine forest, overlooks the valley below, provides gorgeous views of the distant hills and valleys, as well as a view of the city of Beitar Illit. It runs parallel to a blue-marked jeep trail a bit above it. The trail emerges in front of the ruins of Khirbet Jumjum (חורבת ג'ומג'ום) ❷.

To view the ruins, take the path straight ahead up the hill.

Jumjum was a fortified Jewish town in the Second Temple period up to the Bar Kochba Revolt, and was also inhabited during the Byzantine and Mamluke periods. It is worthwhile going to the top of the hill to view the ruins. Excavations in 2005 and 2008 uncovered ossuaries, burial caves and winepresses. Go to the left when you get to the top to look for a ritual bath (mikvah), a water cistern and remains of an olive press. The view from the top of the hill is spectacular.

After descending from Khirbet Jumjum you have two options:

Hike A (shorter):

Go through the open area in the fence and take an immediate left onto a path that initially parallels the jeep trail on the other side of the fence. Follow this trail on the outside of the vineyard until it meets the blue-marked paved road. Then turn left up the hill.

Towards the top of the hill, the blue-marked trail comes to an intersection. Take the right fork onto the blue-marked jeep trail, and this will lead you to the pool of Ein Huvela ❹.

Unlike the other pools in this area, the main pool of Ein Huvela is enclosed and functions as a mikvah for the male residents of Bat Ayin and other nearby areas. Enter the pool and you will get a wonderful spiritual and physical jolt (the water is very cold). The source of the spring can be reached from the pool by crawling through the narrow tunnel near the mikvah. Across the road from the mikvah is a vendor offering pita and hummus that is open in the afternoon and evening. They do not serve dairy – so forget the latte.

Hike B (longer):

By the base of the hill of Khirbet Jumjum is a bicycle trail on your right (as you are facing away from the ruin) indicated by a red bicycle trail sign. This will take you to the next valley along. Close to the bottom of the valley, it joins with a green-marked jeep trail. Turn left here and you will come to Ein Livna ❸.

Ein Livna is only a small pool, but at 2.5 meters it is quite deep. Take this into consideration before you jump in. There are picnic tables close to the pool.

From Ein Livna continue ascending up the valley. The settlement of Bat Ayin is on your right. This settlement was founded in 1989 and now has a population of over

The ruins of Khirbet Jumjum are on top of the hill

one thousand people. At the top of the hill you will see a footpath that climbs up to Ein Huvela.

From Ein Huvela to your car (continuation of both hikes):

From Ein Huvela, continue up the blue-marked trail to the left of the pool. At the next intersection turn left, and at the intersection after this turn right onto the continuation of the blue-marked trail.

When you come to a paved road turn right. Your car is a short distance past the Gavna events center.

Nearby Places of Interest:

Gush Etzion Heritage Center is in Kibbutz Kfar Etzion and is a memorial to the people who gave their lives protecting the communities of the Etzion Bloc during Israel's War of Independence. A very moving sound and light show is shown in Hebrew or English. This site was declared a National Heritage Project by Israeli Prime Minister Benjamin Netanyahu. It is open Sunday to Thursday in the summer from 9 am–5 pm and in the winter from 9 am–4 pm. It is advisable to call beforehand. Their phone number is: (02) 993-5160 or (02) 993-8308.

Gush Etzion Winery is at the Gush Etzion Junction. Visitors can visit the wine production area and taste the wines in the Visitors Center. Tours are daily by appointment only, Sundays through Thursday from 10 am–5 pm and Fridays 9 am–1 pm. Their phone number is: (02) 930-9220.

Deer Land Park: This has a nature reserve, petting zoo, climbing wall, 360 degree swings, bungee trampoline, paintball, archery, marksmanship, horseriding, 4 x 4 jeep rides, and a 400-meter-long zipline that crosses the valley at a height of 120 meters. It is open in the summer from 9:30 am–5 pm and 9:30 am–1 pm on Fridays. In the winter from 9:30 am–4:30 pm, 9:30 am–12:30 pm on Fridays. Their phone number is: (02) 570-9768.

The Lone Oak Tree is located just outside the town of Alon Shvut. Relax by the tree and listen to the recording.

The Workshop Gush Etzion is at Rosh Tzurim. Design and make Judaica objects with specialized woodworking tools in a 2.5 hour session that is suitable for everyone age 6 and over. Their phone number is: (054) 678-5813.

Oz veGaon Nature Preserve: This was established by members of "Women in Green" as a response to the murder of three youths by terrorists in 2014. The preserve overlooks the Gush Etzion junction and is 300 meters from kibbutz Migdal Oz. There is playground equipment, picnic area, camping area, synagogue and event hall. Tel: (050) 550-0834.

34 Nahal Tekoa

The views of the wadi are absolutely stunning on this wonderful hike along the bank of Nahal Tekoa. The Hariton Cave is also worth exploring. Return to the starting point via the settlement of Tekoa.

TIME: 2.5 hours

DISTANCE: 4.75 km

TYPE OF HIKE:
Circular

DIFFICULTY:
An easy trail along the side of the wadi, but a few areas are slightly difficult. The entrance to Hariton Cave is on a rock ledge, but there are metal supports fixed to the rock to help you climb up. Bring a flashlight and appropriate clothing if you intend crawling in the cave. The final ascent from the bank of the wadi is minimally difficult with some climbing on rocks.

STARTING POINT:
The intersection of the road to the Hariton Cave and Derech Hashalom. The junction is recognizable by white huts on the left, and a sign that points to רפואות חדרים to the right and חוות סוסים straight ahead down the hill.

DRIVING DIRECTION AND PARKING:
Enter "Hariton Cave" into Waze. This will direct you to a parking lot by the start of the footpath along the side of the wadi. However, this approach road, although paved, has a

continued

lot of potholes and it is better to park on the side of of Derech Hashalom just before the approach road becomes difficult to drive on (see map on page 252).

(see map on page 252).

PUBLIC TRANSPORT:
There are buses from Jerusalem. Enter "האישה החכמה" into Moovit. This bus stop is about a five minute walk from the start of the hike.

SECURITY:
The Jewish settlements in this area are in an island surrounded by Arab villages. However, Route 398 to Tekoa is usually regarded as being safe. Bedouin are forbidden to graze in the wadi. Nevertheless, it may be advisable not to go alone unless there are people around. For concerns before or during the hike call: (02) 626-9797.

AMOS-COUNTRY

Sometime between 760 and 750 BCE, God called upon the prophet Amos to leave his home town of Tekoa in the southern kingdom of Judah to prophesy about the social injustices and eventual destruction of the northern kingdom of Israel. He therefore moved to Bethel, then the capital of the northern kingdom and the royal residence of Jereboam II. However, he was denounced by the head priest to the king Jereboam II and forced to leave Bethel. His book was written when he returned to Tekoa. In this book, he emphasizes that he is not a professional prophet, but that he received a calling. This is also the pattern for prophets such as Hosea, Isaiah, Jeremiah and Ezekiel. Amos was an older contemporary of Hosea and Isaiah.

The site of the biblical Tekoa is Tel Takua, which is about 2 km east of modern-day Tekoa. This Tel also contains ruins from Roman, Byzantine, Crusader and Mamluke times. The present-day settlement of Tekoa began as a military-sponsored Nahal outpost in 1975 and changed to a civilian settlement in 1977. Adjacent to Tekoa is the Arab village of Tuqu, which was established in 1948 by Bedouin tribesmen.

At the time of Amos' prophesying, both the northern and southern kingdoms had become prosperous because of the non-interference of the great powers of Assyria and Egypt. However, this wealth was not spread evenly and the poor were being oppressed: "*Therefore, because you have trodden on the poor and the burden of grain you take from him, houses of hewn stone you have built but you shall not dwell therein... For I know that your transgressions are many and your sins are mighty; you who oppress the just, taking ransom and turning aside the needy in the gate*" (Amos 5:11-12).

The writing of Amos seems to downplay the role of ritual and the sacrificial cult: "*I hate, I despise your festivals, and I will not smell the sacrifices of your assemblies. Even though you offer up to Me your burnt offerings and your meal offerings, I will not accept them and the peace offerings of your fattened cattle I will not regard... but let justice well up as waters and righteousness as a mighty stream*" (Amos 5:21-24).

Nevertheless, reading into the words of Amos the ideas of a religious reformer is probably inappropriate, and he was as much bound to the Mosaic Law as the other prophets. Rather, he was probably pointing out how the rich were covering up the social injustices rampant in their society with false piety. He may also have been emphasizing the people's duplicity in their straying after foreign gods: "*For they rejected God's Torah, and they did not keep His statues and their lies misled them, which their forefathers followed*" (Amos 2:4).

Amos was a sheep herder and not surprisingly, he spoke and wrote in terms he was familiar with from his daily work at the edge of the wilderness. He wrote: "The pastures of the shepherds will wither and the best of the fertile feeds will dry up." (Amos 1:2). And "*Just as a shepherd can rescue from the mouth of a lion but two legs or the cartilage of an ear, so will the children of Israel dwelling in Samaria be saved in the corner of a bed or in the corner of a couch*" (i.e., very few

will be saved) (Amos 3:12). He also used analogies from the agriculture work he saw around him: "*Behold, I will oppress your dwelling place as a wagon full of sheaves is oppressed*" (i.e., from its weight) (Amos 2:13).

At the conclusion of his book he envisions a new reality with Israel's redemption: "*Behold days are coming, says the Lord, that the plowman shall meet the reaper and the treader of the grapes the one who carries the seed, and the mountains shall drip sweet wine and all the hills shall melt. And I will return the captivity of My people Israel; and they will rebuild desolate cities and settle them: they will plant vineyards and drink their wine; they will cultivate gardens and eat their fruits*" (Amos 9:13-15).

If Amos were to show up today and take a walk from biblical Tekoa to the settlement of Tekoa, he would not be surprised at what he sees!

WHO WAS HARITON?

Chariton, or Hariton the Confessor as he is known, was an important figure in the monastic movement and his name comes up a lot during this hike.

He was born in Asia Minor at the end of the 3rd century CE. We know quite a bit about him because a monk in the 6th century wrote an anonymous book about his life. Hariton was persecuted because of his Christian beliefs and tortured, but was later released from prison. He subsequently went on a pilgrimage to Jerusalem in 275 CE, but was abducted by bandits. He managed to escape from them and decided to remain as a hermit in the cave in which he was captured in

the upper part of Wadi Qelt. He founded what is called a "laura." This consisted of a group of cells or caves where the monks would spend time in solitude, a church, and perhaps a central dining room for times when the monks would eat together. His monastery in Nahal Tekoa is the third he established. His monasteries became extremely popular and people flocked to them. Hariton was later made a saint.

The Judean Desert was a convenient location for these types of monasteries, since, although in remote locations, they were still close to civilization. Other monasteries subsequently established in the

Judean Desert include the monastery of Saint Euthymius (377-473 CE) in the Mishor Adumim section of Ma'ale Adumim, the laura of Saint Sabba the Sanctified in the Kidron Valley (died in 532 CE), and that of Saint Gerasimus in the Jordan Valley in the 5th century. In the 4th century, in particular, monasteries also became popular in the deserts of Egypt and Syria, as Christian ascetics rejected the worldly values of society and attempted to recreate the simple values of the early Christians. The word "hermit" comes from the Greek word for wilderness.

THE HIKE

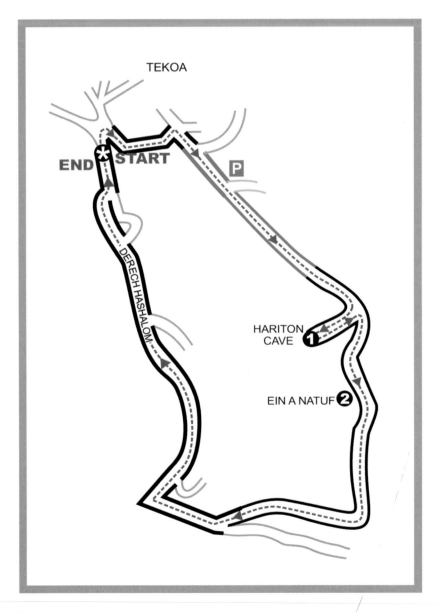

From its junction with Derech Hashalom, walk down the paved path towards the horse farm. This road soon becomes a paved blue-marked trail that ends at a parking lot by a large empty pool. This may have been the main water supply of the Hariton Monastery. The footpath, which is black-marked, begins from here.

Eventually, you will come to a junction. Straight ahead leads to the Hariton Cave ❶. If you wish to explore the caves there are metal supports on the rock to help you climb up to the ledge.

Hariton Cave is the largest known karst limestone cave in Israel. The entire system has been mapped. You can easily enter the first chamber, although to go further requires some crawling. Despite its name, these caves were not part of the Hariton Monastery; they used a cave further along the wadi. However, it was used by Jews during the Bar Kochba Revolt. Its three to four km length and fifty-five "rooms" made it an ideal hideout from the Romans.

Return to the junction and descend on the black-marked trail. The buildings you see on the other side of the wadi are those of the Jewish settlement of Nokdim.

You will soon come to two small pools called Mayan A Natuf ❷. They fill up from drips of water from the cliff above. These pools were also a water source for the Hariton Monastery. There is a water cistern below the pools, but it has been closed since a member of the settlements died here.

A short distance after this can be seen caves in the rock cliff used by the Hariton Monastery.

The black-marked footpath eventually ascends to the main road. There is parking area here and a picnic bench. At the paved road, which is also black-marked, turn right. You will now be walking through the settlement of Tekoa.

At the top of the hill, turn left at the intersection and continue straight ahead to your car.

These pools, Mayan A Natuf, are formed from water dripping from the rocks above

Nearby Places of Interest:

Sde Bar: See page 241.

Herodium: See chapter 32 on page 235.

THE
JUDEAN
DESERT
AND
JORDAN
VALLEY

THE JUDEAN DESERT

The most popular sites for visitors to the Judean Desert are oases, and it is very easy to imagine that this desert is full of springs and streams. But the very opposite is the case. There are only a few springs in the Judean Desert, and it is their rarity (and also their beauty) that make them popular tourist sites.

This area is a desert because it is in a rain shadow. The prevailing winds lose their moisture on the windward side of the central mountain range. Air rises over the mountains, it cools, and water condenses from the clouds that are formed. As the wind descends on the other side of the mountain range, the air warms and dries out, and there is a paucity of rain.

Unlike the Judean Mountains to the west of the central mountain range that consist of limestone, the slopes of the Judean Desert are composed predominantly of chalk. Both are sedimentary rocks formed when this area was a vast ocean, but they have different properties. Chalk is a soft rock and is relatively impermeable to water. Because of this, there are no shallow aquifers. Moreover, because rainwater remains on the surface and the slopes are steep, rainfall can lead to sudden flash floods as the water speeds down the erosion-formed steep canyons towards the Dead Sea. Therefore never, never go hiking in the Judean Desert if there is a likelihood of rain. If you are in a park, the wardens will close it, but if you are not in a park the responsibility is on you.

Despite being a desert, the Judean Desert is not devoid of vegetation. Close to the watershed line, towards the top of the mountain range, there is sufficient rain to support agriculture. Further towards the desert, there is often enough grass on the hillsides and wadis to support shepherding.

Throughout history the Judean Desert has been a convenient place to escape to, whether it was from enemies or from civilization. It was convenient because it was not that far from the country's major centers. For David escaping from King Saul, Ein Gedi was an excellent place to hide with his fighters. A monk in the Byzantine period could communicate with God in a cave close to a desert monastery, but it was nevertheless a relatively short journey for a meeting with the bishop in Jerusalem or to stock up on provisions. This is why a number of well-known monasteries were established here during the Byzantine period. If you were a sect anticipating the soon arrival of the End of Days, you could disconnect from civilization and live in Qumran, but still be close to population centers where you could sell your manuscripts and catch up on news. If you were Herod, you could prepare an impregnable stronghold in Massada in case the going got tough, but still live in luxurious palaces in Jerusalem and Herodium. And if you were zealots and survivors from the Great Revolt against Rome, you could hope to hide away from the Romans in that very same fortress. Unfortunately for them, that plan didn't work out.

See page 5 for a map of the location of hikes in the Judean Desert.

35 Ein Prat Nature Reserve

Hike among luscious foliage by a stream in the Judean Desert that flows even in the middle of the summer. Picnic in a Eucalyptus grove by a beautiful spring while your kids play in the water. Swim in the Palm Pool. All this and more you will find in the gorgeous Ein Prat Nature Reserve just a short distance from Jerusalem.

NAHAL PRAT, ANATOT AND JEREMIAH

Nahal Prat is a wadi that descends a distance of 28 km from close to Jerusalem to Jericho and then to the Jordan River. Ein Prat is one of three springs within this wadi. Ein Prat is the closest of these springs to Jerusalem and is

TIME:
Allow about 2-3 hours to explore, swim and relax

THE NATURE RESERVE:
The Park is open from 8 am—5 pm during the summer and until 4 pm from October to March all days of the week except Friday and holiday eves when it closes one hour earlier. There is an admission charge. Adjacent to the lower parking lot is a station for information, hot and cold drinks and snacks, a WC, and faucet with drinking water.

DRIVING DIRECTIONS AND PARKING:
Enter "Ein Prat" into Waze and click on "Ein Prat Nature Reserve." Initially, you will enter the settlement of Almon (also known as Anatot). Follow the signs and descend to Ein Prat. Park in the lower parking lot by the ranger station. If it is full, you will have to park in the upper parking lot and walk down to the stream.

SECURITY:
Ein Prat is in area C outside the Green Line. You will be passing Arab villages to get there, but the roads are well traveled and there should be no concerns. The Nature Reserve has park rangers and is quite safe.

below the settlement of Almon. Ein Mabu'a is further along the wadi close to Alon, which is on the Allon Road; and the third spring is Ein Qelt below Mitzpe Yericho. All these springs can be visited.

Water flows constantly from these springs. Until 1970 Ein Prat was used for supplying water to parts of Jerusalem. The present-day park offices, store and WC's were built in 1927 and were formerly the pumping station and purification center. Water from Ein Mabu'a was added a few years later to this water supply. The eucalyptus trees in the park are not indigenous but were planted by the British to provide shade for the workers in the pumping station. The water in the shallow stream is great for kids to play in and these eucalyptus trees now provide shade for family picnicking.

Nahal Prat was formerly the border between the tribe of Benjamin to its north and the territory of Judah to its south. The Arab village of Anata, which is on the other side of Route 437 from the settlement of Almon is probably the site of the Levitical village of Anatot, which was in the territory of Benjamin. The prophet and priest Jeremiah lived in this town towards the end of the kingdom of Judah, and he was witness to the destruction of Jerusalem in 586 BCE by the Babylonians. Jeremiah had clearly seen the moral disintegration of nearby Jerusalem, its attraction to idol worship, and its likely destruction by Babylon, the great power of the day. He tried unsuccessfully to turn the people from their ways.

Jeremiah was very familiar with nearby Nahal Prat. In the book of Jeremiah, he describes God commanding him to place a garment in the spring of Ein Prat, and when it became rotten and of no use, he compared this to Jerusalem and its fate (Jeremiah 13:6-7). Nevertheless, his prophecies were not all gloom and doom. Imprisoned at the very time that Jerusalem was being besieged by the Babylonians, the word of God came to him to buy his uncle's field in Anatot, since he was the closest relative to redeem it. Logically, this was a ridiculous thing to do. Nevertheless, the purchase was made in front of the prisoners in the prison yard and the deed was placed in an earthen vessel. "*For so says the Lord of hosts, the God of Israel: Houses and fields and vineyards shall be purchased again in this land*" (Jeremiah 32:15).

Consider the following activities and hikes in the Nature Reserve:

1. Picnicking in the eucalyptus grove and playing in the stream

Cross over the stream using the stones or the wooden bridge. On the other side are numerous picnic benches under shade. The kids will enjoy playing in the shallow flowing water. Cross over the stream using the stones or the wooden bridge. On the other side are numerous picnic benches under shade. The kids will enjoy playing in the shallow flowing water. Having appropriate shoes for walking on the stones can be helpful.

2. Swimming in the Palm Pool

The best place for swimming is in the Palm Pool, which is a short distance from the parking lot on the other side of the stream. The water is at a constant temperature of 20 degrees C whatever the season. It is quite deep at 2.5 meters. There are steps to go down. A lifeguard is always present, even in the winter. The pool was built by the British to hold the water from a small spring that emerges here.

3. A short circular walk to the Faran/ Hariton Monastery

This easy thirty minute circular walk climbs up to the monastery.

The path starts behind the information office. Follow the blue trail until you come to a fork by the ruins of a flourmill. Take the left fork marked to Faran Monastery (Haritoun) up the hill. This will take you to just outside the monastery. You are advised not to enter the cave you pass because of the danger of becoming infected with tick-borne relapsing fever (TBRF).

Return by the blue-marked trail, and this will bring you close to the source of the Ein Prat spring.

Turn right onto the blue trail, and walk past some beautiful pools back to the ranger's office.

The Faran or Hariton monastery was started by the monk Hariton at the end of the 4th century CE. This was the first monastery to be built in the Judean Desert. Hariton would subsequently establish two other monasteries in the Judean Desert. The monks lived in seclusion for most of the week, but gathered together on Saturday and Sunday for prayer. This monastery was destroyed during the Persian invasion of 614 CE. The Greek Orthodox Church rebuilt a church over the Byzantine ruins. The monastery was abandoned in the 1980's, but monks reestablished it in the 1990's, and the monastery is again in use. A visit can be arranged by calling (02) 539-9074.

4. A circular hike to Tel Fara and the Waterfall Pool

This sixty minute, about 2 km circular walk visits Tel Fara and the Waterfall Pool. There is swimming along this route in the Palm Pool and also in the Waterfall Pool, so you may want to leave additional time for this. You will need to cross the shallow stream, stepping on rocks. This is not difficult to do, although a walking stick can be helpful to keep your balance.

From the parking area, cross over the stream either on the rocks or on the wooden bridge slightly further along. After passing through the eucalyptus grove, turn right onto the black-marked trail. You will soon come to the Palm Pool.

Shortly after the pool you will come to a fork. Take the left fork onto the black-marked trail. It is indicated by a sign "לתל פארה" (To Tel Fara). This easy path takes you around the side and then back of the Tel to its top. At the top of the Tel continue following the black markings. There are great views ahead of you.

Tel Fara was the site of a settlement in the Late Bronze and Iron Age periods, which is also the time of the Israelite settlement. The city located here has not been definitely identified, although it may have been the Benjamite city of Para mentioned in the book of Joshua (18:23). There is not a lot to see on top of the Tel other than rocks, but there are impressive views of the nahal and nearby settlements of Kfar Adumim and Mitzpe Yericho.

The quickest way down from the Tel is to continue on the black-marked trail as a circular walk. This route is minimally difficult at its lower section and you will need to climb on rocks, but is not at all dangerous. Alternatively, you can return by the

route you came up on, which is easier but a bit longer. Once you reach the path by the stream turn left and continue on the black-marked trail. The path soon leads through reeds to the stream, which you will cross over on stones.

Once you have crossed the stream, turn left and you will immediately see the Waterfall Pool. This is a beautiful pool and reasonably deep – halfway up to an adult male's chest – but not big enough to do much in the way of swimming. There is not a lot of shared room for you and the fish, and you may feel fish touching you. Be careful when you come out of the pool as the wet rock can be slippery.

Return to the lower parking lot on the red-marked path on the same side of the stream.

5. An incredible hike from the entrance of Almon to Ein Prat

For the more adventurous, this hike is highly recommended – but you will need a second car. The trail descends from close to the entrance to the settlement of Almon along the bank of the wadi to Ein Prat. The footpath is just minimally difficult with easy rock climbing and takes about two hours. Drive both your cars down to Ein Prat. One car is left in the parking lot by the nahal to bring you back, and the other returns and parks just outside the entrance to the settlement. It will take you about thirty minutes to get the cars in place.

The footpath, which is to the left of the entrance to Almon as your face the settlement, is not indicated from the main road. It begins very close to the security fence of the settlement at the far corner of the adjacent field. Enter the field close to the security fence and after about five minutes of walking the security fence turns inwards. Ahead of you is a green marker on a stone. Continue down the side of the wadi following the green markers.

Close to Ein Prat you will come to a T-junction with a green-marked trail. Turn left down the hill and this will lead you past the Hariton Monastery. From there continue on the blue trail to the spring. An easy path from here takes you to the parking lot and your second car:

6. Hiking to Ein Mabu'a

It is possible to walk from the Waterfall Pool to the next spring along, Ein Mabu'a. This three hour or so hike is for experienced hikers only. You will need to have a car waiting for you at Ein Mabu'a to take you back. Arranging the cars for this can take some time. You should coordinate your walk with the office at Ein Prat.

Nearby Places of Interest:

The Tel of Almon/Almit: *Just after turning from Route 437 to Almon, on the left side of the road, is a hill with the ruins of the Iron Age Levitical village of Almon. It is mentioned in the book of Joshua:* "And from the tribe of Benjamin.... Anatot and its open land and Almon and its open land... all the cities of the sons of Aaron the priests" *(Joshua 21:17-18). Park on the side of the road and walk up. There is not much to see at the top except ruins of water cisterns and wine presses, but you are treading on ancient Jewish history. The views are impressive.*

Eretz Bereshit (Genesis Land): *Experience life as it was in Biblical times. Visitors are greeted by Eliezer, Abraham's manservant, and by a train of camels, and are then led to Abraham's tent where they experience his legendary hospitality. Fresh pita making and shepherding are among the different workshops offered. There are kosher meals and other activities. There is an admission charge. Directions: Turn off Route 1 onto Route 458. The turning to Eretz Bereshit is on your right shortly before the settlement of Alon. Their phone number is: (02) 997-4477.*

Ptil Tekhelet: *is at the entrance to Kfar Adumim and offers factory tours in English and Hebrew on how the dye extracted from a sea snail is being used again to provide the blue color to the fringes worn by many Jews at the corners of their prayer shawl or garments. Tours need to be booked in advance by calling (02) 590-0577. There is an admission charge.*

Canaan Tours at the Dead Sea: is located by the Sonol Station just outside Kfar Adumim and offers a variety of attractions in the Judean Desert – jeep rides, ATV rides, rappelling, camel, horseback and donkey rides, and navigation activities. All attractions and activities are suitable for children. One, two or four-hour trails can be arranged. Advanced booking is required. Open Sunday– Thursday: 9 am–5 pm, Friday 8 am–2 pm. Their phone number is: (02) 535-5351.

Lookout by Mitzpe Yericho: The Dead Sea Balcony Lookout in Mitzpe Yericho offers spectacular views over the Judean Desert, the city of Jericho, the Arava, and the tip of the Dead Sea. On a clear day you can see the hills of Moab. Take the turn to Mitzpe Yericho, and the next turn on the right to the entrance to the settlement. Continue straight until you come to a T-junction. Follow the signs to the Dead Sea Balcony Lookout. This takes you on a somewhat long and windy road, but you will eventually reach the top of the hill and the observation point. Park in the parking area. Head to the open building facing Jericho. You can listen to a recording in Hebrew or English describing the biblical significance of Jericho. There is also a sign identifying the places that you can see, including the settlements of Vered Yericho and Kibbutz Almog. Walk around the hill for more views of the desert. There is no entrance fee.

Museum of the Good Samaritan: This museum is in a 19th century Turkish building and contains an impressive collection of mosaics from Jewish, Samaritan and Christian synagogues and churches from Judea, Samaria and Gaza. It is close to the traditional site of the Inn of the Good Samaritan mentioned in the New Testament. It is probably also the site of the Biblical Ma'ale Adumim, which was on the border between the tribes of Judah and Benjamin. It is open Sunday to Thursday 9 am–3 pm, Friday and holiday eves 8 am–4 pm. There is an admission charge. Their phone number is: (02) 633-8230. Directions: Turn off Route 1 to the right shortly after the entrance to Kfar Adumim and follow the road sign.

36 Ein Mabu'a

Ein Mabu'a is a stunningly beautiful oasis in Nahal Prat only a short distance from Jerusalem. There is a pool for swimming, and you can hike along the path adjacent to the stream or wade in its shallow water even in the middle of summer. There is no admission charge.

TIME:
Allow several hours for swimming and hiking

DISTANCE:
About 3.5 km

TYPE OF HIKE:
There and back the same way

DIFFICULTY: The dirt footpath is easy walking. You will need to cross the shallow stream on two occasions, and a walking stick can be helpful to maintain your balance on the rocks.

STARTING POINT:
The parking lot at Ein Mabu'a.

DRIVING DIRECTIONS AND PARKING:
Enter "Ein Mabu'a" into Waze. The parking lot is at the bottom of the wadi.

PUBLIC TRANSPORT:
There is no convenient public transport to Ein Mabu'a.

SECURITY: Although the three springs in Nachal Prat are in area C beyond the Green Line, Ein Mabu'a is regarded as being quite safe. It has park rangers and there are usually plenty of people around.

264

SWIMMING AND HIKING

Descend from the parking lot and go past the store to the pool of Ein Mabu'a. The pool is not that big and you may have to share it with a lot of people, particularly in the middle of the summer, but it's fantastic for a swim on a hot day. WC's close to the pool can be used for changing.

Do not be surprised if the pool suddenly empties on you, especially in the summer. It's not a park ranger playing a joke. The pool is fed by an underground basin that empties into the pool by a siphon effect. Once the basin is emptied, it needs to refill before more water can be released. This is fairly rapid in the winter, but can take longer in the summer. In the meantime, water in the pool discharges into the stream and the pool empties. You will pass other pools as you walk along the stream, although they are not as large and deep as this one.

The hiking trail is alongside the stream and you will need to cross this on several occasions on conveniently placed rocks. A walking stick can be helpful to keep your balance. If you prefer, you can walk part of the trail in the water instead of hiking, so bring the right footwear if you intend doing this.

Return to your car the way you came.

It is possible to hike from Ein Mabu'a to Wadi Kelt along the wadi, although you need to be an experienced hiker. It takes about five hours and you will need to have a second car waiting for you at Mitzpe Yericho. Do not go alone and tell the park ranger where you are going.

> *Nearby Places of Interest:*
> **Eretz Bereshit (Genesis Land)** – *see page 261.*

37 Nahal Og

I f climbing up a high vertical cliff on metal rungs will send you into a panic attack – this hike is not for you. But otherwise, this circular hike through Nahal Og with steep cliffs on either side and returning on a path with impressive views over the Judean Desert and Dead Sea is quite spectacular. Understandably, it is a popular hike with Israelis, including for children.

TIME:
About 1.5 to 2 hours.

DISTANCE:
Just over 2.5 Km

TYPE OF HIKE:
Circular

DIFFICULTY:
There are 5 climbs up the cliff face on metal rungs. The cliff is fairly high for two of them, but the climb is short for the other three. Since most people prefer climbing up rungs rather than climbing down them, this circular hike is arranged accordingly. Apart from this, hiking along the wadi bed and the jeep trails on top of the cliffs is very easy, with just a few areas of climbing over large boulders.

STARTING POINT:
The parking lot a bit beyond the entrance to Kibbutz Almog. By the parking lot are two picnic tables, although without shade. At the other side of the parking lot is a shaded observation structure with a long stone bench.

DRIVING DIRECTIONS:
Enter "Almog Kibbutz" into Waze. The turn-off to the kibbutz is just before the Sonol

continued

gas station at Almog Junction and is signposted. Continue past the entrance to the kibbutz to the parking lot.

PUBLIC TRANSPORT: Buses from the Jerusalem Central Bus station stop at the Almog Junction. Enter "Almog Gas Station" into Moovit. From here it's a 1.6 Km walk to the start of the hike, passing the entrance to Kibbutz Almog.

SECURITY: This area is beyond the Green Line in area C. Nevertheless, there are no close Arab villages and the area can be regarded as being safe.

THE DEAD SEA – DEAD AND STILL DYING

The Dead Sea is located at the lowest point on earth. It is the deepest hypersaline lake in the world. It is six times saltier than the ocean – and it is in deep trouble.

The Dead Sea is part of the Jordan Rift Valley, which in turn is part of the Syria-African Rift that extends through the eastern part of Africa and into Turkey. The Jordan Rift Valley includes the Hula Valley, the Sea of Galilee, the Jordan Valley, the Dead Sea and the Arava. This valley resulted from the moving apart of two tectonic plates – the African Plate and the Arabian Plate – leading to a thinning of the earth's crust.

The sources of water for the Dead Sea have been the Jordan River, rivers on the eastern side of the lake, and subterranean springs that enter into and around the lake. However, most river water is now siphoned off for agriculture. Industrial potash production from the Dead Sea Works also leads to water evaporation. As a result of this and normal water evaporation from the high ambient temperature, the level of the Dead Sea has been receding at a rate of about 1.5 meters a year. This is equivalent to six hundred Olympic pools of water being emptied every day. As a result of this, the peninsula that formerly ended in the middle of the lake has become a land bridge. The ground water level has also dropped and this is flushing out brine near the shoreline leading to sinkholes. In fact, it is dangerous to get too close to the Dead Sea in many parts of the Israeli side of the lake. Sink holes are not a problem on the Jordanian side because the cliffs descend steeply into the lake.

There are currently no viable plans to save the Dead Sea. Bringing in water from the Mediterranean would change the nature of the lake. Gypsum (calcium sulfate) would be deposited and this could turn the Dead Sea white. There is currently a plan budgeted by the World Bank and signed onto by Israel, Jordan and the Palestine Authority to feed in hypersaline water. Water will be brought by channels from the Red Sea to a power station in Jordan and some of the water will be desalinated. The power and de-salinated water will be shared among the parties and the hypersaline water from the desalination plant will be fed into the Dead Sea. However, as one article stated: "*The Dead Sea will next decade be swallowing waters it never tasted and thus launch a new chapter in its history.*" Nevertheless, the amount of water from the desalination plant will not be that great and this will not solve the Dead Sea's problems.

Despite all this, there is no reason not to benefit from this unique and remarkable area. Sunlight at the Dead Sea has weaker ultraviolet radiation than at sea level and the atmospheric pressure is slightly higher. The atmosphere also has a slightly higher oxygen content and less allergens. These factors probably account for the health benefits claimed for visiting the Dead Sea area, including healing of psoriasis lesions.

THE HIKE

From the far end of the parking lot, take the trail towards the wadi. You will shortly come to a signpost. Take the green-marked trail to "Lower Wadi Og".

After just under an hour of hiking along the wadi, you will come to another signpost. Follow the black-marked jeep trail to "Almog Junction".

After 15 minutes or so you will come to another fork. Take the right branch, which is a blue-marked foot-path signposted to "Kibbutz Almog". From this trail are great views of Nahal Og, the hills of the Judean desert, and the Dead Sea. This path will take you back to the parking lot.

38 Qumran

An Essene sect lived in Qumran over two thousand years ago, and much has been discovered about how they led their lives here and what they believed. After viewing the movie and ruins, consider taking a short hike into the mountains above Qumran for a wonderful view of the Dead Sea and surrounding area. Round off the day with a visit to the beautiful oasis of Enot Tsukim, only an eight minute drive away, for a swim, picnic and short nature walk (see the next chapter 39 on page 273).

TIME:
About an hour for viewing the movie and viewing the ruins. The hike is an additional hour there and back

DISTANCE:
Just under 1 km for the ruins and 2 km for the hike

DIFFICULTY:
Easy walking around the ruins. The walk into the mountains is just minimally difficult.

STARTING POINT:
The parking lot at Qumran.

DRIVING DIRECTIONS:
Enter "Qumran" into Waze.

PUBLIC TRANSPORTATION:
Enter "Qumran" into Moovit and click on "Khirbat Kumran." Bus 487 leaves frequently from the Jerusalem Central Bus Station and stops at the junction for Kibbutz Qalya and Qumran. It is about a seven minute walk from the bus stop to the entrance to Qumran.

ADMISSION DETAILS:
Summer: Sunday–Thursday and Saturday 8 am–5 pm, Friday and holiday eves 8 am–4 pm.

continued

View of Qumran, the Dead Sea, and the Mountains of Moab from the mountains above Qumran

OVERVIEW

THE SECTARIANS OF QUMRAN AND THEIR PREPARATIONS FOR THE WORLD TO COME

In 1947, two Bedouin shepherds found a small collection of ancient scrolls in a cave in the Judean desert. This led to the discovery of fragments of over nine hundred scrolls written by Jews at the end of the Second Temple period. Among these scrolls were the oldest extant copies of parts of the Hebrew Bible, as well as literature describing the beliefs and practices of an unusual Jewish sect. The discovery of the "Dead Sea Scrolls" that were placed in the caves around Qumran for safekeeping, or possibly to hide them from the Romans, has been one of the most important discoveries in modern Biblical research. About five decades after the scrolls were discovered, the home of the sectarians who authored them was excavated in nearby Qumran.

According to the Jewish historian Josephus, there were three main groups of Jews at the end of the Second Temple period – Pharisees, Sadducees and Essenes. The Pharisees were Sages whose ideas and rulings were based on the Jewish Oral Tradition. These were recorded in the Mishnah and Talmud and form the basis of Rabbinic Judaism. The Sadducees did not accept the Jewish Oral Tradition and based their practices on their understanding of the written Bible. They also rejected key doctrines accepted by the Pharisees, such as the concepts of an afterlife, messianic redemption, and resurrection of the dead. The Sadducees were very influential politically and for a time controlled the high Priesthood in the Temple.

The Essenes were an ascetic sect that lived in Jerusalem and other cities, numbering about four thousand people. Most researchers believe that a group of Essene priests, who were probably an extreme group, came to Qumran in the late Hellenistic-Roman period. The Roman historian Pliny the Elder writes, *"On the west side of the Dead Sea, but out of range of noxious exhalations of the coast, is the solitary tribe of the Essenes..."* He goes on to describe a group of celibate men living together, focusing on their interpretation of spirituality, renouncing material comforts, and pooling their resources as an economic collective.

What motivated these people to leave Jerusalem and live in the desert?

This was a time of heightened Messianic expectations among the Jewish people, and this Qumran sect believed that a final apocalyptic battle between the forces of light and darkness was imminent and that this would usher in the perfection of the Messianic era. They viewed the priesthood in Jerusalem as corrupt and they broke away to lead a pure and ascetic existence in preparation for the End of Days.

Based on what we know from the descriptions in their scrolls, they ate their meals together in a communal dining hall in total silence. The ruins of this room can be seen at this site. Meals were preceded by ritual immersion, just as food from the Temple was eaten by priests in a state of ritual purity. This would explain the large number of ritual baths found at Qumran. They also donned special white clothing for their meals, and this may have been regarded as a substitute for the sacrificial service in the Temple. They spent much of their time in prayer and studying Jewish texts, and supported themselves with scribal work and agriculture. The

Essene calendar for the Jewish festivals was different from that of the Pharisees and Sadducees, in that it was based solely on the solar calendar and not the solar-adjusted lunar calendar used by other Jews.

Qumran was first settled at the time of the Hasmonean kings John Hyrcanus or Alexander Jannaeus, towards the end of the second century BCE. The site was abandoned during the time of Herod following an earthquake, but was resettled after about a quarter of a century. It remained in use until it was destroyed by the Romans during the Great Revolt of 68 CE.

In general, Judaism does not value asceticism, and the ideas of the Esssenes had little influence on mainstream Judaism. Jesus was not an Essene, but Christianity may well have been influenced by the asceticism and messianic ideas of this sect. The movie shown here suggests that John the Baptist visited Qumran, and some believe he spent as long as two years here. John the Baptist baptized Jesus, and according to the Christian gospels, this was when Jesus was proclaimed as the Messiah.

TOURING THE SITE

First view the short movie with its impressive photography to appreciate the lifestyle of the people who lived in Qumran. You can request that the movie be shown in English.

The exit from the movie theatre leads directly to a small museum that depicts different aspects of the beliefs of this Qumran sect and their daily routine.

After leaving the museum, proceed to the covered octagonal structure and from here you can ascend the wooden stairs or go on the pathway with rails for a self-directed tour. There are informative signs along the way. Look also at the views. To the east are spectacular views of the Dead Sea and the mountains of Moab beyond this. To the west are the mountains and wadis of the Judean Desert.

A HIKE INTO THE MOUNTAINS

A fun thing to do is to hike to one of the caves above the settlement, and from this elevation there are even more spectacular views. There is no chance of finding scrolls here, but your kids may enjoy a make-believe search for them!

Head out towards the hills of the Judean Desert, but instead of continuing straight on the green trail, cross the aqueduct by a small bridge shortly after leaving Qumran. The path is unmarked except for two white arrows.

You will eventually come to a large open cave(see picture above). If you want to explore it you will need to climb to its entrance, and this is slightly difficult. Much easier is to keep on walking up the rocky path and within a few minutes you will come to another smaller cave.

Continue ascending for a few more minutes and you will reach a plateau from which you can view the surrounding area.

Return the way you came.

39 Enot Tsukim/ Ein Feshkha for Swimming and Nature Stroll

Enot Tsukim/Ein Feshkha is the lowest Nature Reserve in the world and a beautiful place for swimming, picnicking and a nature stroll. The mountains of the Judean Desert provide a spectacular backdrop to your activities. The Palm Pool for adult swimming is only open on certain days, and not at all during the winter, but the kid's wading pools are open all year long.

DRIVING DIRECTIONS:
Enter "Ein Feshkha" into Waze and click on "עינות צוקים עין פשח׳ה." It is about an eight minute drive from Qumran.

PUBLIC TRANSPORT:
The nature reserve is serviced by the reasonably frequent bus 486 from the Jerusalem Central Bus Station. This bus can also be used for the short journey between Qumran and Enot Tsukim from the Kibbutz Kalia Junction.

TICKET
ADMIT ONE

ADMISSION DETAILS:
The Park is open in the summer April through to September from 8 am—5 pm, and in October through March 8 am—4 pm. On Friday and holiday eves closing is 1 hour earlier. The site is open on Saturday. There is an admission charge. A combined ticket for Qumran and Enot Tsukim can also be purchased. More details about the park are available on their website.

SECURITY:
This area is outside the Green Line and in area C. The roads to and by the Dead Sea are well traveled and safe. The pools are popular for Israelis and Palestinians, and there is peaceful but separate co-existence between them.

SWIMMING:
Enot Tsukim has a number of fresh water pools. The first two
continued

pools will be adequate for most families, so park in the first parking lot. The shallow Reed Pool is close by and is great for kids. If you prefer less crowding, then go to the second parking lot. All these pools have concrete bottoms and no footwear is needed. The Palm Pool is good for adult swimming and has a deep and shallower section. There is also a chair device for lowering the disabled into the water.

NOTE THE TIMES WHEN THE PALM POOL IS OPEN:

It is open all week during July and August, except for Wednesdays when it closed for cleaning. During the rest of the summer it is open on Friday and Saturday only. It is closed during the winter. This is the only pool for adult swimming. All the pools have plenty of picnic benches with shade. WC's close to the pools can be used for changing. A kiosk sells cold drinks and is open during popular times.

WALKING:

Do take a nature walk on the paths. A brochure with a map is available in English at the park entrance. The paths and pools are clearly marked. The route is about 2 km and takes about forty-five minutes to complete. There are also free tours of the Hidden Reserve in Hebrew from June to September on Fridays (10 am and noon) and Saturdays (10 am, noon and 2 pm) that last about one hour. The area covered is an extensive part of the reserve otherwise closed to the public. A tour with no additional charge is also available in English on Fridays and Saturdays. This needs to be arranged in advance as it will only take place if there is sufficient demand. Their phone number for current information is: (02) 994-2355.

40 Nahal David, Ein Gedi Spring and Ancient Synagogue at Ein Gedi

Most visitors to Ein Gedi walk no further than along Nahal David – but they are missing out on fantastic hikes, interesting sites, and exceptional views of the Dead Sea and Mountains of Moab. This hike visits the waterfalls of Nahal David and then ascends to Ein Gedi Spring. The Dodim Cave can also be visited. There has been settlement and agriculture in this area for thousands of years and you will see the ruins of a Chalcolithic temple and an ancient synagogue in a Jewish village from Roman and Byzantine times.

TIME:
About 2.5 hours

DISTANCE: About 7.5 km

TYPE OF HIKE: Circular

DIFFICULTY: The trail is minimally difficult, but there are handrails at challenging points.

STARTING POINT:
The entrance to Nahal David in the Ein Gedi Reserve. There are shaded benches by the store close to the entrance to the reserve and additional shaded picnic benches adjacent to the parking area.

DRIVING DIRECTIONS AND PARKING:
Enter "Ein Gedi Reserve" into Waze. The entrance to the Ein Gedi Nature Reserve is clearly marked from Route 90. There is free parking outside the entrance to Nahal David.

PUBLIC TRANSPORTATION:
Enter "Ein Gedi " into Moovit and click on "Ein Gedi National Park." Buses 486 and 444 leave from the Jerusalem Central Bus Station and stop outside the Nahal David Field

continued

OVERVIEW

WHEN WAS THE CHALCOLITHIC PERIOD?

The temple at Ein Gedi is thought to have been constructed during the Chalcolithic Period. This was a period between the Stone Age and Bronze Age, and extended from about 4300 BCE to 3300 BCE. It was a time of transition between simple farming communities and more complex sociopolitical communities. The term is applied not just to one culture but to a mosaic of cultural entities. Chalcolithic means copper, and a feature of this period was the widespread use of this metal. Bronze was not yet in use. In fact, many copper cultic objects were found in a cave 11 Km south of Ein Gedi, and it has been speculated that they were hidden there when the temple was abandoned because of approaching danger. This temple may have served a number of Chalcolothic communities in the area.

Most Chalcolithic settlements were abandoned at the end of the Chalcolithic Period and new people moved into the country during the Early Bronze Age. The Middle Bronze Age, beginning in about 2100 BCE, is probably the time that the Canaanites and other tribes mentioned in the Bible settled in Canaan, and also the time that the Biblical patriarchs travelled throughout the country.

THE HIKE

Follow the crowds to the scenic waterfalls of Nahal David. At the fork above the Lower Waterfall take the right branch, the Waterfall Trail. This crosses the stream on a wooden bridge. Shortly before the Upper Waterfall it crosses the stream again on a wooden bridge.

After viewing David's Waterfall, the signs direct you towards the exit of the reserve. Follow this path. Shortly, you will see a path on the right signposted to "En Gedi Spring."

This path ascends to Shulamit's Spring. Shortly after the spring is an intersection. [At this point you may wish to visit the Dodim Cave. It will add about three quarter of an hour to your hike. At the end of this trail you will need to go down a short cliff face on metal rungs to reach the cave. After visiting the cave, return back to the intersection just beyond Shulamit's Spring.]

Continue up the hill to the next intersection. From here take the right fork in the direction of the Chalcolithic Temple. There are a few footpaths to the temple, but the one on the far right is the easiest to walk up.

This pagan temple is worth exploring. On its southern wall is an entrance with a gate house. Proceed through the courtyard to the main building adjacent to the northern wall and enter through an entrance on its southern wall. Facing you is a hoof-shaped niche surrounded by a stone fence. Within it were found animal bones, sherds, ashes, and a clay statuette of a bull. It may well have contained an altar. Notice the round piece of white limestone on the ground, which could have been the base for a statue of the deity. Stone benches are laid out along the walls. The temple shows no signs of destruction and was probably abandoned.

From the top of the hill follow the sign down to En Gedi Spring. The pool is just beyond the signpost and on the black-marked trail. If there are no crowds, you may be fortunate to see Nubian ibex drinking in the pool. Nubian ibex are wild goats that became almost extinct as a result of hunting. They

School. From here it is only a short walk to the Nature Reserve.

TICKET
ADMIT ONE

ADMISSION:
The reservation is open from 8 am–4 pm in the winter and 8 am–5 pm in the summer. It closes one hour earlier on Friday and holiday eves. A brochure is available in Hebrew or English and it contains a clear map that can be used to follow this hike. The admission fee includes admission to the ancient synagogue. Retain your ticket for this. Their phone number is (08) 658-4285.

A Nubian ibex at Ein Gedi Spring

David's Waterfall in Nahal David

were rescued by the Nature Protection movement and the Wild Animal Protection Law of 1955. Next to the spring is a flourmill from the Mamluke period.

Continue on the black-marked trail down the hill. You will pass a small stream leading from the spring. Further on, you will cross a jeep trail. Continue on this black-marked trail. Towards the end of this trail is a memorial on the left to six youths from HaShomer HaTzair who were killed in 1946 when one of their own grenades blew up.

When you come to a paved road turn left. Just before the bottling factory is a concrete covered footpath on the left and this will lead you to the ruins of an ancient Jewish settlement and synagogue.

Close to the entrance of this site are WC's, shaded picnic benches, a cooled water fountain, and a store selling cold drinks and ice cream. There is also a model of how the buildings of the Jewish community would have looked. Some homes have been excavated and you can now walk between the houses in an excavated area adjacent to the synagogue. This street will lead you to the Synagogue.

The ruins you see are from the late Roman and Byzantine periods (3rd to 6th centuries CE). Beneath them are the remains of an even earlier Second Temple Jewish settlement that extended to the foot of Tel Goren. The mosaic floors of the synagogue are quite impressive and indicate the prosperity of this community. This prosperity was based on a secret. In fact, an inscription on the synagogue mosaic floor pronounces a curse on anyone who reveals it. And the secret? The people here grew a plant from which a highly valued perfume was extracted. To this day the plant has not been identified, although not for lack of trying. The Jewish settlement was destroyed by fire. Coins were found in the ruins from the reign of the Emperor Justian the First, and the destruction was probably from persecution during this time.

Exit the site and turn right on the paved road. A concrete footpath on the right shortly after exiting the synagogue will bring you to the parking lot and your car.

Nearby Places of Interest:

*A visit to the very beautiful **Botanical Garden at Kibbutz Ein Gedi** is highly recommended. It is only a few kilometers along Route 90. In actuality, the entire kibbutz is one large, impressive botanical garden! After passing through the kibbutz entrance, go to to the*

adjacent office and for a small charge you are provided with a map containing information about advised stops and lookouts. The brochure also provides descriptions of the plants. In the kibbutz hotel there is a kosher cafe for coffee or a dairy meal.

*A visit to **Masada** is also a must. It is a distance of 20 km and about an eighteen minute drive from Ein Gedi along Route 90.*

41 Ein Gedi – Nahal Arugot

Most visitors to Ein Gedi head to Nahal David, but there are also other wonderful hikes in the area. Hiking through Nahal Arugot you will pass by luxuriant vegetation framed between towering cliffs. Walking through the stream in hot weather to the Hidden Waterfall is also a lot of fun. A longer hike will bring you to swimming in the upper pools.

TIME:
2 to 3 hours

DISTANCE:
About 6 km

TYPE OF HIKE:
Partially circular

DIFFICULTY:
Most of the trail is fairly easy, but a few areas are slightly difficult. Bring footwear suitable for walking through shallow water. Walking sticks can be helpful for balance in the stream.

STARTING POINT:
The entrance to Nahal Arugot. There is free parking here and also cold water, WC's, and in the summer a coffee bar.

ADMISSION:
The Reserve is open from 8 am—4 pm in the winter and 8 am—5 pm in the summer. It closes one hour earlier on Friday and holiday eves. There is an entrance fee.

DRIVING DIRECTIONS:
Enter "Ein Gedi Reserve" into Waze. From Route 90, go past the turning to Nahal David, and continue for a few minutes to the next traffic circle from where you turn off to Nahal Arugot.

continued

Enter "Ein Gedi " into
Moovit and click on "Ein
Gedi National Park." Buses
486 and 444 leave from the
Jerusalem Central Bus Station
and stop outside the Nahal
David Field School. From
here it is about a twenty-five
minute walk to Nahal Arugot.

THE HIKE

Follow the red trail overlooking the wadi.

You will soon come to a blue-marked trail on your left that descends into the wadi. However, this section of the blue trail is fairly short and entails climbing up two sets of metal rungs to get back onto the red trail. So, unless the kids are insistent or you need to cool off because of the hot weather, you can easily give this a miss and continue along the red trail.

After a while you will come to a fork and again meet the blue-marked trail on the left. Take this trail through the wadi to the Hidden Waterfall. Resign yourself to getting your feet wet. (It is also possible at this fork to take the red trail to the Upper Pools. This will make your hike about an hour longer, is uphill, and is slightly more difficult. You will again meet the blue trail and will be wading through water at this point. The reward is swimming in the Upper Pools).

To return to the park entrance, go back the way you came on the blue-marked trail, and this leads onto the red trail.

After some distance you have the option of taking the blue trail to the Hidden Waterfall. This trail descends to the wadi and then parallels the red trail. Some of the time you will be wading through shallow water and this is a lot of fun. This trail eventually joins the red trail to the park entrance.

The Hidden Waterfall

Nearby Places of Interest:

Botanical Garden *at Kibbutz Ein Gedi – see page 279.*

42 Qasr El Yahud National Park

ADMISSION DETAILS:
Summer hours for Sunday to Thursday and Saturday are 8 am–4 pm and Friday and eve of holidays 8 am–3 pm. Winter hours Sunday to Thursday and Saturday 8 am–3 pm, Friday and holiday eves 8 am–2 pm. Last admission is one hour before the site closes. There is no admission charge. Their phone number is: (02) 650-8444.

continued

Qasr el Yahud has significance to Christians and Jews. It is also one of the few places where Israelis can see the River Jordan close up. But don't be too disappointed! Before the age of modern agriculture, the Jordan River, fed by rain and melted snow from Mt. Hermon, would have been at least half a mile wide in the spring. All you see today is a muddy-looking narrow stream. In the 1930's, a dam was built next to Kibbutz Degania at the southern edge of Lake Kinneret, and Jordan and Israel began diverting water from the river, primarily for agricultural use. This led to a 98% decrease in water flow.

DRIVING DIRECTIONS AND PARKING:
Enter "Qasr el Yahud" into Waze. Shortly after leaving the intersection with Route 1, you will see the turn off from Route 90 to Qasr el Yahud on the right. The building on your right is the fortified monastery of St. John. You can also see ruins of Churches from the 5th and 6th century CE. Continue until you come to the free parking lot.

JOSHUA AND JESUS AT THE RIVER JORDAN

In this area opposite Jericho, the Children of Israel crossed the River Jordan into the land of Canaan under the leadership of Joshua. They arrived at about the time of Passover when the River Jordan was at its fullest – "*And the Jordan is full on its banks all the days of the harvest*" (Joshua 3:15).

The Jordan River has two terraces and both can be easily identified. The upper terrace is known as "*Kikar Hayarden*" (the Plain of the Jordan) and the lower one, which is where the River Jordan meanders today, is called "*Gaon Hayarden.*" Because of its heat and humidity, the lower terrace was once full of dense vegetation and wild animals. The Israelites crossed the River Jordan in the spring, when it had probably overflowed onto the upper terrace.

As when the Israelites left Sinai, the Ark of the Covenant was carried before the people (Numbers 10:33). As soon as the priests, who were in front and carrying the ark, stepped into the River Jordan, the river ceased flowing: "*Upon the arrival of the bearers of the Ark and the feet of the priests, bearers of the Ark, were immersed in the edge of the water... the waters descending*

from upstream stood, they rose up in one column, far from the city of Adam which is near Tzarsan; and those descending to the sea of the plain, the Dead Sea, ceased flowing, they were cut off, and the people crossed opposite Jericho" (Joshua 3:15-16).

Even in modern times, the Jordan has become blocked a number of times by mudslides or earthquakes. Nevertheless, the Bible points out that what happened was far from being fortuitous: "*It was when the priests, bearers of the Ark of God, ascended from the Jordan and the soles of the priests' feet were uprooted to the shore, the waters of the Jordan returned to their place and stretched to all its banks as before*" (Joshua 4:18).

Adam is in the location of the present-day Adam Bridge, a distance of just over 40 km from Jericho. There is a Tel close to where the bridge is now, and this is probably the site of the ancient city of Adam. The Israelites now had a large length of dry river bed on which they could cross and the camp "*hastened and crossed.*"

As narrated in the New Testament (Matthew 3:1-17 and Mark 1:4-9), Jesus was baptized by John the Baptist, and this is when it was revealed

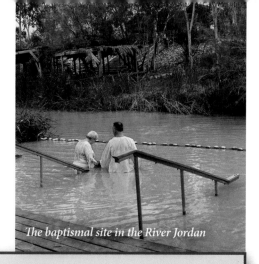

that he was the messiah. The actual site of his baptism is difficult to determine from the New Testament. Nevertheless, this present location has become established as the baptismal site where Christians come to renew their faith.

The baptismal site in the River Jordan

Nearby Places of Interest:

The Jordan Valley Monument: *This monument, which looks like a giant anti-aircraft gun pointing to the sky, was designed by the artist Yigal Turmakin and constructed from old parts of armored vehicles, tanks and guns. It is a memorial to Israeli soldiers who died in the Jordan Valley, particularly those who died in the "Period of Pursuits." In a War of Attrition, between 1967-1970, many attempts were made by Arab terrorists to infiltrate into Israel. This area of the Jordan Valley became known as the "Land of Pursuits" because the Israel Defense Force successfully pursued infiltrators deep into Jordan to prevent them from crossing over the river. A list of over four hundred soldiers killed in attacks is etched in stone next to the monument. Also, within the adjoining park are plaques with the names of the twenty-one communities established here. Some are named after soldiers killed in the area (such as Argamon, an acronym of two commanders), while others have Biblical names (Gilgal, Patzael, and Gitit). Directions: Enter "Habika Memorial" into Waze and click on "אנדרטת הבקעה." The turn off from Route 90 is shortly after Tzomet P'zael and Route 505 and shortly before the Delek gas station at Mifgash Habika. The first gate may be locked. If so, continue to the second gate and there is a road that will lead you to the monument on top of the hill.*

The Oren Farm in Netiv HaGedud: *This farm offers insights into the life of an agricultural family in the Jordan Valley. Argan oil, which is derived from nuts of the Argan tree, is manufactured and sold here. This oil is said to have very healthful properties, particularly in relation to the skin, and is used in prestige anti-aging creams. A short movie is shown and there are refreshments. There is an admission charge. Call Silvi Oren at (054) 232-6116 to book a visit. Driving directions: enter "משק אורן" into Waze and click on "משק אורן-תיירות חקלאית." Shortly after Jericho turn left from Route 90 onto the turn for Gilgal and Netiv HaGedud.*

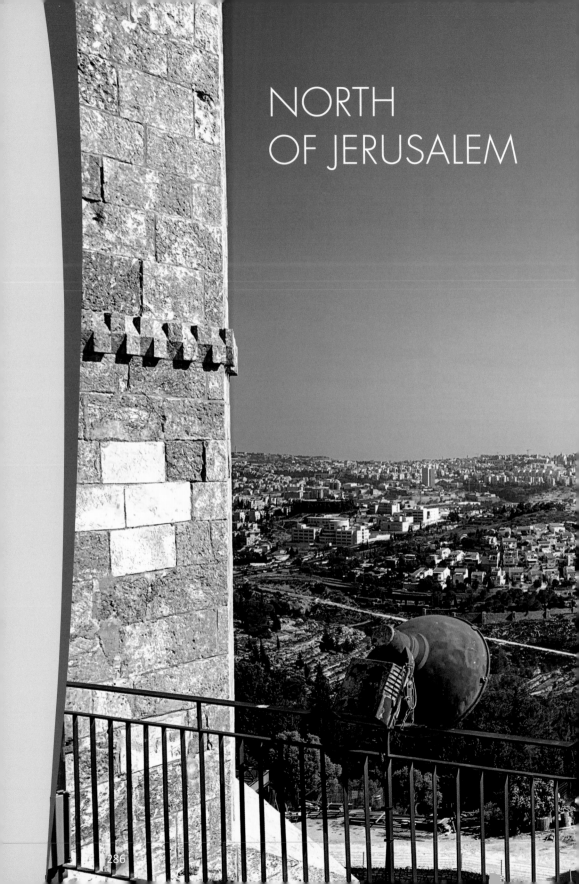

NORTH
OF JERUSALEM

43 Nebi Samuel National Park

The views of Jerusalem from the roof of the mosque at Nebi Samuel are exceptional. In fact, the Crusaders of the First Crusade were so overcome at their first sight of Jerusalem from here that they called the hill "Montjoie." This site also contains interesting Second Temple period ruins, the tomb of Samuel, and picnic areas by Hannah's Spring.

View of Ramot and Jerusalem from the roof of the mosque

TIME:
About 90 minutes

DIFFICULTY: Easy walking. The two flights of stairs to the observation area on the roof of the mosque are quite steep.

SECURITY: Nebi Samuel is beyond the Green Line but within the security barrier and is a popular place for visitors and worshipers.

ADMISSION DETAILS:
The archaeological site is open 8 am—4 pm in the winter and until 5 pm during the summer. There is no entrance fee. The synagogue is open for prayer Sunday through Wednesday and on Shabbat except between the hours 2 am—4 am. There are WC's close to the entrance of the park and cold water. Their phone number is: (03) 794-2481.

DRIVING DIRECTIONS AND PARKING: Enter "Nebi Samuel National Park" into Waze. There is free parking by the entrance to the park.

PUBLIC TRANSPORT:
Enter "Nebi Samuel National Park" into Moovit. The nearest bus stop is at Tzomet Nebi Samuel, which is about an eight minute walk from the park. Bus numbers 131 and 132 leave from Binyanei Ha'umah in Jerusalem.

SAMUEL-TERRITORY

According to tradition, Nebi Samuel is where the prophet Samuel is buried. However, this is debatable. The tradition that this site is his place of burial probably arose in Byzantine times, as the Christians were keen on linking stories in the Bible to Jerusalem and its approaches.

The Book of Samuel records that Samuel was buried in his hometown of Ramah (Samuel I 25:1, 28:3). His family were Levites and Ramah was a Levite town within the territory of Benjamin. Ramah is mentioned a number of times in the Bible and may well have been where the Arab village of Er-Ram is today, about 8 km north of Jerusalem.

It has been suggested that Nebi Samuel is the site of the ancient town of Mitzpah. If this is correct, then Samuel would have visited here frequently. From his hometown Ramah, Samuel would make a yearly circuit within the tribal territories of Benjamin and Ephraim to adjudicate cases, and this would have included Mitzpah: "*And from year to year he would set forth and go around to Bethel, and Gilgal and Mitzpah, and he would judge Israel in all these places. And his return was to Ramah, for there was his house...*" (Samuel I 7:16-17).

Mitzpah means "a lookout" in Hebrew, and Nebi Samuel has the highest elevation in the area. It also has a spring, and this would have permitted habitation. However, while excavations have found evidence of settlement from First and Second Temple times, no ruins have been found from the time of the Judges.

A church was built on the top of the hill during the Byzantine period, and this was destroyed during the early Muslim period. The Crusaders set up a network of way-stations for Christian pilgrims traveling to Jerusalem during the time of the Crusader Kingdom of Jerusalem (1099 to 1187 CE), and they built a church, monastery and fortress on this hill. This fortress was destroyed by the Mamlukes when they brought the Crusader kingdom to an end and a mosque was built on its ruins. The present mosque dates from the 18th century from the Ottoman period.

Because of its elevation, Nebi Samuel has been a staging point for attacks on Jerusalem. There were battles here with the Turks when the British conquered Palestine during the First World War. The Jordanians bombarded Jerusalem from Nebi Samuel during Israel's War of Independence. The Palmach attempted to capture its height, but were unsuccessful, and suffered many casualties in the attempt. It remained in Jordanian hands until the Six Day War.

TOURING THE PARK

From the entrance to the park, walk to the left of the mosque to view ruins from Second Temple times. This area has been extensively excavated and it is possible to identify a mikvah, oven and winepress. As you go around the mosque, you will see quarry areas, which were also used as a moat for the fortress. The wall in front of the mosque is the base of the wall of the former Crusader fortress. At the back of the

Ruins of the gate of the Crusader fortress

mosque are the ruins of the entrance to the fortress.

Pass through the open gate to descend to the orchard. The orchard is planted on terraces, and contains mulberry, olive and fig trees. There are picnic benches throughout the orchard. Hanna's Spring is at the bottom of the park within a cave. The spring is named after Samuel's mother. There is no pool here and the water is quite shallow.

On your return, take the path to the left to examine the ruins of the Crusader hostel.

The highlight of this site are the views from the roof of the mosque, including those of Jerusalem. The stairs to the roof are on your immediate left as you enter the mosque.

After returning to ground level, you can visit Samuel's tomb by passing through the doorway on the far right and descending to the synagogue. The tomb was originally in a cave carved into a rock beneath the main building. There are separate entrances for men and women.

Places to Visit North of Jerusalem:

The following places north of Jerusalem are worth visiting, although they are not in the immediate neighborhood of Nebi Samuel:

__Psagot Winery__ is currently in Kokhav Ya'akov about 18 km north of Jerusalem (although it will be moving to another nearby location). A one hour tour is available, and this includes a movie about their wine-making process, a thirty minute movie about how the calls of history influenced a young man to give up his profession and join his family's wine-making business, and a view of the landscape from the balcony of the visitor center. This is followed by tasting of some of Psagot's wines. Tours are available in Hebrew and English and other languages. There is an admission charge. The visitor center is open Sunday to Thursday 9 am–5 pm (last tour 3:30 pm) and Friday 9 am–1 pm. Call (02) 997-9333 to arrange a tour. Driving directions: Enter "Psagot Winery" into Waze. Public transport: Several buses go from Jerusalem to the gas station at Kokhav Ya'akov and from here it is about a nine minute walk to the winery.

__Ancient Shilo__ is about 43 km from Jerusalem in the settlement of Shilo. This is where the Tabernacle was located for 369 years during the time of the Judges. The place where the Tabernacle could have been located has even been identified. This site offers archaeological tours, a wonderful light and sound experience overlooking the Tabernacle location, and archaeological finds. It is open Sunday to Thursday 8 am–4 pm and Fridays 8 am–1 pm. A guided tour is recommended and should be reserved in advance by calling (02) 578-9111 or e-mailing visit@telshiloj.org.il.

POOLS IN AND AROUND JERUSALEM

The summers in Israel are long and hot. What better way is there to relax and cool down than at a pool?

Nevertheless, finding somewhere suitable for you and your family is a bit like choosing a vacation resort, and you need to plan according to your requirements. Do you need a wading pool for your toddler, a children's pool for your kids, a waterslide to keep the kids occupied, lap swimming for yourself, a pool with a spectacular view, or separate-sex swimming?

The information provided in the following chapters is designed to help you with your decision.

Many Jerusalem hotels have outdoor swimming pools that are open to the public. However, unless you are a guest at the hotel, admission is often pricey and they are not therefore included in this section.

The seasons and times that the swimming pools are open and that are provided in the following chapters should be regarded as a general guide only and should be checked with the facility as changes do occur.

There are two ways to get to Ein Lavan by public transport. The quickest way is to take a bus to the Biblical Zoo. A more scenic way is to take a bus to the Ora Intersection (the bus stop before Hadassah Medical Center) and to walk down the hill to the pools:

FROM THE BIBLICAL ZOO OR AQUARIUM:

Enter "Jerusalem Biblical Zoo" or "אקווריום" into Moovit. From the Zoo, walk through its parking lot and past the Aquarium. The entrance to Ein Lavan is where the paved road comes to an end and changes to a jeep trail. It's about a fifteen minute walk from the zoo.

FROM ORA INTERSECTION (TZOMET ORA):

Take the bus to Tzomet Ora. Just beyond the first roundabout after Tzomet Ora on the Mesho'a Ora Rd. (i.e. in the direction away from Hadassah Medical Center and Route 369) is a brown sign on the road indicating "White Valley," and after this a paved road with a pedestrian and cyclist sign. This paved path soon turns into a jeep road. You will pass an ancient wine fermentation area and mikvah on your right. A mosaic sign "עין לבן" points down the valley. There are many interconnected paths in this area, but follow the jeep trail marked with either a blue-marker or a Shvil Yisrael-marker and you will not go wrong. After some distance, you will see the Ein Lavan Park below you. Look out for a footpath on your left indicated by a Schvil Yisrael marking leading to Ein

continued

44 Ein Lavan

Ein Lavan is one of the most delightful spring-fed pools in the Jerusalem area, and is an ideal place for a family picnic or trip with the grandkids. There are two pools – one suitable for children and the other for toddlers. There is no entrance fee.

Both pools are about four meters long. The depth of the larger pool is about half a meter and a bit higher in the winter. It's great for kids to swim in, but too shallow for adults. The water is not particularly cold. There is smooth concrete on the bottom so footware is not needed. Entry into the pool is via steps. On the terrace above is a shallow pool for smaller children (photo below). Its depth is to just below the knees of an average-height male. There are steps to enter, and it has a smooth and sometimes somewhat slippery concrete bottom.

Below the pools are terraced areas for relaxing and picnicking, with some shaded areas. The shaded areas are taken up quickly during the summer so you may be without shade. The ground surface is dirt, and only some areas have grass. So, you might want to bring ground-covering or chairs. There are no picnic tables, drinking water, WC's, or designated changing area.

Nearby Places of Interest:

The Pool of Ein Haniya: *see chapter 45 "The Spring-fed Pool of Ein Haniya" on next page.*

The Jerusalem Biblical Zoo – *see chapter 19 "The Gorgeous Jerusalem Biblical Zoo" on page 168.*

The Israel Aquarium – *see page 170.*

Lavan. When the footpath comes to a paved road with railings follow it to the right and very soon you will come to steps leading into the park.

DRIVING DIRECTIONS AND PARKING:
Enter "Ein Lavan" into Waze. This will take you through the parking lot of the Biblical Zoo and past the Israel Aquarium. Continue on this paved road until it ends at a gravel jeep path by the entrance to Ein Lavan. There is parking on the side of the road. Ascend to the pools via the steps. There is a paved road just before this that can be used for a wheelchair or stroller.

45 The Spring-Fed Pool of Ein Haniya

Ein Haniya, which is in the Emeq Refaim valley and close to the Jerusalem Biblical Zoo, is a large, deep pool in which an adult can easily swim mini-laps. The area around the pool has recently been renovated. There is no admission charge.

OVERVIEW

EIN HANIYA IN THE CHRISTIAN TRADITION

Ein Haniya is thought to be the site where the apostle Philip baptized the Ethiopian eunuch (Acts 8:26-39). Accordingly, it is often called the Philip Pool. According to Christian tradition, this eunuch brought Christianity to Ethiopia. Despite its Arab neighbors, Ethiopia has managed to survive as a predominantly Christian country.

Above the pool are the ruins of a Byzantine church surrounding a Roman-era fountain. The pool is fed by a spring that emerges from two caves in the area of these ruins. Enter "עין ח'נייה" into Waze for driving directions. For walking directions from Ein Lavan, see page 192.

46 The Zippori Center in the Jerusalem Forest

This swimming pool is tucked away in a beautiful location in the Jerusalem Forest, although at a distance from public transport. It is open June to August. There are reserved hours for women's separate swimming several days a week. Therefore, men and women should check on times before showing up.

> The pool is Olympic size, and there is also a children's pool. Seating is plastic chairs, but there may be deckchairs near the pool. There are grassy areas adjacent to the pool and plenty of shaded areas. There are impressive views of the Jerusalem Forest and Ein Kerem.

Nearby Places of Interest:

Yad Vashem – see page 145.

Herzl Museum – see page 145.

DRIVING DIRECTIONS AND PARKING:
Enter "Zippori Center, Jerusalem" into Waze and click מרכז הנופש ציפורי יער חס ירושלים. There is free parking adjacent to the pool.

PUBLIC TRANSPORT:
Take the light rail to Mount Herzl, and from here it is about a thirty-five minute walk (1.7 mile) to the Zippori Center. From Mt. Herzl walk along Hazikaron St. in the direction of Yad Vashem. Where the road branches to Yad Vashem keep to the left and after some distance there is a turn on the left signposted to the Zippori Center.

HOURS OF OPERATION:
Check on hours by calling (02) 675-3002.

SPORTS CENTER FACILITIES

The outdoor pool
has no deep end and there
is therefore no separation
between kids and adults.
An outdoor water slide is
operative in the summer. The
lawn is spacious and is rich
green even in the middle of
the summer. Large umbrellas
provide plenty of shade,
and there are deckchairs
and plastic chairs. There are
beautiful views of Bethlehem
from the grounds. Inside the
building and close to the
outdoor pool is a large and
impressive toddler and kid's
pool with fountains and fun
theme characters. Inside

continued

47 The Sports Center at Ramat Rachel

The sports facility at Ramat Rachel has been renovated and is now a top-notch sports center. It has a large outdoor pool with lanes for laps. Before leaving the area, consider visiting the Archaeological Park opposite the Sports Center and the statue of Rachel opposite the hotel.

OVERVIEW

ABOUT KIBBUTZ RAMAT RACHEL

The kibbutz was established by ten people on a hilltop in 1929. It was completely burnt down during the Arab riots of 1929, but the members returned a year later and rebuilt it. With the fall of Gush Etzion during the War of Independence, the kibbutz became the southernmost Jewish outpost in the defense of Jerusalem. Completely isolated, it changed hands several times.

Ruins of a casement wall of the Royal Palace in the Archeological Park

It was finally relieved by the Palmach and the settlers themselves, and the kibbutz members were eventually able to return. The kibbutz remained in an isolated position adjacent to the border with Jordan until the Six Day War.

The kibbutz members were socialists and communists who believed in manual labor, and when the kibbutz was set up they worked on building projects in Jerusalem and as stone cutters. Today, the kibbutz has four hundred members and is involved in hi-tech, agriculture (especially cherries), and the hotel industry. As Jerusalem has expanded, it has surrounded the kibbutz.

While at the kibbutz, leave time to visit the Archaeological Park and the statue of Rachel:

The Archaeological Park: This well-known archaeological park is directly across from the entrance to the Sports Center. The site was discovered when the kibbutz started digging to construct a water tower. The largest remains are that of a palace and citadel from the period of the late Judean monarchy. There are ruins of a casement wall from the 8th century BCE, and ruins of a royal citadel or palace that enclosed much of the hill from the 7th to 6th century BCE. A seal impression was found with an inscription to Eliaqim, steward of Yochin, who is believed to have been an official of King Jehoiachin, one of the kings of Judah. There were also finds from the Persian and Hellenenistic periods. The Roman Tenth Legion had a military camp here when stationed in Jerusalem. The Byzantines built a church on this site, and the hill was also inhabited during the early Islamic period. The ruins are marked with explanations. The views of Jerusalem from the hill are impressive.

Statue of the biblical matriarch Rachel: Consider also visiting the statue of the biblical Rachel on the lawn outside the hotel. She has a torch in one hand and two children are holding her other hand. On the statue are the words from Jeremiah 31:17: "Your children will return to their own land." The actual sentences from the book of Jeremiah read: "A voice is heard on high, lamentation, bitter weeping, Rachel weeping for her children... So says the Lord: Refrain your voice from weeping and your eyes from tears... And there is hope for your future, says the Lord, and the children shall return to their own border" (Jeremiah 31:14-17). In this statue, she is protecting two children while staring into the distance waiting for others to come. The kibbutz overlooks Rachel's Tomb and is named Ramat Rachel after her presumed burial place.

the building is an indoor pool, Jacuzzi, two saunas, a large exercise room with a multitude of exercise machines, a dairy cafe, and a store for drinks and snacks. The indoor pool is heated in the winter. Their phone number is: (02) 670-2920.

HOURS OF OPERATION:

Sunday to Thursday: 5:30 am—10:45 pm, Friday: 5:30 am—4:45 pm. In the summer until 5:45 pm. Holiday eves until 3:45 pm, and Saturday and holidays: 7:30 am—9:15 pm.

PUBLIC TRANSPORT:

Enter "Ramat Rachel" into Moovit. Buses stop outside the hotel. Buses also stop at Givat Hamatos on Derech Chevron, which is a ten minute walk to the kibbutz, and this includes buses from the Jerusalem Central Bus Station.

DRIVING DIRECTIONS AND PARKING:

The Sports Center is in Kibbutz Ramat Rachel adjacent to its hotel. Facing the hotel, the pool is to its right. Enter "רמת רחל מלון" into Waze. There is a large free parking area by the entrance to the Sports Center.

48 Ein Hemed National Park (Aqua Bella) – Swimming and Picnicking, and Fortified Crusader Home

E in Hemed is a national park in the Judean Mountains that has a natural pool for kid's swimming, green lawns, plenty of picnic benches, and a play area with swings and slides. There are also ruins of a fortified Crusader farmhouse and observation area. In sum, a great place for families to swim, play, picnic and explore.

TO THE FORTIFIED HOUSE

From the parking lot there are two paths to the park. Take the path to the right and you will shortly come to the main spring of Ein Hemed on your left.

Cross the lawn and continue to the left on the concrete path. Go down to the stream, cross over it on the last bridge and this will lead you to the ruins of the fortified house.

This fortified house was built by the Hospitaller Knights during the period of the Crusader Kingdom of Jerusalem (1099 to 1187 CE).

It is one of thirty-one fortresses built in Israel. This particular strong-hold was built between 1140 to 1160, at the same time that the nearby Belmont fortress was built on Tel Tzubah and the Emaus fortress was built at Latrun. It was one of a string of fortresses designed to control the main road to Jerusalem and provide services to Christian pilgrims visiting Jerusalem. The agricultural community around the fortress was run in a European-type feudal system through an agent. (See also the essay "Crusades and Castles" on page 209).

TO THE OBSERVATION AREA

Above the lawn area where three paths join up opposite terraces and picnic benches is a broad footpath going up the hill. This leads to an observation area providing views over the nearby Arab village of Naquba, the village of Abu Ghosh on the far side of Route 1, and the Judean Mountains in the distance.

TIME: Allow about 30-60 minutes for exploration

DISTANCE: 1.25 km to the Crusader home and back from the parking lot. The paths are suitable for a stroller and are wheelchair accessible

DRIVING DIRECTIONS: Enter "Ein Hemed National Park" into Waze.

PUBLIC TRANSPORT: Enter "En Hemed" into Moovit. There are frequent buses from Binyanei Ha'umah in Jerusalem and bus stops are no more than a five to ten minute walk from the park.

DETAILS OF THE PARK: The Park is open Sunday to Thursday and Saturday from 8 am—4 pm in the winter, and 8 am—5 pm in the summer. On Friday and holiday eves, 8 am—3 pm or 4 pm. There is an admission charge. There are WC's close to the parking lot and also by the fortress. Don't forget to request a brochure, which is also available in English.

THE POOLS here are part of the Kisalon Stream, a tributary of Sorek Valley. The main pool was created by damming up the stream. Spring water issues from a crack in the rock in the upper side of the pool. The water is recirculated during the summer to prevent it drying up.

DRIVING DIRECTIONS: Enter "Shoresh" into Waze. Signs at the entrance to the moshav direct you to the pool.

PUBLIC TRANSPORT: Enter "Shoresh" into Moovit. There are infrequent buses to the moshav and more frequent buses to the "Shoresh Interchange" (מחלף שורש), which is 2 km away and about a half hour (uphill) walk to the moshav.

ADMISSION DETAILS: This pool has a long season from Pesach to Succot. It is open from 9 am—6 pm during July and August, and otherwise from 9 am—5 pm. Their phone number is: (02) 533-8338.

49 Swimming in Shoresh in the Judean Mountains

There is something magical about swimming in the pool in Shoresh perched high in the Judean Mountains and surrounded by breathtaking views.

This is not a large facility and sometimes it can get a bit crowded. The deep end of the swimming pool is separated off from a kid's area at the shallow end and adults can swim laps without interference. There is a very nice wading pool for toddlers, which is partially shaded and has a slide and fountains. Around the pool are natural and artificial lawns, plastic chairs and deckchairs, and a reasonable amount of shade from trees and umbrellas. The snack bar sells cold and hot drinks and ice cream. An inflatable slide and inflated dragon are brought to the pool a few hours a week.

50 The Country Club in Ma'ale Adumim, the Most Beautiful City in Israel

The facilities of this country club are open to the general public, although not the exercise facilities. Admission for non-residents of Ma'ale Adumim is twice that for residents, but swimming in the outdoor pool in the summer and indoor pool throughout the year can still be worthwhile. Ma'ale Adumim has been voted the most beautiful city in Israel on three successive years by the "Mo'atzah LeYisrael Yafa."

The Country Club has a large outdoor pool and toddler's wading pool with a fountain that are open in the summer, and a large indoor pool open all year. There are no deckchairs, but plenty of plastic chairs, a grass lawn, and lots of shaded areas around the outdoor pool. Barbecue grills are available (there is a request not to use them on Shabbat) and a cold-water fountain. Admission includes use of the sauna and the adjacent indoor pool. There is also a snack bar when the outdoor pool is open. From the grounds you can see East Jerusalem and the Mount of Olives Ridge. There are times for separate sex swimming every day for the indoor pool, but not the outdoor pool. The indoor pool has designated times for family swimming and lap swimming for adults.

Nearby Places of Interest:

In Ma'ale Adumim:

Moshe Castel Museum at 1 Kikar HaMuseon contains the artwork of the well-known Israeli artist Moshe Castel. It is open Sunday to Thursday 10 am–5 pm and Friday 10 am–2 pm. It is closed on Shabbat, eves of holidays and holidays, except for Chol Hamoed Succot and Pesach. There is an admission charge, with a special price for families. For information call (02) 535-7000. The Castel Waffle Bar on the museum grounds serves dairy meals and operates on a different schedule than the art museum.

Park Shamir: This Park with a lake is located at the beginning of the Central Entrance to Ma'ale Adumim. Enter "פארק שמיר" on Waze. There is no charge for entrance to the park. It has grass lawns for picnicking, although no benches or chairs. Two quality restaurants overlook the lake.

Close to Ma'ale Adumim:

Museum of the Good Samaritan – see page 262.

Ptil Tekhelet – see page 261.

Lookout at Mitzpe Yericho – see page 262.

DIRECTIONS AND PARKING:
Enter "Derech Midbar Yehuda 1" into Waze and click on "Derech Midbar Yehuda 1, Ma'ale Adumim." There is a free parking lot outside the building and street parking on Derech Midbar Yehuda if it is full.

PUBLIC TRANSPORT:
There are frequent buses from Jerusalem. Enter "קאנטרי קלאב מעלה אדומים" into Moovit. The Country Club is only a short distance from the bus stop.

ADMISSION DETAILS:
Call (02) 591-3444 or (02) 591-3111 for the pool schedule and admission charges or view their website.

ADMISSION DETAILS:

The park is open from 8.00 AM-5.00 PM during the summer and until 4.00 PM from October to March all days of week except Friday and holiday eves when it closes one hour earlier. There is an admission charge. Adjacent to the lower parking lot is a station for information, hot and cold drinks and snacks, a WC, and faucet with drinking water.

DRIVING DIRECTIONS AND PARKING:

Enter "Ein Prat" into Waze and click on "Ein Prat Nature Reserve". Initially, you will enter the settlement of Almon (also known as Anatot). Follow the signs and descend to Ein Prat. Park in the lower parking lot by the ranger station. If it is full, park in the upper parking lot and walk down to the stream.

SECURITY:

The 3 springs in Nachal Prat are in area C and beyond the Green Line. However, Ein Prat is regarded as being safe. It has park rangers and there are usually plenty of people around.

51 The Palm Pool at Ein Prat

E in Prat is in the Judean Desert and only a short distance from Jerusalem. It is a wonderful place for a refreshing swim. The biggest pool is the Palm Pool, which is a short distance from the parking lot on the far side of the stream. Young children will enjoy wading in the shallow stream by the Eucalyptus Grove. There are also great hikes in the Nature Reserve (see page 259).

52 The Artesian Pool at Ein Mabu'a

E in Mabu'a is a beautiful oasis in the Judean Desert close to Jerusalem that has cool flowing water throughout the year. The best swimming is in the artesian pool. There is no admission charge.

Descend from the parking lot and go past the store to the pool. The pool is not that big and you may have to share it with a lot of people, particularly in the middle of the summer, but it's fantastic for cooling down on a hot day. There are WC's close to the pool that can be used for changing.

Do not be surprised if the artersian pool suddenly empties on you, especially in the summer. The pool is fed by from an underground basin that empties into the pool by a siphon effect. Once the basin is emptied, it needs to refill before more water can be released. This is fairly rapid in the winter, but can take longer in the summer. In the meantime, the water in the pool discharges into the stream and the pool empties.

There are other pools along the stream, although they are not as large and deep as the artersian pool.

For details about hiking in Ein Mabu'a see chapter 36 "Ein Mabu'a" on page 263.

> ### *Nearby Places of Interest:*
> *Eretz Bereshit (Genesis Land) – see page 261.*

DRIVING DIRECTIONS AND PARKING:
Enter "Ein Mabu'a" into Waze. Take Route 1 from Jerusalem in the direction of the Dead Sea and shortly past Mishor Adumim take the turn off to Ma'ale Mikhmas/Kfar Adumim/Allon Road on the left. At the roundabout at the entrance to Kfar Adumim take the first right onto the Allon Road (Route 458). This is a windy but beautiful road that passes Eretz Bereshit and then the settlement of Allon. After about 4 km and a seven to eight minute drive from the entrance to Kfar Adumim you will come to the parking lot for Ein Mabu'a at the bottom of the wadi.

PUBLIC TRANSPORT:
There is no convenient public transport.

SECURITY:
The three springs in Nachal Prat are in area C and beyond the Green Line. However, Ein Mabu'a is regarded as being safe. It has park rangers and there are usually plenty of people around.

53 Swimming at Enot Tsukim/Ein Feshka by the Dead Sea

Enot Tsukim/Ein Feshkha is a stunning oasis by the Dead Sea with wading pools, and adult and kid swimming in the Palm Pool – although the Palm Pool is only open at certain times during the summer and not at all during the winter.

Enot Tsukim has a number of fresh water pools, such as the Reed Pool which is shallow and great for kids. All these pools have concrete bottoms and no footwear is needed.

The Palm Pool is suitable for adult swimming in the deep section and the shallower section is appropriate for kids. There is a chair device for lowering the disabled into the water. However, it is closed for much of the year. It is open

all week during July and August, except for Wednesday when it closed for cleaning. During the rest of the summer it is open on Friday and Saturday only. It is closed throughout the winter. Their phone number for current information is: (02) 994-2355.

All the pools have plenty of picnic benches with shade. WC's close to the pools can be used for changing. A kiosk sells cold drinks and is open during popular times.

Short and longer hikes are also available here – see page 273 in chapter 39 "Enot Tsukim/ Ein Feshka for Swimming and Nature Stroll."

Nearby Places of Interest:

*Nearby **Qumran** is well worth a visit (see chapter 38 "Qumran" on page 269). This chapter also describes a short walk into the mountains by Qumran.*

ADMISSION DETAILS:
The Park is open in the summer April through to September from 8 am–5 pm, and in October through March 8 am–4 pm. On Friday and holiday eves closing is 1 hour earlier. The site is open on Saturday. There is an admission charge. A combined ticket for Qumran and Enot Tsukim is available. Their phone number is: (02) 994-2355.

DRIVING DIRECTIONS:
Enter "Ein Feshkha" into Waze and click on "עינות צוקים עין פשח'ה."

PUBLIC TRANSPORT:
The nature reserve is serviced by the reasonably frequent bus 486 from the Jerusalem Central Bus Station. This bus can also be used for the short journey between Qumran and Enot Tsukim from the Kibbutz Kalia Junction.

SECURITY: This area is outside the Green Line and in area C. The roads to and around the Dead Sea are well traveled and safe. The pools are popular for Israelis and Palestinians, but there should be no concerns regarding security.

ADMISSION DETAILS:

The pool has a long season. In July and August, the pool is open from 9 am and closes on Mondays at 9 pm, on Tuesdays at 5 pm, on Wednesdays at 9 pm, on Thursdays at 7 pm, and Fridays and Saturdays at 6 pm.

Admission on Fridays and Saturdays is for families only (adults plus children). The pool is closed on Sundays. In May, June and September the pool is open from 3 pm and the closing time varies. On Saturday it is open 9 am–6 pm. Call beforehand to check on times, prices, and when there are activities for children: (072) 372-6465.

DRIVING DIRECTIONS AND PARKING

and parking: Enter "Swimming pool, Mesilat Zion" into Waze. There is free parking just before the entrance to the moshav in front of the pool.

PUBLIC TRANSPORT:

Enter "Mesilat Zion" into Moovit. Bus 415 leaves from the Jerusalem Central Bus Station in the direction of Beit Shemesh and stops at the Mesilat Zion intersection. From here it is a thirteen minute walk to the moshav.

54 Mesilat Zion Swimming Pool

This swimming pool, which has a long season, is located at the entrance to the moshav Mesilat Zion, close to Beit Shemesh. In addition to swimming, it has many activities for kids, such as table top games, inflatable slides, climbing equipment and a tree top walk.

There is a large outdoor pool. The shallow end is shaded. A toddler's pool is in semi-shade. There are real and artificial grassy areas with plenty of trees and other areas with shade. A cafe is open on weekends for cold and hot drinks and ice cream.

For the children, there are free table top games such as air hockey, foosball and ping pong in the pool area. There is also a climbing wall, climbing equipment, an omega from an adjoining wall into the pool, and at set times, an inflatable water slide and other inflatable slides. A seventy meter treetop walk on rope bridges is open on set activity days. In short, if you are kid – there is never a dull moment!

55 Outdoor Trips in Jerusalem Suitable For a Stroller and Wheelchair

ON THE TEMPLE MOUNT (see chapter 5 on page 52)

The Temple was destroyed almost two thousand years ago, but the Temple Mount is still considered holy in Judaism. There are two aims to this walk. Firstly, to understand the main Muslim buildings on the Temple Mount. And secondly, to conjure up the Temple that once stood here based on the structures that are currently standing, historical information and archaeological findings.

NACHLA'OT AND MAHANE YEHUDA MARKET ("THE *SHUK*") (see chapter 8 on page 85)

The neighborhoods of Nachla'ot were some of the first residential areas to be built outside the Old City walls and they still retain their old-world charm. There was a strong feeling of community in these new estates and many of the people who lived here remember this very fondly. The walk ends at the famous, bustling Mahane Yehuda market.

GIVAT RAM – BIRDS, ROSES, THE SUPREME COURT AND KNESSET (see chapter 11 on page 114)

This circular walk should be fun for all ages. It includes the Jerusalem Bird Observatory, the Rose Garden, the menorah outside the Knesset, the Supreme Court building, and the Biblical displays on the roof of Cinema City, including Noah's ark. Free tours of the Supreme Court building and the Knesset are available in English. After the walk consider visiting one of the nearby museums – the Israel Museum and Shrine of the Book, the Bible Lands Museum, or the Bloomfield Science Museum.

THE HAREDI NEIGHBORHOODS OF ZIKHRON MOSHE AND MEAH SHEARIM (see chapter 12 on page 123)

About one-third of Jerusalem's population belongs to the sector known as haredim, often called "ultra-Orthodox Jews." In this walk through the neighborhoods of Zikhron Moshe, Geulah and Meah Shearim you will see the people who live here and view the outside of some important Hasidic centers. The main commercial arteries for Jerusalem's haredi community also provide plenty of opportunities for shopping.

The Sherover and Haas Promenades and Water Supply System for Second Temple Jerusalem (see chapter 13 on page 131)

Nothing surpasses the Sherover and Haas Promenades for views of the Temple Mount, the Old City, and the surrounding hills. Understandably, the observation area on the Haas Promenade has become a popular place for tourist groups. We will also explore the shafts under the Armon Hanatziv mountain range that were part of the water supply system for Jerusalem during the time of the Second Temple. The early part of the walk is appropriate for a wheelchair, but the incline to the Haas Promenade may be too steep to go further.

Pioneers of Modern Jerusalem – Eliezer ben-Yehuda, Rav Abraham Isaac Kook and Dr. Abraham Ticho (see chapter 15 on page 146)

The appearance of a cosmopolitan, intellectual and Zionistic neighborhood outside the Old City walls was an important stage in the early development of modern Jerusalem. This walk views the homes of three influential Zionist figures who lived and set the tone for this new neighborhood, now in the center of Jerusalem – the first Ashkenazi Chief Rabbi of Palestine Rabbi Abraham Isaac Kook ("Rav Kook"), the linguist Eliezer Ben-Yehuda, and the ophthalmologist Dr. Abraham Ticho. The exhibition in Beit HaRav Kook is not accessible for wheelchairs because of the stairs.

The German Colony and Liberty Bell Park (see chapter 16 on page 154)

Old Templer homes and quaint streets and alleys are the main attractions in this walk through the German Colony, which starts at the First Station (the old Railway station) and ends at the Liberty Bell Park, with its replica of the Philadelphia Liberty Bell.

The Gorgeous Jerusalem Biblical Zoo (see chapter 19 on page 168)

The Tisch Family Zoological Gardens, popularly called the Jerusalem Biblical Zoo must be one of the prettiest places in Israel. It contains numerous species from around the world, including animals indigenous to Israel, and animals that were once indigenous to Israel, such as the Persian leopard and Nile crocodile. All are displayed in a beautifully landscaped park with a large duck and swan filled lake, green lawns, flowing streams, attractive flowerbeds and interesting paths. Most of the paths are paved.

The Jerusalem Botanical Gardens (see chapter 20 on page 172)

Explore colorful paths in the areas of Southern Africa, Australia, Asia, Europe, North America and the Mediterranean, with over six thousand plants and trees from around the globe. The scenic pools, waterfalls, tree walk, and Tropical Conservatory with exotic plants are sure to engage your interest. The numerous multi-colored blossoms after the winter rains are quite inspiring. Most of the paths are paved.